BRITONS,
To Arms!
The Story of the British
Volunteer Soldier

The Volunteer tradition – G.A.L. Keck, Lieutenant-Colonel Commandant of 'Prince Albert's Own' Regiment of Leicestershire Yeomanry, 1856. His personal service in the Yeomanry, from first becoming a cornet in 1798 until his death in 1860, saw the emergence of the great Volunteer Force of the Napoleonic wars and its revival half a century later in the Rifle Volunteer Movement of 1859. Keck served as commanding officer for fifty-seven years which, if an exceptional example of long service, was not in its nature so unusual.

BRITONS, *To Arms!*

The Story of the British Volunteer Soldier and
the Volunteer Tradition in Leicestershire and
Rutland

GLENN A. STEPPLER

ALAN SUTTON

For Carrie

First published in the United Kingdom in 1992
Alan Sutton Publishing Ltd · Phoenix Mill · Far Thrupp
Stroud · Gloucestershire
in association with
Leicestershire County Council Museums, Arts and Records Service

First published in the United States of America in 1992
Alan Sutton Publishing Inc. · Wolfeboro Falls · NH 03896–0848

Copyright Glenn A. Steppler, 1992

British Library Cataloguing in Publication Data

Steppler, Glenn A.
  Britons to Arms: Story of the Volunteer Soldier
  I. Title
  940.48341

  ISBN 0–7509–0057–1

Library of Congress Cataloging in Publication Data applied for

Typeset in Bembo 10/12.
Typesetting and origination by
Alan Sutton Publishing Limited.
Printed in Great Britain by
Billing & Sons Ltd, Worcester

Contents

List of
Illustrations

Photographic Acknowledgements

Except where indicated, all illustrations are from the collections of Leicestershire Museums, Arts and Records Service. Copyright resides with the owners in all cases.

Acknowledgements

I must thank Leicestershire Museums, Arts and Records Service for providing the opportunity to study the British Volunteer. The current Director, Tim Schadla-Hall, has always backed my endeavours with his personal support, while Tim Clough, Keeper of the Rutland County Museum, has spent a great deal of his time preparing the text for publication. I would also like to make special mention of the assistance received from Robin Jenkins at the Leicestershire Record Office, from Jane Legget, formerly at the Newarke Houses Museum, and from Peter Stoddart at Humberstone, who made things much easier. Steve Thursfield and Catherine Lines are to be especially thanked for their photographic support in preparing the illustrations. Outside Leicestershire, I would like to acknowledge help received from Peter Harrington of the Anne S.K. Brown Collection in Rhode Island, from W.Y. Carman and from D.H. Stanley. Ian Beckett very kindly read and commented on an earlier draft when first finished in 1989. The final word of thanks, however, must go to those who have shared the author's daily tribulations, both real and imaginary, when, like the man himself, the 'Volunteer Book' has persistently re-emerged. My wife Carolyn was at my side when, in November 1983, over a pint in an Oxford pub, G.A. Chinnery first invited me to take part in Leicestershire Museums' Volunteer Soldier project, and she has given her support ever since.

Introduction

There is no country on the face of earth to which the principle of citizen-soldiership is so well adapted as our own, for the freedom possessed by Britons is of so general and real a character as to cause the humblest in the land to feel deeply the necessity of preserving the safety and independence of the nation of which he is a part.

The Volunteer's Book of Facts (London 1863), p. 14

. . . so long as every man is his own soldier, England need not fear the thousand ills of invasion; her integrity is ensured, and she will remain safe on her sea-girt throne.

Wimbledon Annual (London 1869), p. 8

The Victorians were immensely proud of their nation and their heritage – and in the early 1860s many were also worried by the prospect, or more precisely the feasibility, of a sudden cross-Channel attack by the French. Historically, their fears were hardly novel, nor was their response. The threat of invasion has been a recurrent theme in British history, and while the principal defence of Britain's 'sea-girt throne' has rested traditionally on naval power, a large measure of reliance has also been placed on 'the principle of citizen-soldiership', the idea that every man should be his own soldier. The need for a large army on the continental European model has been consistently rejected as an unnecessary expense and a threat to civil liberties, attitudes which have fostered a preference for amateur, and temporary, forces. From the late eighteenth century these were the Militia, the Volunteers and the Yeomanry, collectively the 'auxiliary forces'. Created as need arose in moments of peril, these auxiliary forces have served not only as a bulwark against invasion itself, but also as a means of policing to ensure local domestic tranquillity. On various occasions, the Militia (the 'Old Constitutional Force'), and to a lesser extent the Volunteers, have been seen not only as a counterpoise to the regular army, but even suggested as an alternative.

While the principle of citizen-soldiership may be said to have applied generally to service in the auxiliary forces, there have nonetheless been two distinct elements: those forces raised largely through compulsion, and those which have been formed by more or less spontaneous offers of voluntary service. The former, from the mid sixteenth century, have been represented by a succession of Militia forces, the latter by the recurring phenomenon of Volunteers, of whom the mounted arm emerged as the Yeomanry at the end of the eighteenth century. It is the latter, the Volunteers (including the Yeomanry), who are the subject of this book.

In its origin, the Militia was a creation of national government, imposed as it were on the counties. Service in the Militia involved an element of compulsion. The rules and regulations which governed it were laid down by parliamentary statute, and its discipline when in training or on service soon became that of the regular army. When actually mobilized, militia units would serve outside their own county, and on occasion some regiments, of their own choice, even served outside Great Britain.

In the eighteenth century the Militia was a local force insofar as it bore a county title and was raised, mustered and trained in that county. It was administered under the county Lieutenancy, and its officers were drawn locally from those with the requisite property qualification. Its rank and file, however, quickly became an army of substitutes, as those balloted men who could afford it took advantage of the option of hiring another to serve in their place. Nor was the choice of substitutes confined to the regiment's particular county – they could be drawn from adjacent counties, and often were. The Militia's formal legal existence was not continuous. After lapsing in 1604, it was revived in 1648, and persisted until 1735. In 1757, a 'New Militia' was created and soon embodied to face the threat of invasion. After 1815 it was little seen. Its permanent staff was cut to the bone, musters were few, and in 1831 it ceased altogether, though officers continued to be appointed. During the Napoleonic Wars, additional Militia forces appeared briefly, a Supplementary Militia and a Local Militia. At the Militia's final resurrection in 1852, enlistment was made voluntary, though the power to hold a ballot if necessary was kept in reserve. In 1908, at the reorganization of the auxiliary forces, the Militia officially disappeared. Being excluded from the new Territorial Force, it formed instead a Special Reserve.

The Militia had a chequered existence, but that of the Volunteer element of the auxiliary forces was often even more ephemeral. In contrast to the Militia, the Volunteers were often solely the result of local initiative, and if sometimes they were encouraged by the government, on other occasions they appeared, and persisted, despite active discouragement. Their formation was expressly for immediate local defence and security, the latter very often being the more important. Their character could be highly individualistic, very much in the fashion of a club with its own rules of conduct and membership. Government attempts to create uniformity never met with complete success. Until Britain's final great struggle with France (1793–1815), British Volunteer forces existed only as temporary short lived bodies, raised spontaneously through local efforts to answer the needs of a particular crisis. When the cause of their assembly subsided, they were quickly dissolved. Throughout the eighteenth century the threat of invasion, of insurrection, and of local disorder repeatedly prompted the appearance of local Volunteer companies. Quite unlike the Militia, they existed without any formal statutory recognition. Where the government sought to control them at all, it was by attempting to graft them onto the Militia. Statutory recognition as a separate type of military force, distinct from both the Militia and the regular army, may be traced to 1782 when Lord Shelburne's ministry made a brief attempt to create autonomous Volunteer corps. The scheme was imperfect, and was only to come to full fruition in 1794, when events again moved the government itself to call for the services of Volunteers. Even so, the experience of much of the huge Volunteer Force raised during the French Revolutionary and Napoleonic Wars followed the old pattern of local bodies raised on an ad hoc basis and soon disbanded when the immediate crisis had passed. The one notable exception was the Yeomanry, the mounted arm of the Volunteer Force. The Yeomanry was retained, and with its continuation after 1815 the Volunteer became a permanent member of county society.

The Yeomanry regiments continued into the twentieth century, but in 1859 the sudden emergence of a nationwide Rifle Volunteer movement added a new force of Volunteers of considerable size. To the surprise of their critics, these new Rifle Volunteers, ostensibly the result of 'panic' over French threats and the realization of the feasibility of an invasion, did not fade away with the passing of the crisis, but like the Yeomanry found a permanent niche in British society. In 1908 the Yeomanry and the Rifle Volunteers were brought together in the new Territorial Force.

Through many changes, and two world wars, the Territorials have carried forward amateur, part-time military service on the voluntary principle into the late twentieth century. Through the Yeomanry they can trace a direct link to the Volunteers raised under the parliamentary Act of 1794, but the Territorials have not been the only expression of voluntary citizen-soldiership in more recent times. The threat of invasion in both world wars produced afresh new forces of temporary, local Volunteers. The Volunteer Training Corps of 1914 and the Home Guard of 1940 have been the latest manifestations of those Volunteers of much earlier times, whose brief existence was in direct response to a specific challenge.

Just as the part-time Volunteer has been a recurring figure in British history, so too there has been a common pattern to many of his experiences. Although the armed Volunteer stepping forward to defend his country might appear as the ultimate expression of patriotism, his relations with those who govern have often been uneasy. Frequently an unsolicited addition to the nation's armed forces, the Volunteer has often been seen by government ministers as an awkward, even troublesome character whose very presence disrupted military planning. He has been hard to control and his role difficult to define, problems made worse by doubts about his military effectiveness, and occasionally even his political loyalties. The Volunteer ideal was self-sufficiency (a state hardly ever achieved), but its corollary was independence. The Volunteer, though he might request government aid, indeed feel entitled to such assistance, also insisted on his own autonomy: he would make his own rules and set his own standards. But the government, while certainly wishing to encourage the Volunteer to bear his own expense, also desired a measure of control over his activities, and where aid was granted, it was in return for more uniformity under central direction. The Volunteer, while resenting outside interference, has nonetheless repeatedly pressed his requests for assistance, and has always believed himself deserving of more than he received.

Doubts have often been expressed about the real motive of the Volunteer in taking up arms. Simply patriotism, or something else? Fear of domestic unrest and a threat to his own stake in the social order? A defiant statement of political loyalties? Or merely an attempt to avoid more uncomfortable service in the Militia or the regular army? The pursuit of social prestige, or simply a desire for recreation enjoyed with friends? The differing circumstances under which Volunteer forces have appeared have suggested various answers. The composition of Volunteer corps may offer some indication, but the evidence is often fragmentary. A frequently expressed ideal of those who advocated the use of Volunteers (and also the Militia), was that they should be based on a wide spectrum of society, especially including the middle and upper elements of society, precisely those who did not normally enlist in the regular army or the Militia. Men of superior social status did come forward as Volunteers, but their presence in any numbers was generally of very limited duration. The pressure of other commitments and the pull of other interests soon took them away, and volunteer soldiering, like soldiering in the regular army and in the Militia, fell largely to those of more humble status. Nevertheless, a wide variety of social backgrounds was often encountered. Not only could Volunteer corps differ greatly from one to another, but so too could companies or troops within the same corps.

The Volunteer has always struggled to find the time and the resources to train himself adequately. His activities have always had to be fitted into civilian life, and those of a military nature balanced against those of a social character, the latter being so often necessary for his continuing at all. The club-like atmosphere of many corps has been no accident. Suitable officers and instructors, most especially in rural areas, have often been difficult to find, and the rural Volunteer has always found his isolation from comrades a major obstacle to attaining proficiency. The Volunteer has often been caught in a cross-fire of criticism from regular professional soldiers and from his fellow citizens. He has frequently been involved in controlling civil disorder, an unpopular task which readily branded him as a partisan in local disputes. Nonetheless, though disdained and ridiculed by some in his community, he has also been referred to with pride by others.

The history of the Volunteer is a particularly interesting one. His experience has touched the world of the regular soldier, though he himself has remained a civilian, a local man, a neighbour, an acquaintance. His experience, and that of others in the auxiliary forces, offers many possible insights for the historian: a different vantage point from which to view the military history of the nation, but also another perspective on its social and political history. At the local level it allows the historian another point of entry into county or even parish affairs. The possibilities are there, but sadly are hardly realized. Only very recently have some scholars begun to take a serious look at the history of the part-time soldier. As yet the field is open for investigation, and is one in which the study of local history must play an important part, for the citizen-soldier can only be properly understood in the setting of his particular community. Studies of the Napoleonic Volunteer Force and the nineteenth century Yeomanry, and their eighteenth century predecessors, are obviously themes of national significance, but the complete picture can only be built up from local examples.

This study, arising from research done for Leicestershire Museums, Arts and Records Service for a new gallery on the Volunteer Soldier in the Rutland County Museum, is divided between a short general history of the British Volunteer and a detailed account of the experience of two English midland counties, Leicestershire and Rutland. In being thus divided it offers both a general context and a specific example, emphasizing the national importance of Britain's Volunteer tradition, while reminding us of its intensely local character. In a small way, it is to be hoped that this study can make a contribution to, and perhaps encourage others to pursue further, the history of a distinctly British response to danger.

G.A.S.
Hendon, 30 August 1989

PART ONE

THE STORY OF THE BRITISH VOLUNTEER

CHAPTER ONE

The Eighteenth Century

Before 1700

'Citizen' and 'soldier' have been synonymous for much of human history. The Anglo-Saxons expected the ordinary citizen to undertake military service in emergencies, and the obligation was preserved in successive medieval legislation. The counties could be called upon to provide men for service at home and, very occasionally, for service abroad, and alongside this national force there remained into the reign of Henry VIII quasi-feudal levies (especially for campaigns abroad) raised by the aristocracy and the gentry. Increasingly, however, the Tudors looked for their soldiers to the nation as a whole. In 1558, the first Militia statutes classified the population according to wealth and laid down a scale of weapons and equipment which each class of person was to provide. The new Lords Lieutenant of the counties were given authority over these forces, being charged with the responsibility of holding regular musters and of raising levies when needed.

In lieu of a permanent, standing force, the immediate military strength of the nation resided in the Militia – but the Militia was an unwieldy institution. In the seventeenth century, in the wake of domestic strife, civil war and threats of foreign invasion, there appeared, if only for short periods of time, many independent bodies of Volunteers. By the late seventeenth century such organized bodies, raised by known supporters of the government, were even proposed as an alternative to both the newly created standing army (which had emerged during the Civil War) and the Militia. Indeed the ineffectiveness of the Militia in dealing with emergencies, and the small size of the new standing army, often made the raising of independent bodies of Volunteers a necessity for local defence and security.

Despite a fairly elaborate reorganization at the restoration of the monarchy in 1660, the Militia, which numbered as many as 90,000 men, was inefficient. Nor could the political loyalty of such a disparate and scattered force be taken for granted. Enthusiasm for the Militia which had been evident in the first years of the Restoration began to wane. After a burst of activity during the second Dutch War of 1665–7, lack of funds and the disinterest of many lieutenancies led to its internal decay. Musters were not called, and the force soon became ill trained and poorly equipped. Although in theory the Militia forces might still play an effective strategic role, it was hardly surprising that their performance in battle (in 1685 and again in 1717) was dismal. The Militia, being increasingly difficult to assemble, had lost its one intended advantage, that of being a force always ready to respond. In emergency, it often seemed easier simply to raise Volunteers, and a noticeable preference for such Volunteers was evident during the invasion scare of 1690.

Defending the Community

Despite the double threat of Jacobite insurrection and foreign invasion, the early decades of the eighteenth century brought very little change in the country's defensive preparations. Jacobite schemes to restore the Stuart monarchy fermented rebellion at home and raised the spectre of French intervention. To meet the danger the government turned first to the Militia, but it was the creation of voluntary Defence Associations and independent bodies of Volunteers, raised by spontaneous local initiative, that provided the most effective response. The pattern established during the first Jacobite insurrection of 1715 was followed again thirty years later during the second, more serious threat.

By the autumn of 1745, having become ever more deeply involved in the War of the Austrian Succession (1740–8), Britain faced a crisis of grave proportions. While a victorious Jacobite army in Scotland threatened the north of England, a French invasion across the Channel was hourly expected. Part of the regular army was committed to a campaign in Flanders, while at home the Militia once again proved weak and ineffective, 'so burthensome and inefficient, that it has been generally laid aside'. In some counties, especially in the north, the inhabitants 'entered into general Associations and Subscriptions for raising a force for their own defence'.[1] At York a meeting of some 800 of the principal nobility, clergy and gentry of the area adopted measures for local defence. A Defence Association was formed, and by the end of September the Yorkshire county subscription had raised £20,000 and commissions for forty-one companies had been given out. At Hull four artillery companies were formed and the leading burgesses raised another twelve 'independent companies of gentlemen volunteers'. Altogether the East Riding alone raised twenty-three volunteer companies of infantry and artillery.[2]

Elsewhere in the country, there was similar activity. Town corporations formed their own Defence Associations and raised Volunteers for their immediate protection. County-wide subscriptions produced funds from which the Lords Lieutenant could pay and provide for such forces as were authorized to be raised for the defence of their counties. In Carlisle, Newcastle, Whitehaven, Liverpool, Nottingham, Bristol, Exeter and London, citizens came forward to enrol themselves as Volunteers for local defence. The forces raised were not confined to companies of infantry and artillery. Mounted corps also appeared, just as they had on previous occasions. The Duke of Montagu, who took command of one such corps, the Northamptonshire Association, in 1744, had previously formed several Associations into mounted troops during the rising of 1715.[3]

A threatened French invasion, a hostile Highland army and a possible insurrection would seem powerful inducements in bringing men out as Volunteers, particularly those with enough social status to have property to lose. Yet some contemporaries insisted that the true motive behind many subscriptions and associations was solely a desire by self-interested individuals to win ministerial favour.[4] Whatever the truth, it is certain that the Volunteers in those Defence Associations raised under the auspices of town corporations included both 'the better sort of people' (those tradesmen and others who considered themselves entitled to be called 'gentlemen'), and their social inferiors, the 'common men'.[5] Those of middling and upper social standing who initiated the subscriptions and associations sought to enrol their more humble neighbours. As they saw it, 'gentlemen' might come forward from a sense of duty and to set an example for others but, as such sentiments were not expected from those of lower rank, pay and clothing, paid for from subscription funds, had also to be offered.[6] If such material blandishments were ineffective, there was still a possibility that some of the 'common men' might be prompted to enrol as a means of avoiding the Press Acts then in force to find recruits for the regular army. All members might serve on foot, but the conscious social superiority of the 'better sort of people' usually led to the creation of distinct and separate companies.

The mounted corps were of a quite different character, clearly foreshadowing the mounted Yeomanry force which was to come into existence at the end of the eighteenth century. Even earlier forebears are discernible in the mounted Volunteers of 1660–1. The Yorkshire Light

Horse, raised in September 1745, was the creation of 'a number of fox-hunting gentlemen and yeomen of the county', described by another observer as the local 'bucks'. They were reported to be mounted 'on tip-top hunters', the gentlemen subscribers forming the first rank, the second and third ranks being composed of their servants. Major-General Oglethorpe was invited to become their colonel and the regiment soon obtained the King's permission to call themselves 'The Royal Regiment of Hunters'.[7] The Northampton Association, formed in April 1744 'to fight in defence of His Majesty's Crown, the Protestant Religion and the Liberties of Great Britain, against Popery and French Slavery', was similar. The original undertaking was signed by 530 'substantial free-holders, yeomen, and yeomen's sons etc' who considered themselves 'more to be depended upon than any millitia [sic]'. When required, members were to appear mounted, and would do so entirely at their own expense. Being all Volunteers, they would 'come out of their own good will and zeal for the King and Government, whereas the millitia [sic] consist of men sent by the disaffected as well as by the well affected'.[8]

The Defence Associations of 1744–5 were highly independent, auto-nomous bodies, and the government was quite content to leave them as such. Those formed under the auspices of municipal corporations were assured that they would 'be subject to no other regulations with regard to military services than such as would be established by the Corporations, at whose expense they were raised and subsisted'.[9] Subscription funds formed the basis of their finances. Individuals, depending on their own means, either provided their own clothing and equipment, or were clothed and accoutred from the common fund. Arms were usually supplied by the government, but the local procurement of a makeshift collection of weapons might also be necessary. Members might agree to forego any pay, or might only be paid if actually called out on service; but there could also be provision for a daily subsistence pay, even though not on service, to come from the subscription money at a rate commen-surate with that of the regular army. The Exeter Association stipulated a pay of 9d. per day for privates when called out and on duty within the county of the city of Exeter, but if on actual service elsewhere it was to be one shilling per day. When only exercising, the men would still receive 1s. 2d. per day. Within the same corps some members might accept pay, while others did not. Those Exeter tradesmen who con-sidered themselves to be 'gentlemen' and who had agreed to clothe themselves and accept no pay were said to disclaim those of lesser means, who drew upon the subscription fund for pay and clothing, as a 'Set of Mercenaries'. The 'common men' in the Association were made to take the 'military oath' in order, it was claimed, 'to prevent their selling the

Cloaths which was purchas'd for them at the Expence of the Subscribers'. Those who provided their own uniforms undertook no oath whatsoever.[10]

In the absence of government control there was a considerable variation in the nature and extent of service agreed to by the Associations. While many were formed primarily to protect local property, check unruly behaviour and keep the disaffected in line, others had specific military objectives in mind. The Royal Regiment of Hunters had been raised to 'harass the Rebels in their March, and give Intelligence of their Motions to the King's Forces, and remove every thing which may be of Service to the Enemy'. While the foot companies which formed the Exeter Association were to serve 'in and throughout the Counties of Exon and Devon only', the members of the Northampton Association agreed 'to Serve within the Realm, where ever His Majesty's Service shall require'. The period of service was also variable. Those at Exeter agreed to serve for six months, or 'till the present Rebellion or the reasonable apprehension of a Invasion, is at an end'.[11]

Early in 1746 the French gave up their invasion plans and in April the Jacobite army was decisively beaten at Culloden. The crisis which had created such panic in the last months of 1745 vanished, and with it the Defence Associations and Volunteer companies it had spawned. The Volunteers of the Defence Associations had at least been of some service, but raising the Militia had been a failure. The Volunteer companies had stiffened morale and like the old Militia had acted as a kind of police, protecting property, checking local disaffection, riot and disorder – and some corps, like the Royal Regiment of Hunters, had provided direct assistance to the regular forces. The experience of such perilous times was not soon forgotten.

Militiaman or Volunteer?

Britain's increasing strategic isolation in the wars from 1739 onwards led to serious thinking and debate on defence, and finally to the birth of a 'New Militia' in the 1750s. The navy seemed too weak to counter every possible threat of invasion and the land forces were ill prepared to deal with a determined enemy when once ashore. In particular the surprise French naval concentration off the English coast in 1744 and the success of the Jacobite army in penetrating England in 1745 had caused great alarm. There arose an agitation for the reform of the Militia, which having reached a climax in 1756 (during the next war with France) was finally successful in 1757.[12]

The Militia reforms carried out in 1757–8 during the Seven Years War (1756–63) were extremely important not only for the Militia, but ultimately for both the regular army and the Volunteers. The New Militia Act of 1757 altered entirely the basis on which the Militia was to be raised. The liability formerly imposed on individual property owners, or groups of owners, to supply men, horses and arms was transferred to the counties, each of which was assigned a definite quota of men. The county quota was apportioned among the various parishes, whose inhabitants aged 18 to 45 years were then made subject to possible selection by balloting. Those chosen by lot were to serve three years (later increased to five years), but even if selected, a balloted man was still given the option of providing, or paying £10 for the provision of, a substitute. The reformers further aimed at bringing the Militia to a new standard of efficiency. The annual training requirements were made more stringent (twenty-eight days) and when embodied or on training (and after 1761, at all times), the whole force was made subject to the Mutiny Act, which with the Articles of War governed the discipline of the regular army. Once embodied the New Militia could be sent to serve anywhere in the Kingdom.[13]

The government hoped that the New Militia would provide an inexpensive bolster to national defence in an emergency, and perhaps make offensive action by the regular armed forces easier, in particular by relieving the army of certain home duties. Initially, however, raising the New Militia ran into problems. The implementation of a first ballot was greeted by rioting among both the poorer and the middling classes. More serious in the long term, however, was the reluctance of the county gentry (and many Lords Lieutenant) to undertake the laborious task of raising the new force and serving as its officers (for a property qualification was required of all Militia officers). It took another invasion scare, in 1759, to bring the New Militia into being, but even then Wales and the Midlands, with exception of Leicestershire, Rutland and Warwickshire, remained an extensive area of apathy.[14] Not until 1778, spurred on by yet another war, was the task of raising the New Militia completed in all counties.

The reform of the Militia was of great importance to the future of the Volunteer. After 1745 government ministers had occasionally thought of using temporary levies of Volunteers as part of the solution to the country's defence problems, but the New Militia Act of 1757 did not make any reference to that notion. It was not however forgotten. In 1758 further legislation (to explain the Act of 1757) empowered the parishes to offer Volunteers towards the quotas, in place of balloted men. In effect such Volunteers would be Militia substitutes, who were not to act on their own but were to be incorporated with the Militia. They would have to submit to the same discipline as the Militia, their sole reward for volunteering being exemption from the Militia ballot. Significantly the new legislation of 1758 seemed also to acknowledge the possibility of independent bodies of Volunteers still being formed outside the Militia. The fact that Militia captains, if ordered on actual service, were authorized to augment their companies by any number of persons who might volunteer to serve with them and who already appeared to be sufficiently trained and disciplined, and who were also provided with proper clothes, accoutrements and arms, seemed to assume the existence of military formations quite separate from both the Militia and the regular army. This indeed proved to be the case when in 1759 Volunteer corps were again formed on a local basis.[15]

The existence of distinct Volunteer corps, independent from the Militia, was thus not clearly addressed in the Militia reforms of 1757–8. However, the new measures did in fact sow the seeds, if quite unintentionally, for the eventual emergence of a Volunteer force in its own right. By allowing Volunteers to count towards the parish quotas, they also set a precedent which would cause much trouble some fifty years later when government ministers came to rationalize the nation's manpower needs in the midst of its greatest war with France. The substitution clause, by which balloted men could discharge their duty through hired substitutes, soon created a Militia force composed largely of long-serving substitutes – men very like those of the regular army and subject to the same code of discipline. Moreover the manner in which the Militia was deployed when once embodied in wartime made them very much like the regulars. While legally confined to serve within Great Britain, almost invariably Militia regiments were used outside their own counties. This was primarily because of their strategic deployment in defence of the whole country against invasion, but also patly to prevent their collusion in local disturbances against unpopular government measures. In effect the New Militia did not solve the immediate needs of local security and defence in wartime, nor did it draw forth the wide range of recruits originally envisaged. The answer to these problems was the creation of temporary, short service, Volunteer corps. Ultimately, by the end of the eighteenth century, the New Militia proved readily convertible into a reserve from which to augment the regular army, and this finally enabled the government to develop what became the classic nineteenth century pattern: Volunteers for local and temporary defence, and a Militia reserve from which the regular army could recruit.

Rebellion in America once more forced government ministers to consider the defence posture of the country. The American Revolution (1775–83) was at first a distant colonial war which posed no direct threat to the British Isles, but following the surrender of a British army at

Saratoga in 1777 Britain's continental enemies began to join in, forcing the government to make extensive preparations for home defence. France's entry into the war early in 1778 provided the final stimulus necessary to raise the Militia in those English counties still in default, and Parliament passed further legislation for its regulation. The Militia Act of 1778 moved ever closer to the recognition of a separate and distinct force of Volunteers, for it not only empowered Militia battalions to accept Volunteers, as had been done in 1758, but it also offered a choice – the Volunteers were 'either to be incorporated into other companies, or to be formed into a distinct company'.[16] In the latter case they would also be commanded by their own officers. Although the Volunteers under this new Act were still not recognized as having an existence apart from the Militia, the permission to create their own distinct companies within it was an important precedent.

The following year (1779) the threat of an invasion from France led to yet another Militia bill as the government sought Parliament's authority to double the size of the Militia, then set at 30,000 men, by ballot. The ensuing debate produced a great range of opinions on the question of raising new forces by ballot or by volunteering. While Sir George Young wanted a return to the 'old tradition' of arming the whole country, General Burgoyne proposed arming the 'Yeomanry', and Earl Nugent hoped for a return to the 'traditional' expedient of Volunteers organized by county meetings as in 1745.[17] The Militia Act of 1779 as finally passed by Parliament suspended the compulsory ballot in favour of raising Volunteers who were to form additional companies to the existing Militia regiments. As in 1758 and 1778, these Volunteers were not to be independent of the Militia, but rather were to be formed for the express purpose of augmenting that force. Since they came under the regulations which governed the Militia, it was clear that they could not claim any of the privileges in training or of self-government which would be enjoyed by those whose services might be accepted by the government on the understanding that they were an independent corps of Volunteers. In the final result the augmentation of the Militia by Volunteer companies was a dismal affair – by March 1780 only fourteen companies had been raised. By the end of 1782 the Militia establishment totalled 37,178 rank and file, still wanting 3,009 to complete it.[18]

The number of Volunteers coming forward to form additional companies in the Militia might be few but many others offered their services in independent Volunteer corps. Spurred on by the threat of invasion from the combined fleets of France and Spain there were many spontaneous offers to raise subscriptions and to form Volunteer companies. The county of Middlesex and the City of Westminster together formed some 24 companies of Volunteers, each of 60 privates, the officers commissioned by the King. The deputy lieutenants and justices of the peace for the Tower Royalty followed suit with another 6 companies, and a further 4 companies (300 men) were formed by the 'Master Artificers employed under His Majesty's Board of Works and at Somerset House'. A group of London's leading merchants and bankers formed themselves into a troop of 'Light Horse Volunteers', 50 strong, for the protection of the city and immediate area. More Volunteer companies were found elsewhere, in areas under immediate threat of attack – 24 companies (about 1,400 men) in Devon, and later 17 companies (about 1,000 men) in Sussex for coastal defence. In the south and west, Volunteer Associations were formed for local defence. By the end of the year about 150 Volunteer companies had been raised.[19] Indeed at the peak of the crisis in July and August 1779 the government had been anxious to restrict the number of Volunteer corps, accepting only those approved by the Lords Lieutenant. While the parliamentary opposition immediately accused the government of arming only its political friends, the government itself faced something of a dilemma. Though ever fearful of arming the disaffected, government ministers found it awkward to refuse offers and were compelled to declare that there was 'no objection to any man's providing arms at his own expense and preparing himself by learning the Military Exercise for repelling any hostile attempt that might be made upon his coast. In such an emergency it is the duty of every good subject to arm himself in the best manner he is able, and be ready to assist Government in the Defence of his Country.'[20]

With the French fleet cruising along the south coast the crisis of 1779 reached its height. The Militia were hastily embodied and marched to the coast. The Volunteer companies were told to be ready to assist the army on the shortest notice and the public were advised by proclamation on the removal of all cattle and draught animals from threatened coastal areas. The crisis, however, was soon over, and by the end of the year the danger of invasion seemed so remote that most of the Volunteer companies were disbanded.

In Ireland the invasion scare of 1779 had carried affairs in a very different direction. With no Militia and no money to raise one, the panic had produced a spontaneous Volunteer movement. Brushing aside the British government's chronic distrust of any widespread arming of the Irish people, there emerged a full blown Volunteer army – cavalry, infantry and artillery – of as many as 40,000 men, overwhelmingly Protestant but including Catholics.[21] Nor was this United Army of Irish Volunteers in any mood simply to disband at the passing of the crisis. On the contrary they remained in being and used their presence and their great popularity to achieve political concessions from the British government. Despite an eventual decline in numbers after 1785 the Irish Volunteer Force continued in existence. In the 1790s, much revived through the republican climate generated by the French Revolution, the Volunteers were again able to make their voice heard in Irish politics. The movement was only checked by the creation of an effective Irish Militia and a general augmentation of Ireland's regular military establishment.

The emergence of a large Volunteer army in Ireland in the 1780s proved prophetic for the future of the Volunteer in Britain. In 1782 Lord Shelburne's Government passed an Act 'for the encouragement and disciplining of such corps or companies of men as shall voluntarily enrol themselves for the defence of their towns or coasts, or for the general defence of the Kingdom during the present war'. Concurrently a plan was circulated for the consideration of the principal towns, proposing that each might raise a battalion of infantry, to exercise regularly in spare time and to be called out only in the event of an invasion. It appeared that such battalions were to be raised by voluntary enlistment and were to be distinct from the existing Militia and the regular army. Reception of the plan was very mixed, some thinking it too dangerous to arm the urban poor, others wanting a simple augmentation of the Militia. Any serious test of such ideas was cut short by the sudden collapse of Shelburne's Government and the end of the war[22] – but they were soon to be revived. The next trial of Britain's strength was close at hand, and with it the final emergence of a distinct British Volunteer Force.

CHAPTER TWO

The French Wars, 1793–1815

True Volunteers

On 1 February 1793 the new revolutionary government of France declared war on Britain. Almost immediately the British government began receiving offers of voluntary service. Within the first three weeks the government had received 'a great number of letters . . . from different Persons residing chiefly upon the coast opposite to France, wherein they have signified their Readiness of embodying themselves in order to resist any incursions which may be attempted to be made by the Enemy . . .'. In London it was reported that 'In all the counties fronting the French coast, the Gentlemen are now mounting themselves on horseback, and are determined to act as a patrole [sic], to establish a chain of Communication and to defend their property against all attack'.[23] Requests for arms and accoutrements were granted and the first Volunteers began to form. The protracted struggle which ensued was hardly expected – more than twenty years of almost incessant warfare. In the course of this struggle, indeed almost from the outset, the Volunteer finally achieved unequivocal recognition as a separate class of soldier, distinct from the Militiaman and the regular soldier. There followed much debate on the proper role and composition of the Volunteer Force. In the years immediately after the great invasion scare of 1803, when the number of Volunteers greatly outnumbered both the Militia and the regular army, such considerations became acute.

From the start there were hopes to establish some control over the creation of Volunteer corps, based on precedents from the previous American war. But not until March 1794 was a definite plan proposed to the country's Lords Lieutenant. In an accompanying circular which suggested the desirability of opening county subscriptions to support the raising of auxiliary forces, the government noted its intention to follow former practice by adding Volunteers to the Militia (as individuals or in whole companies), to raise regiments of Fencible Cavalry ('Fencibles' being regulars who were raised for home defence duties only), and also to raise independent Volunteer corps for local defence, especially in the towns and in districts contiguous to the coast. In addition to the Fencible Cavalry, there were to be further mounted units consisting of 'Gentlemen and Yeomanry', or such persons as they could bring forward, to serve within a particular county or district. These mounted Volunteers were to be embodied in the event of an actual invasion, but were also to be liable to be called out to suppress local disorder and riot.[24]

Finally in April 1794 Parliament gave statutory sanction to a distinct Volunteer Force by passing an Act 'for encouraging and disciplining such corps or companies of men as shall voluntarily enrol themselves for the defence of their counties, towns, or coasts, or for the general defence of the Kingdom during the present war'.[25] The new Act's link with previous legislation on Volunteers was unmistakable, its title virtually identical to that passed in 1782 towards the end of the American war. But, whereas the Act of 1782 had produced only a few corps in the maritime counties, the results of the 1794 Act were very different. Running concurrently with Parliament's new Act to encourage and regulate the Volunteers was a new system of augmentation of the Militia by ballot. The two measures became closely related, for the creation of a substantial Volunteer Force, at the expense of the Militia, was given great impetus by expressly exempting Volunteers from Militia service if balloted. Already in May 1794 the War Office could list some thirty-two different mounted Yeomanry corps and a further seventy-two companies of Volunteers serving on foot as infantry or artillery.[26] Ironically, as will appear later, the first mounted Yeomanry corps to be formed under the new Act was not from a coastal county, but rather from the Midlands, from Rutland, England's smallest county. The offer of service made by the Earl of Winchelsea's three troops of 'Gentlemen and Yeomanry' from Rutland was recommended by the government as a model, and was quickly taken up in Kent and in Surrey. Within a few weeks there was hardly a county without its own corps of Volunteer cavalry.

Significantly, almost all of those offering to volunteer made reference to their intention to resist both the foreign and the domestic enemies of the state. Local security and the maintenance of order had always been prominent features of eighteenth-century volunteering, and the enrolment of Volunteers in 1794, though certainly precipitated by the military threat of a foreign power, had also a political flavour. Government supporters were prominent in the formation of many corps, denouncing French Jacobinism and striving to create a 'party of order' at the expense of their Radical opponents.[27]

The possibility of French coastal raids had been feared from the very outset of the war in 1793, and by the beginning of 1794 this had developed into a genuine fear of invasion. By the end of 1796 the government's military advisers felt an invasion very likely, and against a background of serious manpower shortages in the regular army, the government was most anxious to increase Britain's auxiliary forces for home defence. The creation of a Supplementary Militia and a Provisional Cavalry (to be based on a levy from all those who paid the horse tax of one horse in ten), were authorized by Parliament but produced very mixed results. The Supplementary Militia, although it did not reach its projected strength of 60,000 men, was deemed a success, but the Provisional Cavalry proved difficult to raise and almost impossible to train, its growth stunted by allowing voluntary troops of Yeomanry to count in making up the county quotas.[28] In the meantime the excitement caused by the landing of a small French force in Pembrokeshire the following February prompted the government to suggest, in March 1797, that each parish might form an Armed Association for local defence and security. The idea was well received, and at the same time a new wave of Volunteers came forward.

A year later, in April 1798, the threat of a French invasion reached a new pitch. The government, believing that drastic measures were needed, gave further encouragement to the creation of local forces by passing an Act 'for applying in the most expeditious manner, and with the greatest effect, the voluntary services of the King's loyal subjects for the defence of the Kingdom'. The avowed purpose of the Act was to give 'a general direction to the zeal of the country', drawing into service as many people as possible but still allowing for personal choice between armed or unarmed service. The principal result of the Act was the creation of more Armed Associations, a continuation of the process started in March 1797. This, however, was not the only result, for within weeks of passing the new Act the government was again receiving numerous offers of voluntary service. In particular there were now many offers from landowners and their tenantry to form corps of Yeomanry Cavalry in lieu of the compulsory levy for the Provisional Cavalry. By 1 June 1798 the strength of the Yeomanry and other Volunteer cavalry corps in Great Britian was claimed to be 19,190. By the end of 1800 the total was 24,000, with another 87,000 men (all ranks) serving in Volunteer infantry and artillery corps. These totals did not include those men enrolled in the parish Armed Associations.[29]

A peace was finally concluded with France in March 1802, and its ratification ended the services of the Volunteers and curtailed the Acts of Parliament under which they had been formed. The Peace of Amiens, however, was to prove only a brief respite, and the likelihood of renewed hostilities induced the government to be more hesitant than usual in cutting back the inflated strength of its wartime forces. Despite the peace, the government wished to continue the services of at least some of the Volunteer Corps, particularly the mounted ones. Quite apart from a long established belief in the utility of cavalry in repelling a foreign invader, the Yeomanry corps were proving a valuable force in controlling internal disorder. Nor was the example of the Irish Yeomanry in the rebellion of 1798 lost on government ministers. As early as August 1799 the Secretary for War, Henry Dundas, had been thinking of extending the services of the Yeomanry beyond the 'period of a general peace'.[30] In June 1802 Parliament passed legislation which permitted the King to retain the services of those Yeomanry and Volunteer corps which wished to continue, but only on condition that they serve without pay. According to Charles Yorke, the Home Secretary, it was his wish:

> . . . to see the spirit of valour flourish among our countrymen . . . [and] that every one of them should, as in the days of our ancestors, have his helmet and his sword suspended over his chimney ready to put on and his horse prepared to bear him against the first enemy that shall dare to invade his native land.[31]

The actual effect of the government's new Act was somewhat different. Although apparently wishing to encourage the Volunteers, at the same time the government sought to minimize any expense. Insistence on a no pay clause sharply reduced the number of Volunteer infantry corps willing, or able, to serve under such conditions. The mounted Yeomanry corps, most of which were already serving without pay, were less affected, but they too soon objected to plans to reduce their government allowances as well. The 'Public Spirit', warned Colonel Stevens of the Eastern Regiment of Somersetshire Yeomanry, had been pushed '. . . to the utmost, it would be unwise to drive it till it is exhausted'.[32] Some concessions followed, and by the end of the year the majority of the Yeomanry and of the Volunteer cavalry corps had offered to continue their service in accord with the Act of June 1802.

A Formidable Army?

By the end of March 1803 the renewal of hostilities looked very close, and the government embodied the Militia and again invited offers of voluntary service. Its position on pay for Volunteer corps was modified and government clerks were soon inundated with offers to renew old corps and form new ones, particularly from coastal areas which felt threatened. In May the war with France recommenced and Britons were again faced with the possibility of foreign invasion. The government took immediate steps to rebuild and expand the Volunteer Force. The result was an unparalleled number of Volunteers – a total of 380,000 in Great Britain and another 70,000 in Ireland – but it was a success gained only with considerable confusion and government embarrassment. In June the government laid down a code of regulations for Volunteers, defining service and pay – the 'June Allowances'. In July as part of its plans to co-opt as many people as possible into the defence preparations, Parliament passed a Levy en Masse Act, which in effect empowered the government to drill all able-bodied men regardless of their objections or preferences. As Lord Sheffield observed, the Act produced 'much disgust at the idea of being forced to exercise',[33] but in fact compulsion was not the government's true design. For, concurrently, great encouragement was given to Volunteers by pledging the suspension of the Act if enough men came forward to enrol in Volunteer corps. By mid-August the number enrolling in such corps reached the point where the King was authorized to suspend compulsory training. That same month a second, and quite different code of regulations, was ordered for Volunteer corps – the 'August Allowances'. There were then two different codes applicable to Volunteers, depending on when they had been formed, and to this confusion was added still more.

Having encouraged Volunteers by ordering a Levy en Masse, the government was soon swamped with offers. Caught off balance, the government then tried to limit the numbers of Volunteers allowed in each county to six times the strength of the old Militia. The uproar of complaint which followed quickly forced the government to change its course: all offers from Volunteers were to be accepted but those over the new quota were to be supernumeraries 'without any allowance of pay, arms or clothing and without claim to exemption from any ballot'.[34] In the counties there was much confusion over the government's intentions, and many would-be Volunteers were discouraged by lengthy delays in answering their offers of service.

Underlying such confusion was the fact that from 1803 until the final cessation of hostilities in 1815 successive governments, while fighting shy of outright conscription, laboured to find a balance between the regular forces needed for offensive action overseas and those forces required only for home defence. Government measures had to provide manpower for very different types of service, and confusion followed in the wake of parliamentary Acts and sets of instructions which ran simultaneously, seemed to cover the same ground, yet were aimed at raising forces for very different purposes. The Addington Government's new sets of Volunteer regulations, together with the Levy en Masse Act, were accompanied by an Army of Reserve Act (passed in June 1803), designed to create by ballot yet another force, not a part of the Militia, to provide recruits for the regular army.[35]

For government ministers trying to make the best use of available manpower, the very success of the Volunteers in producing an unprecedented number of armed men was itself a problem. According to returns in 1804 there were then in Great Britain 87,000 regulars, 80,000 Militiamen – and 343,000 Volunteers (mounted and on foot). To those advocating a stronger regular army and Militia, the success of Britain's 'new military system', the Volunteers, already seemed out of control. When the threat of invasion receded, criticism of the Volunteer Force soon followed. The Volunteers, by being exempt from serving in the Militia and the Army of Reserve, were thought to be hurting recruitment for both the Militia and the regular army. Indeed the army not only drew on the Army of Reserve but was also receiving substantial numbers of men from the Militia, if only sporadically in large batches.[36] The Volunteers had become an integral part of Britain's military organization and would have to be included in any solution to the manpower needs of the regular forces and the Militia.

Pitt took office for the last time in 1804. A Volunteer Consolidation Act of May 1804 brought some improvement in the regulation of the Volunteers themselves, but an attempt to bolster the regular army through the creation of yet another new force, the Permanent Additional Force, was a failure. The Permanent Additional Force Act merged the Army of Reserve and the Supplementary Militia, and compelled each parish to produce a quota of recruits (without a ballot), with the ultimate aim of supplying men to the regular army through second battalions of existing regiments. Neither the promise of a guinea for each man enlisted, nor the threat of a £20 fine for each man short, proved an adequate stimulus, and in May 1806, after Pitt's death, the Act was repealed. In twenty-three months only 13,000 men had been produced, far different from the 20,000 in two months originally hoped for.

During the summer of 1806, most of the Volunteer corps had been reported as fit to act alongside the regular army.[37] This proved to be the apogee of their achievements, for the new government, Grenville's 'Ministry of All the Talents', soon moved to dismantle much of what had been accomplished. William Windham, Secretary for War and the Colonies, had little sympathy for the Volunteers, though himself a

Volunteer colonel. In Parliament he castigated the Volunteers: they were excessively expensive, their exemption from the Militia service hurt both the Militia and the regular army, and they were useless as soldiers, 'painted cherries which none but simple birds would take for real fruit'.[38] Although hesitant to abolish the Volunteers outright, Windham nevertheless destroyed much that was good in the force in the name of economy, yet without the great savings predicted. Allowances were reduced and the system of Inspecting Field Officers, which had been so valuable in bringing the Volunteers to proficiency, was ended. Windham introduced a new General Training Act, by which he hoped to train all able-bodied men of military age, enrolling 200,000 men each year. He hoped the Volunteer Force could ultimately be dispensed with entirely.

Windham's Training Act proved unworkable and was never enforced, but the damage done to the Volunteers was considerable. From a strength of 330,116 in 1805, the number of Volunteers fell by 90,000 men to 240,000 effectives according to the last inspections of 1807. Nor was their state of discipline maintained. According to Viscount Castlereagh, Windham's successor in the new administration of the Duke of Portland, the Volunteers had become a 'fleeting and inapplicable mass'.[39] Castlereagh had much to repair and, most importantly, he was finally able to end much of the confusion which had persisted in the recruitment of Britain's land forces, particularly those for home defence. In so doing he set all of Britain's military forces on a firmer footing.

Castlereagh's first task was to strengthen the regular army, which he accomplished by procuring a large draft of volunteers from the Militia. In its turn the Militia was then replenished by a revival of the ballot, suspended during Windham's term of office. The task however could not stop there. Britain still relied heavily on the Volunteers for home defence and that very imperfect force would now have to be reorganized. Castlereagh's aim was to make good the diminished number of Volunteers by creating a new force – the Local Militia – which he intended would ultimately absorb the Volunteers. Enlistment was to be voluntary in the first instance, but where necessary the ballot would be used, but with no substitutes allowed – a significant departure from all previous legislation to raise Militiamen. As soon as the Local Militia was brought into being, in 1808, pressure was put on the Volunteers. Volunteer corps were invited to transfer bodily into the new force in return for a bounty of two guineas per man, and inefficient corps were now disbanded and swept into the ballot. In March 1809 the bounty was abolished and in June the Volunteers were given a further push when they were told they could expect no further clothing allowances from the government.[40]

After one year there were already 250 regiments in the new Local Militia. The force consisted of 195,161 men, of whom 125,000 had transferred from Volunteer corps. From 1809 the number of Volunteers dwindled, until in March 1812 the strength of the Volunteer Force (all arms) was reported as only 68,643 effective rank and file, some 30,000 below establishment. The following year, in March 1813, the Volunteer infantry corps, with only a few exceptions, were dissolved, their weapons being required to arm the Prussians in their renewed struggle against Napoleon.[41] But the Yeomanry, the mounted arm of the Volunteer Force, still numbering some 19,207 rank and file in 1812, was left untouched.

A Nation in Arms

Such Volunteers as were raised in 1745, 1759 or 1779 had been quickly disbanded, but those raised during the final great struggle with France (1793–1815) not only came out in unprecedented numbers but also remained ready for active service for a much longer period of time. Perhaps one man in five served in some branch of the nation's armed forces during that conflict, and in the early years of the nineteenth century the decided majority of them did so in Volunteer corps.

The vast numbers of men serving as Volunteers in the early nineteenth century were drawn from every social group and occupation. To counter the menace of a French invasion, the government appealed to all citizens and made deliberate efforts to secure the active support of as many as possible. The Armed Associations of 1798 appeared at the instigation of government and were to include all 'householders' – quite unlike the Defence Associations of the 1740s which had been raised through local initiative and run by town corporations. Proposals for Associations and Volunteer corps came from all levels of society, from Flintshire miners and from London lawyers. Indeed the social distance between companies of the same corps could be marked. Lord Sheffield's proposed 'Legion' for the Northern Division of the Rape of Pevensey offered a fair cross-section of local society. The Legion was to consist of a rifle company composed of 'Upwards of seventy persons of property in the large parish of Rother-field'; another company, of skirmishers, was 'to be formed from Ashdown Forest and of Smugglers, Poachers . . . and unsightly men', and eight battalion companies were to be formed of men whose low status would make it necessary to supply them with uniforms, without which 'they will not be respectable in their own eyes, nor will the Gentlemen like to serve with them'. In addition there were to be two troops of cavalry whom Sheffield wished to be made up only from those who 'can afford to mount, clothe, and equip themselves'.[42]

The need for internal security, social control and the fear of domestic rebellion encouraged those of superior social status to take up arms as Volunteers, just as they had in the 1740s. The Duke of Richmond noted that his Volunteer corps of Sussex Light Horse Artillery was particularly useful 'for the preservation of internal order', and since it had been raised in 1798 'nothing like tumult has been seen, to which there had before appeared some disposition in this neighbourhood'. Lord Sheffield's North Pevensey Legion was required to keep in check that 'bad breed of Smugglers, Poachers, Foresters, and Farmers' Servants, who, in the case of confusion, are more to be dreaded than the march of a French Army . . .'.[43] But underlying everything was the fear of invasion, which in 1803–5 reached a peak, eventually bringing out an unparalleled number of Volunteers. Attack seemed imminent and the gravity of the situation without equal. Napoleon's insatiable lust for conquest and the unspeakable excesses of previous French campaigns were expounded to the full in the most lurid imagery.

National pride and a determined resolution to resist motivated many of those who enrolled as Volunteers, but the appeal of voluntary service could also be one of cynical self-interest. In 1803 there was no spontaneous rush to arms. Rather it was the government's Levy en Masse, which by threatening to make military service compulsory, encouraged men to choose the more compatible alternative of becoming Volunteers. In 1799 an officer of the Surrey Militia reported that enrolment in the county's Volunteers was mainly just a way of assuring escape from the Militia service.[44] Volunteering not only gained a man an exemption if balloted, but could also be cheaper than hiring a substitute. Moreover the government also offered immunity from the annual hair powder tax, and if a mounted Volunteer, from the horse tax. The exemption of the Volunteer from other forms of compulsory service remained a strong inducement to become one, though in fairness it should also be acknowledged that there were some Volunteer corps (about 7,000 men in all) who gave up the exemption of their own accord.[45]

The ideal Volunteer Force for both Windham and Castlereagh was one composed 'of a higher class of life, of such description of men as it would not be proper to mix with soldiers of the Line, and whom no one would wish to see obliged to serve in the condition of a common soldier in a regular regiment'. Such Volunteer corps would be chiefly confined 'to the great towns and populous manufacturing districts' and would 'naturally consist of persons in business, and in easy circumstances, who will resort to these corps to escape service in other modes less consistent with their habits and avocations'.[46] Such ideals however were never attained. From the start it was believed that the Volunteer Force was hurting army recruitment by 'locking up' too many of the 'artisan and peasant classes'. The 'right and proper spirit' of the first Volunteers 'dwindled down to little else than exemption from other services'. As those of better education and higher social standing dropped out, the force increasingly recruited lower down the social scale, taking in even greater numbers of artisans and labourers. One disgruntled gentleman described what he felt had happened in Norwich:

> When the volunteers were first raised, I subscribed like other people, as it was conceived that the subscribers were to bear all the expense; and numbers of people enrolled themselves. But when pay was allowed, a new set of men joined, who found that when work was short the Volunteers' pay, added to casual employment, would enable them to live. Half of them are rank revolutionists. Half of them meet in a court at the back of my house, where I hear them damning the King and Parliament. They command their officers and declare openly they will do what they please.[47]

Mounted corps, true to the pattern of their eighteenth century predecessors, were substantially different from those which served on foot, and, from the government's viewpoint, more reliable. The rural based Yeomanry Force was officered by the local aristocracy and landed gentry, the rank and file being provided by their tenant farmers and other small landowners. More precisely, the other ranks consisted 'in most of the Yeomanry Troops, of the younger Brothers, sons and Servants of Farmers who were not in business'. This allowed for a certain flexibility, making the force more available than might have been the case otherwise. By contrast, the rank and file of the Duke of Richmond's troop of Yeomanry artillery was composed principally of his own 'Tenants or neighbours, themselves using considerable Farms or being reputable Tradesmen who could not leave their occupation and were therefore obliged to confine their services within the limit of the County round them'.[48] The social background and circumstances of the Yeomanry could therefore be quite different from that of the Volunteer infantry corps, and set them very much apart from those they were often called upon to police.

Service on Terms

The first terms of service offered by Parliament to Volunteer corps and local Associations, in April 1794, were generous, and would not be repeated. The government undertook to supply a basic set of clothing, arms and accoutrements or, in lieu of these, allowances where corps furnished their own. Officers and men were to be entitled to pay for the two days per week that their corps were to assemble for training. For non-commissioned officers and private men this meant two shillings per week for two days' exercise, six hours each day. In addition the government allowed constant pay for one sergeant-instructor per company or troop. If called out on actual service (in event of an invasion, or to quell local disorders), they were to be subject to military discipline and were to be paid at the same rate as the regular forces. The Act of 1794 also gave Volunteers an exemption from Militia service on their producing a certificate of attendance at their corps' drills for the six weeks prior to the hearing of appeals against the Militia lists.[49]

A few corps, both infantry and cavalry, chose service without pay or assistance of any kind, but most accepted the government's offer of pay and various allowances. Nonetheless, self-help was a prominent feature of the Volunteer corps raised during the wars with France, as it would be again in the Volunteer Force created in 1859–60. Complete self-sufficiency was exceptional – the wealthy and prestigious Light Horse Volunteers of London and Westminster, according to admirers, were turned out 'at the sole expense of the individual, in a manner complete without parallel in any corps that perhaps ever existed in the world.'[50] Typically, Volunteer corps were supported by raising public subscriptions, a process very familiar to communities which had frequently to provide services which national government or the local authorities could not. Men of wealth and some community standing were prominent among those who subscribed, and such corps were run by the subscribers, usually by a committee of the wealthiest members.

Although the Act of 1794 had given the King the authority to employ the Volunteers as he chose in the event of an invasion or internal disorders, it gave no indication on the conditions of service, beyond stating that the force had certain entitlements to pay and would be subject to military discipline if called out. No mention was made of the geographic area in which corps might be required to serve, and most were quick to confine their activities to their immediate locality only. The very restricted areas of service indulged in by most Volunteer corps rendered much of the Volunteer Force quite useless for national defence. To correct this, while at the same time cutting back its expenditure on Volunteer corps, the government introduced new legislation in April 1798. Corps raised before 17 January 1798 continued as they were, but all new corps, both infantry and cavalry, were to enjoy certain advantages of pay, clothing allowance and Militia exemption only by extending their service to the whole of the military district (several adjacent counties) they were in. The allowances were not nearly as generous as before and, to make further savings, the new corps were to be paid for only one day's exercise (of only three hours) per week. Subsequently the allowances were increased, but even so there could be a considerable margin between the allowances and what was actually spent, at least in middle-class corps. Nonetheless many corps forwent all allowances and pay, and as a further gesture of patriotism some even sent money to help the government in defraying defence costs.[51]

All told, volunteering could still be made a fairly soft option, and the Volunteer corps were frequently criticized as merely havens for those wishing to escape Militia service. The cost to the individual could still be less than the price of buying a Militia substitute to serve in his place should he be balloted and the training requirements were minimal. From 1798 it was possible for a corps which had been certified by an Inspecting General Officer as sufficiently disciplined, to dispense with the minimum drill requirement yet still draw pay (even for sick members), this indulgence to continue for as long as the corps had favourable inspection reports (to be done every three months).[52]

The Peace of Amiens in 1802 brought the service of most of the Volunteers to an end. The government invited those corps which so wished to continue to serve, but only on the understanding that they would receive no pay from the government. Such conditions fell with less severity on the Yeomanry and Volunteer cavalry (as most were already serving without pay) than on the Volunteer infantry: the majority of the cavalry continued in service, but comparatively few of the infantry corps. The cavalry's allowances were trimmed further (though not as much as the government would have wished), but in 1803, as the renewal of conflict came closer, the government relented and became more generous. Volunteer corps were reformed, their services being offered upon a great variety of conditions, some accepting pay and allowances, others not, or only in part; nor was there any consistency in their other conditions of service. Government attempts to bring in regulations at first created only further chaos. The June Allowances, followed by the August Allowances, added their own muddle to the confusion by making two different sets of conditions depending on when a corps was raised. To make matters worse, the government's attempts to cut expenditure made the distinctions completely irrational. While those corps on the June Allowances were to be supplied with an adjutant and a permanent instructor, and were to be paid on the basis of eighty-five days' training per year; they could only be ordered to serve within their own military district. But those on the August Allowances, who were denied an allowance for an adjutant and a permanent instructor, and were to be paid for only twenty days, could be ordered to serve anywhere in the Kingdom. Thus it appeared that the least efficient part of the Volunteer Force could be deployed at will wherever needed, but their better trained comrades could not.[53]

The Volunteer Consolidation Act, passed in June 1804 after lengthy debate and many alterations, helped to clarify the regulations and to amend previous legislation, but the Volunteer soldier's terms of service remained a complicated matter.[54] Only in 1806 were the June Allowances effectively swept away in Windham's efforts to reshape the Volunteers. Training allowances were cut, and the number of days drill required was to be twenty-six, to include days of inspection. Nor did Windham offer any guarantee of clothing or pay for the future. His successor Castlereagh restored some of the Volunteers' lost allowances, but his real interest was the creation of a new force, the Local Militia, which he hoped would ultimately supplant the Volunteers. The terms of service in the new force required men to serve for four years, doing twenty-eight days' training each year, either in their own or a neighbouring county. They could be called upon to suppress riots, but not for more than fourteen days' duty, all of which would count towards their annual training time. On assembling for exercise the Local Militiamen would be entitled to one guinea the first year and another guinea in subsequent years for necessaries, and to a further guinea if called out or embodied.[55]

As intended the new Local Militia regiments absorbed a large number of Volunteers, and many of those who declined to transfer were soon disbanded. In March 1813 almost all of the remaining infantry corps were dissolved and, apart from a handful of survivors, only the mounted arm of the Volunteer Force, the Yeomanry, remained. Significantly, new measures were introduced to increase its efficiency. Faced with serious domestic unrest the government, more than ever, appreciated the value of a force which was effective in police work.

CHAPTER THREE

Keeping The Peace, 1795–1870

In the first half of the nineteenth century, Britain not infrequently experienced serious public riot and disorder. Food shortages, rising prices, fluctuating wages, unemployment and, later, agitation for political reform brought together angry and often violent crowds. In a period of quickening industrialism and economic change, workers in the domestic handicraft industries, such as handloom weaving, framework knitting and wool combing, experienced chronic distress and suffered severely from the cyclical depressions which affected the economy. These workers in particular played a prominent part in the unrest, but they were hardly the only working people to be roused to action. Farm labourers, miners, boat hauliers and others also gave vent to their frustration, and to them were added those demanding political reform, most notably the Chartists in the 1830s and 1840s. The period 1811–17, during which the Luddite disturbances convulsed the Midlands, saw the worst effects of economic dislocation and produced the most serious problems of public order. By contrast the disturbances of the Chartist era were far less destructive. Unlike the deliberate machine breaking of the Luddites, much of the disorder of the late 1830s and 1840s was that caused by tumultuous demonstrations and meetings – this was especially true of the Chartist troubles of 1838–40 and 1848.[56]

To police such outbreaks the state had only very imperfect resources. It was completely dependent on the initiative of those who were actually on the spot. The burden of maintaining order fell on local magistrates who were expected to act in person, mustering a sufficient force and leading it to the scene of disorder. But the civil forces available to magistrates – a motley combination of local residents acting as petty or parish constables, Special Constables and 'armed associations' – were completely incapable of dealing with large-scale disruption. In the 1840s, copying the example of London, professional police forces began to appear, but apart from the borough police in a handful of the largest towns, these new provincial police forces made little impact on the difficulties of controlling large, unruly, and possibly violent crowds. Confronted with serious problems of public order, magistrates frequently felt they had only one recourse – to military force.

Military assistance was available from several sources – the regular army, the Militia and the Volunteer forces – and after 1843 a force of Enrolled Pensioners (former soldiers) was also available. The army bore the brunt of requests for aid, supported by the Militia and the Volunteers, neither of which were themselves always reliable as agents of law and order. The Volunteers, especially in the south-west, had proved particularly unreliable during the food rioting in the 1790s and in 1800–1. After the Napoleonic Wars, however, assistance from the Militia, which retained only a skeleton staff, or from the Volunteer infantry corps, almost all of which were disbanded, was negligible. Of the auxiliary forces this left only the mounted Volunteers, the Yeomanry, as an effective aid to the civil power.

Although military in character, the Yeomanry was normally under the direction of the civil authorities. The Home Secretary, not the War Office, decided on its annual strength, and it was his approval which was necessary for any change to the normal routine of once yearly assemblies for six days of permanent duty and an inspection. Yeomanry corps could be ordered into neighbouring counties to counter unrest only on the direction of the Home Office, though for short periods of time this authority might be conferred directly on the military commanders of districts subject to disturbance. At county level the Yeomanry was directly under the control of the Lord Lieutenant. He signed Yeomanry commissions and his authority was required for calling out the various county troops in time of trouble – though in practice his consent might only be formal, in effect allowing the magistrates to call out their local troop directly.[57]

Unlike the Militia, the Yeomanry was a purely voluntary force, officered by the landed gentry and aristocracy and relying heavily for its rank and file on tenant farmers and small landowners. Several local troops, each about 70 men, together formed a county regiment or corps, which nationwide gave a total Yeomanry force of 17,818 in 1817 and 14,274 in 1838. But the geographical distribution of the Yeomanry was far from even. Increasingly as the nineteenth century progressed, the strength of the force came to lie in the Midlands and in the western counties, from the mouth of the Mersey to the borders of Devon and

Cornwall. The Yeomanry were not numerous in the east, the south-east (with the exception of Kent), Wales, or the north (with the exception of Yorkshire and Northumberland). The manufacturing districts of the Midlands possessed a relatively strong body of Yeomanry. In the 1830s Staffordshire, Warwickshire and Worcestershire could muster a total of 25 troops (a force of 1,886 men), while Derbyshire, Leicestershire and Nottinghamshire possessed 20 troops, or 1,450 men. Elsewhere the presence of the Yeomanry might be little noticed: Lancashire could call on only 3 troops (171 men), yet the county's population was larger than that of Staffordshire, Warwickshire and Worcestershire combined. In 1839 Co Durham, important for its mining, did not possess a single troop of Yeomanry, nor did the counties of South Wales (with the exception of Pembrokeshire), scene of the Newport Rising and of the Rebecca Riots (1842). The Yeomanry made an important contribution to the maintenance of public order, but their importance must not be exaggerated. They were not the foundation of every county's defences. In 1828 many rural Yeomanry corps were disbanded in the very counties later affected by the Swing Riots of 1830–1. The principal duties of public order were generally carried out by the regular army.[58]

For dealing with riotous mobs and the policing of large crowds the Yeomanry had many advantages. They were mounted, well armed, reasonably well trained, and were subject to military discipline while acting on public order duties. Like the regular cavalry they were highly mobile, and were available for service anywhere within their county, or in neighbouring counties if needed. But there were also serious disadvantages. Embodying the Yeomanry for service cost the government money, an expense which could be avoided (at least as far as their subsistence was concerned) if regular soldiers were used in their place. There were difficulties if the Yeomanry had to be called out at times which were inconvenient to the farmers of whom it was largely composed. But most importantly it was felt that the presence of the Yeomanry too often exasperated people and tended of itself to produce trouble. On occasions of public disturbance the use of the local Yeomanry seemed to create more animosity than using the regular army, a fact which Lord John Russell attributed to the local connections of the Yeomanry giving them the character of interested parties in disputes. Furthermore it was believed, on the basis of a quite undeserved reputation for savagery which stemmed from the bloody affray of Peterloo in 1819, that the Yeomanry were 'over zealous for cutting and slashing' – a factor which seemed to heighten the intensity of any confrontation, at times subjecting the Yeomanry to particularly vicious treatment. In fact there was often a great reluctance to be involved, the

Yeomanry frequently showing great restraint despite much provocation.[59]

It was not government policy to encourage a too frequent or protracted use of the Yeomanry in the suppression of civil disturbances, but despite this the Yeomanry were frequently called out to assist the civil power. The original conditions of their engagement in 1794 stipulated that Yeomanry corps could be embodied to police 'riots and tumults', and they were soon called out in various parts of England to deal with bread rioting and other disturbances, including the mutinous behaviour of some Militiamen. The Luddite disorders, which lasted intermittently for seven years from March 1811, required frequent and often extended service from the Midlands' Yeomanry corps, acting with detachments from the Militia and the regular army. Yeomanry troops in the west of England were also called out to deal with unrest and rioting, the continuing trouble of these years finally resulting in the Peterloo 'massacre' at Manchester in July 1819. Soon after, owing to the general atmosphere of political unrest, the existing Yeomanry corps were augmented and new corps formed. Incidents of riot and violence among miners and other workers in the Midlands again demanded the attention of local troops of Yeomanry in the 1820s, and in 1824 the entire force offered voluntarily to place themselves on permanent duty. Three years later however, the government, hoping to cut its expenditure, decided to disband all Yeomanry corps which had 'very seldom or never' been called out in support of the civil powers over the preceding ten years. Early in 1828 some twenty-four regiments of Yeomanry were disbanded, most of them to be reconstituted only two years later when trouble flared in the rural areas of the south and west of England.[60]

Civil strife and political agitation continued to plague British society in the 1830s and 1840s. The defeat of the Reform Bill in 1831 sparked off a series of riots, the worst being three days of fire and pillage in Bristol. Other disturbances followed sporadically throughout the 1830s: disorders by boat hauliers on the Severn, election rioting at Frome and in the Staffordshire Potteries. In the West Country, the North Devon Yeomanry varied its usual duties with the occasional stint on 'Wreck Protection Duty', guarding the cargoes of wrecked or stranded vessels from looters. The Yeomanry and the regular army were frequently called in, magistrates perhaps too often tending to over-react, feeling secure only when supported by a strong military presence. Nevertheless, early in 1838, on the very eve of the Chartist troubles, the Yeomanry were again the subject of government retrenchment, their total strength being cut by a quarter. The result was a legacy of disaffection in the minds of many Yeomanry officers, whose uncompromising Toryism did not commend them to the Whig government and its supporters. The reductions, being mostly in the rural areas of southern England, did little to weaken the forces which confronted the Chartists, but not surprisingly General Napier, commanding the military forces in the Midlands, found the local Yeomanry apathetic and uncooperative in the spring of 1839, at precisely the time when their assistance was again needed.[61]

The Chartist troubles of 1839 did encourage the government to suggest the formation of local voluntary associations 'for the protection of life and property', but confusion and misunderstanding wrecked any chance of success. In May 1839, when the officers and men of an extinct Yorkshire Yeomanry corps offered their services they were told that 'associations of a military character' were not intended; apparently the government wished only for a civil force akin to Special Constables.[62] Offers to form Volunteer rifle corps were similarly rejected. The government's suggestion bore little fruit, though voluntary horse patrols did appear in 1842 with official blessing. The Yeomanry, however, were soon redeemed, at least to the extent that the disturbances of 1842 (again inflamed by the Chartists and other agitators) clearly demonstrated their value in dealing with civil strife and caused the government to reverse its policy of cutting the Yeomanry's strength. By the end of 1842 it was decided to increase the force by 950 men, exclusive of officers. This was achieved by restoring to the permanent establishment six troops which had been serving gratuitously since 1838, and also by forming new troops in the north, in the Midlands and in Scotland. In 1850, however, further troops were lost in eastern and south-eastern England, bringing the total Yeomanry force in that year to 13,676 men, slightly below its strength in 1839.[63]

Throughout the 1840s the Yeomanry continued to play a role as an aid to the civil power. The widespread industrial strikes and rioting of 1842, which found the Yeomanry heavily committed in the Midlands, were followed in subsequent years by scattered troubles of a less serious nature. After 1848, the year of the last great Chartist meeting, the number of occasions on which the Yeomanry acted in this capacity dropped sharply, and by the close of the 1850s the Yeomanry had performed their last duties in the maintenance of public order.[64] In contrast to the Yeomanry's active service in the first half of the century, the last decades of the nineteenth century were uneventful. Lack of active employment, however, did not result in wholesale disbandment. The Yeomanry had carried forward, from the days of Napoleon, an unbroken tradition of the local Volunteer, and if there was now peace at home, there were still foreign enemies, and it was fear of hostile intentions from abroad which ensured the continuation of the Volunteer tradition. While the Yeomanry settled into a comfortable niche in county society and enjoyed a domestic tranquillity which made them less controversial, there emerged, quite without precedent in time of peace, a new force of Volunteers – the Rifle Volunteers, considered by many as the wonder of the age.

CHAPTER FOUR

Volunteers and Territorials, *c.* 1850–1914

The Rebirth of the Volunteers

The years 1859–60 witnessed the sudden and quite unexpected rebirth of a large Volunteer Force, consisting principally of infantry and artillery. The spontaneity, wide appeal and size of the new movement, in a time of peace, impressed contemporaries, who were certain that some future historian would 'record the formation of the Volunteers as one of the most remarkable events in the century'.[65] Perhaps even more surprising was the survival of this new Volunteer Force, through many changes, into the twentieth century.

The new enthusiasm for volunteering was sparked by French hostility after an attempt on the life of Napoleon III by an Italian refugee who had connections with England. But the resulting invasion scare of 1859 was also the third of three 'panics' to have stirred the British public since 1848. The underlying cause of these successive scares was an anxious and growing worry over French interest and activity in new technological advances which from 1840 promised to revolutionize naval warfare. The simultaneous development of steam power, the screw propeller, rifled ordnance and armour plate appeared as a direct challenge to the superiority of Britain's navy, and a successful invasion of Britain, regardless of the Royal Navy's best efforts, loomed as a distinct possibility. Such fears were fed by a constant stream of invasion literature and much exacerbated by pessimistic military assessments offered by such eminent authorities as the Duke of Wellington and Sir John Fox Burgoyne.

To make good Britain's military weakness and to secure her from invasion, many urged the creation of Volunteer corps, but this 'popular' solution was not readily accepted by the government or the army. Instead they lay emphasis on augmenting the regular army, improving fortifications and renewing the Militia (which in 1852 was revived by a new Militia Act). The public clamour for Volunteers was hardly new, even if much louder than previously. Periodically from the end of the Napoleonic Wars until the 1850s there had been offers to form Volunteer infantry corps as measures of public security, but these had almost all been rejected by the government as an inappropriate way to handle domestic disorder. Nonetheless a few corps, such as the Duke of Cumberland's Sharpshooters (formed in 1803), had continued to meet, if only infrequently and more in the nature of clubs than military units. But there had also been some isolated examples of Volunteer corps which had received official recognition: a corps at Salisbury and one at Uxbridge (but both disbanded by 1842). In the early 1850s the government seemed more favourably disposed, and accepted the services of an Exeter and South Devon Corps and the Victoria Rifle Corps (started in 1835 as the Victoria Rifle Club), both formed with an eye to preserving domestic order. In addition a number of rifle clubs, some with paramilitary features, had also come into existence, and through the 1850s an increasing number of enthusiasts, most notably Hans Busk, Alfred Richards and Nathaniel Bousfield, advocated the creation of a new Volunteer Force for home defence. In 1859 the popular press, particularly *The Times*, gave widespread publicity to the idea, and the government reluctantly accepted the Volunteers as a convenient and cheap solution to popular agitation, feeling confident that their enthusiasm would be short-lived.[66]

Accordingly, in May 1859, the Secretary of State for War sent out a circular authorizing the creation of Volunteer corps, the provisions for which were taken directly from the former Volunteer Consolidation Act of 1804. At first there seemed to be only a mild response but this changed suddenly in the early winter of 1859 when renewed alarm over French intentions and the exhortation of *The Times* produced a rush of enthusiasm, which was further encouraged the following year by royal patronage and a grand review in London. By 1 October 1860 the new Volunteer Force had enrolled some 119,146 men. According to the *Annual Register* of that year, this 'self-planted institution outgrew first the conception of the government, and then the anticipations of its own most ardent advocates . . . .'.[67]

The new Rifle Volunteer Movement spread to every part of Great Britain, but the enthusiasm for creating Volunteer corps was hardly uniform. The greatest support for the new force was in Scotland, particularly in the Highlands, where an average of 5 per cent of all males aged 15 to 49 years were enrolled in 1862. Least enthusiastic were those living in the Midlands, where only 1.8 per cent of the male population came forward. In most regions the proportion of males serving as Volunteers remained relatively constant to the end of the century, though by 1881 London and the south-eastern counties had relinquished their primacy in Volunteer recruiting in England and Wales to the counties of the south-west.[68]

The majority of men joining the new force enrolled as infantrymen, but there was also a substantial artillery branch. Far less numerous were those who chose to serve as light horse, mounted rifles or engineers. Early enthusiasts visualized a self-sufficient force, 'a second Army, homogeneous in itself and complete in all its branches, but differing entirely in composition and stamp from the Regular Army',[69] but their vision was never to be realized. Any concept of a self-sufficient force was quickly eroded as the government, very reluctantly at first, took on increasingly heavy financial obligations towards the arming, clothing and training of the Volunteers.

Government expenditure on the force rose from £3,000 in 1860 to £627,200 by 1897.[70] In return the government insisted on better organization, stricter control and greater efficiency. As the Volunteers became more dependent on government money, so government control became more rigorous. Already in 1860 the force was being organized into battalions, either 'consolidated' battalions in which companies in close proximity to each other were combined (as in large towns), or 'administrative' battalions which drew together the scattered corps of rural areas for administration only. The club-like atmosphere of the earliest days, when members drew up their own rules and officers were elected, was eventually replaced by stricter military discipline and a closer identification with the regular army.

The social origins of the Rifle Volunteers can be discussed in some detail.[71] Much of the original inspiration behind the Rifle Volunteer movement was founded on the notion that the middle classes of society should have a recognized place in the nation's military forces. The growth of cities and towns had produced a large, and ever increasing, urban middle class but the composition of neither the army, the Militia nor the Yeomanry reflected this fairly. In 1857 the Royal Commission on Purchase had pointed out that the middle classes had 'no place in the British Army under the present system'.[72] The regular army drew a disproportionately large number of its officers from aristocratic and landed families, while the rank and file were predominantly lower working class. The Militia was not so very different, while the Yeomanry was virtually restricted to the landed and farming communities, who alone could afford and manage the upkeep of horses and equipment.

The Rifle Volunteers sought to rectify this imbalance by creating a force which would be essentially middle class, both officers and other ranks. The Rifle Volunteer corps of 1859–60 were clearly intended to be rather exclusive military clubs 'maintaining that exclusiveness by the sheer barrier of expense'.[73] Membership was further restricted by rules on the proposing and seconding of prospective members. However, the initial pattern of middle class participation varied considerably between urban and rural corps, and different again were those who formed mounted corps. Landed interests were not excluded, but the leadership in urban corps came predominantly from professional men, particularly those of the commercial and financial world. In London the level of participation from the educational, medical and clerical professions was even higher. To fill the other ranks in the larger urban areas there was usually a dependence upon clerks, less so on tradesmen. Most metropolitan units appear to have relied on a strong core of lower middle class other ranks. By contrast the rural corps, usually formed in the smaller provincial towns, often drew their highest proportion of officers from the legal profession, and their rank and file predominantly from the local tradesmen, mainly shopkeepers, with a sprinkling of craftsmen. In most cases, units in rural areas were concentrated in the small market towns, due both to the physical difficulty of securing recruits from a widespread farming community and to the inability of agricultural labourers to find either the time or the money to take part. But in some rural areas, a corps might also be raised from the tenantry of a local landowner of great prestige and influence, in the same fashion as had been done earlier in the century during the French wars. Tenantry corps were formed by both the Duke of Northumberland and the Duke of Rutland during the Napoleonic Wars and again in the Victorian era.[74]

Some Volunteers, believing that a force of mounted riflemen would be a more useful auxiliary to their colleagues on foot than the long established Yeomanry, proceeded to form units of Light Horse Volunteers. Farming and hunting communities were the obvious recruiting grounds, the new force lodging itself somewhere above the status of Rifle Volunteers, yet offering a considerably cheaper and less socially exclusive force than the Yeomanry, with whom they nevertheless came into competition. The Light Horse Volunteers never attracted a large number of men and by the mid 1870s most of the original units had disappeared, their costs proving prohibitive to recruits.[75]

The middle-class ideals of the original rifle corps enthusiasts were never fully realized. From the very beginning there were conscious efforts to involve some members of the working class, and purely artisan corps came into existence from the start, the majority in the great urban centres, but also in rural areas (drawn usually from small localized industries). By 1862 over half of the Rifle Volunteer Force were drawn from the working class, predominantly from the upper working class – men who described themselves as mechanics and artisans. The trend continued, the Volunteer Force not only becoming mostly working class (70 per cent of the rank and file in 1904), but its recruits younger in years (17 to 25), and staying in the force for much shorter periods of time, perhaps only three years or less. As time progressed, the Volunteer Force was recruiting lower down the social scale, and the social composition of the rank and file began to converge with that of the regular army and the Militia. According to the *Volunteer Service Gazette*, by 1877 the middle class had simply 'melted away'. Time and other interests were crucial considerations for middle-class recruits and there had been a 'spontaneous extinction of the enthusiasm which had led those men to join'.[76]

Diminishing middle-class support also resulted in a chronic shortage of officers. Finding suitable candidates was a problem of long standing in the auxiliary forces. It had plagued the Militia throughout the eighteenth century and had troubled the Napoleonic Volunteers as well. The Victorian Volunteer Force was no different. As upper middle class elements dropped out it became more difficult to find proper officers. Of necessity men in trade, who might previously have aspired to non-commissioned rank only, had to be accepted for commissions. The commitment of time and the personal expense (for the gap between government grants and actual expenditure fell on the officers) were hardly attractive, while the public image of the Volunteer officer was soon held up to ridicule for alleged low breeding and professional incompetence.[77] As one Surrey captain remarked: 'Society demands consistency. It cannot assimilate the social rank of an officer in Her Majesty's service with one who serves beer over a public house counter, or measures you for a suit of clothes in his shirt sleeves.'[78] The shortage of officers was a serious problem; not only did it affect discipline but some corps simply ceased to exist because of it.

In November 1859 the Mayor of Leicester, addressing the local Volunteers, ascribed 'the highest and purest patriotism' as the motive behind their coming forward to enrol. Many contemporaries would have agreed, but despite the many public pronouncements throughout the existence of the Volunteer Force, it was not patriotism alone which induced men to become Volunteers – and the Volunteers themselves said

so. Patriotism was by no means absent; it was an unmistakable ingredient in the creation of the Volunteer Force, and would be again in the
recruiting surge during the South African War, and in other periods of
crisis as well. And where patriotism was not itself a cause of enrolment,
it might yet prove a consequence of serving. Nevertheless, critics of the
force claimed that the men who joined were social climbers in search of
respectability, attracted by the uniform and military vainglory. While
this might not be dismissed entirely, it would seem unlikely to have been
of importance in later years when volunteering does not appear to have
conferred any superior social distinction at all. But there were other very
good reasons why a man might become a Volunteer. The Volunteers
offered a wide variety of recreational and social activities, with a strong
admixture of patriotism. Rifle shooting was the key recreational attraction of the Volunteer Force (indeed the National Rifle Association had
been established concurrently with the force to encourage and sustain
that interest), but shooting alone was not the sole attraction: competition
prizes were offered in abundance. Drill too was seen more as an
amusement after work than a hardship. The field days and annual camps
were also popular, but there was much more in addition. Cricket, golf
and especially football were offered, as well as the sociable com-
panionship of the corps' club, refreshment and reading rooms.[79]
Patriotism undoubtedly played a part in recruitment, but it was the offer
of a wide variety of recreational and social activities that sustained the
Volunteer Force in the face of much criticism and ridicule of its military
potential.

The middle-class origins of the Victorian Volunteer Force meant that
becoming a Volunteer was not a light undertaking. Members received no
pay, but were themselves expected to pay a subscription and bear the
cost of uniform, arms and accoutrements. Such costs could be prohibitive, especially for working class recruits, and so various schemes were
tried to make easier terms for those who could not afford them: reduced
subscriptions, no entrance fees, instalment payments, special individual
assistance and public appeals for funds were all tried. Finally in 1863 the
government was persuaded to offer financial assistance to the Volunteer
Force. Following the recommendations of a Royal Commission of the
previous year, an annual capitation grant was offered to the corps for
each Volunteer, based on the amount of drill, musketry instruction and
exercise which had been undertaken. To earn the basic 'efficiency' grant
of twenty shillings each Volunteer had to complete nine drills and attend
the annual inspection of his corps. For an additional ten shillings he had
only to fire off sixty rounds at a target. The grants however were to be
spent on 'necessary expenses', defined as the cost of a headquarters, a

drill ground, range, conveyance, postage, stationery, forage, clothing, accoutrements and care of arms. From time to time the formal re-quirements for 'efficiency' were changed, the trend being to increase the number of drills, etc. Overall, however, the regulations of 1863 were relatively little altered for most of the Volunteer Force's existence.[80]

The original concept of a self-sufficient force was quickly eroding even before the introduction of a capitation grant in 1863. At first it was thought that the Volunteers ought to supply their own arms, but already in July 1859 it was conceded that 25 per cent of the effectives would receive rifles at government expense, and by the end of the year the government had agreed to supply the entire force. As the Volunteers became more dependent on government money and assistance, so the demands made on them by government became more rigorous. Finance remained a critical problem for as long as the Volunteer Force existed. The vitality and success of every corps was closely bound up with matters of finance: transport and camp alloances, the pay of adjutants and drill sergeants, the musketry requirements, the cost of uniforms and equipment were all debated with sharp interest. Fund raising activities, balls, bazaars, fêtes and theatrical performances were all used to boost corps funds, but even these and government assistance still frequently left Volunteers out of pocket.[81]

What Role for the Amateur Soldier?

By the end of its first decade there was a feeling that the Volunteer Force was in need of firmer direction. It was 'now time that the true principles of its administration were discovered and applied'. The popular enthusi-asm and praise of its first years, when the Volunteers were found to be 'exceedingly satisfactory' and 'fit for any service in any battlefield', were replaced by doubts and forthright criticism.[82] According to rumour there was said '. . . to be a serious desire on the part of those in authority at the Horse Guards to practically abolish Volunteers'.[83] The Franco-Prussian War provided much food for thought, and from the 1870s the government showed an increasing desire to integrate the Volunteers into the nation's defence plans.

Edward Cardwell's appointment as Secretary for War in December 1868 marked the beginning of this new era. It was not an auspicious start, for his military reforms aroused much animosity and opposition from the Volunteers. His new regulations required from them a higher level of training, laid down standards of proficiency for officers and non-commissioned officers, and tied the amount of government financial assistance to each corps' success in meeting the new requirements. Still more important for the future development of the Volunteer Force were those provisions in the Regulation of the Forces Act of 1871 which transferred control over the Volunteers from the Lord Lieutenant of the county to the Crown, and made the Volunteers subject to the Mutiny Act when brigaded with the regular army or the Militia. Opponents of the new Act declared that such changes would annihilate the Volunteer Force, but more were to follow. In 1872 the government announced its intention to replace the adjutants of the Volunteer Force by regular army officers on five year attachments. In 1873 Cardwell's Localization Scheme was applied to the Volunteers. The scheme divided the country into military sub-districts roughly corresponding to the then existing counties and assigned to each the local Volunteers, two Militia battalions and two 'linked' line battalions. By placing the inspection and training of the Volunteers under the direction of the lieutenant-colonels commanding the new sub-district brigade depots, the future well-being of the Volunteers came to depend heavily on the interest and cooperation of these officers and on those regular officers who also served as adjutants. Cardwell had laid the groundwork for closer ties with the regular army and for further rationalization of the Volunteer Force's role in national defence. Already in May 1872 the Volunteers were ordered to exchange their title of 'Reserve Forces' for that of 'Auxiliary Forces'.[84]

The next important changes to the Volunteer Force stemmed from the investigations of the Bury Committee, appointed in February 1878 with the intention of fully assimilating the Volunteers into the Cardwell system. The Committee wished both to raise the efficiency of the force and to reduce its cost. The consolidation of all existing 'administrative' battalions seemed to offer the best chance of achieving both aims, and a further reduction in cost might be hoped for by encouraging a uniformity in dress. An increase in the number of recruit drills, together with additional camp and travel allowances, were hoped to enhance further the force's military efficiency. In 1880 new efficiency regulations were introduced and guide lines were set down for the consolidation of all remaining administrative battalions. On 1 July 1881 full territorialization came into effect, with each of the 215 Volunteer battalions being assigned to particular regiments of the regular army. Efforts to improve the military efficiency of the force continued. Training requirements were again raised, and supporting services such as a Medical Staff Corps, Submarine Miners and Cyclists were encouraged. By 1888 all Volunteer battalions had been assigned a definite role in the nation's mobilization plan for defence.[85]

After the early years of praise and popularity the Volunteers had undergone a period of criticism and reform. Morale was visibly affected and from 1868 to 1873 the numbers enrolled in the force dropped yearly. To some extent public perception of the utility of the Volunteer Force was tied to the increasingly rapid technological changes which were seen to be altering the nature of warfare, and to the general performance of foreign armies in contemporary conflicts. With the completion of the Cardwell reforms public interest in the Volunteers waned, but as the force entered a more settled period recruiting picked up and the Volunteers became an accepted institution with a strength of some 200,000 members, enrolling about one man for every twelve in the population.[86]

Not until the outbreak of the South African War in 1899 was there a great revival of public interest in the Volunteer Force and its mounted counterpart, the Yeomanry. The war seemed to offer at last a chance for the Volunteer soldier to prove his worth – not that offers to go on foreign service had not been made, and even accepted, before. As early as 1861, on account of the Trent affair, two Volunteer corps had offered to serve in North America, and offers for foreign service had been repeated during the Eastern Crisis of 1877–8. In the 1880s men from the Post Office Volunteers and the Crewe Railway Volunteers had seen service in Egypt.[87] The South African War, however, saw over 30,000 Volunteer soldiers serve overseas – more than 27,000 from the Volunteer Force and another 3,000 from the Yeomanry.

At first the War Office was reluctant to accept offers of service from Volunteers, but the military disasters of Black Week (December 1899) quickly changed official thinking. Some confusion ensued as there was no coherent scheme for dispatching the Volunteers to the theatre of war. Initially a small contingent (finally totalling 1,726 men) drawn from forty-seven different Volunteer corps went out in January 1900 as the City Imperial Volunteers. In October they returned to a triumphant welcome. The majority of the Volunteer Force (over 19,000 men) who were accepted for service during the war made their way to South Africa in special Active Service Companies, attached to regular regiments. A further estimated 7,000 men abandoned their Volunteer status and enlisted directly into the regular army. Another 700 Volunteers joined the Yeomanry, now styled the Imperial Yeomanry, a force raised under War Office instructions.[88]

The performance of the Volunteer soldier in the South African War was generally felt by the public to have been creditable, even if the experts were divided in their opinion on the actual efficiency of the Volunteers in action. Both the Yeomanry and the Volunteer Force experienced a sharp increase in recruits during the war. The response to the war had been enthusiastic; one third of the Yeomanry's 10,000 officers and men had gone to South Africa and another 32,000 new men were recruited. In January 1900, 20,929 men came forward from the Volunteer Force to offer their services, but the fact that one third of them had been rejected (3,528 as medically unfit and 3,333 as inadequately trained) called attention to the auxiliary forces' inability to give the regular army the direct support it might need in a major conflict. The war helped the public image of the Volunteers but at the same time opened a new and vigorous debate on their true role and value. Were they to be considered solely as a force for home defence or should they take on new obligations to serve abroad, becoming a proper army of reserve? Were they sufficiently trained for either role?[89] In the debates which followed the political strength of the Volunteer Force made itself strongly felt.

Since the earliest days of the force, the Volunteers had been well represented in Parliament, at least insofar as a sizable number of MPs were, or had been, Volunteer officers. In the 1870s, at its greatest potential strength, the Volunteer interest could muster as many as 130 MPs with Volunteer connections – though active supporters were far fewer, perhaps only a fifth of that number. Until the mid 1880s Volunteer pressure in Parliament largely failed to influence government measures, but from that time onwards a new generation of Volunteer MPs, increasingly associated with the Conservative Party, pressed the self-interest of the Volunteer Force. In the years immediately after the South African War a small but vociferous group of Volunteer MPs frustrated ministerial plans to reform the force. Volunteer MPs came to monopolize virtually all debates on military affairs and, in March 1907, on the eve of the introduction of Haldane's Bill to create a new Territorial Force, the Volunteers appeared to some politicians as a real menace to any reform.[90]

In the first decade of the twentieth century, government ministers, like their predecessors a century before, grappled with the problem of how to rationalize the nation's requirements for military manpower – and like their predecessors they found the Volunteer Force to be a serious obstruction to their plans. Unease over home defence during the South African War (when Britain was denuded of regular troops) led to the imposition of still greater training and service obligations on the Volunteers, but any more drastic reform of the force was successfully resisted for some years. By the close of the South African War the number of Volunteers was again declining. The force was well below its establishment, lacked cohesion, was deficient in training and equipment, and many corps faced serious financial problems. Yet plans by Arnold-Forster, the Secretary of State for War, to create a more efficient force, by reducing its numbers (culling the inefficient battalions) and ploughing back the money to provide for rifle clubs and such necessities as a transport service, were strenuously opposed by Volunteer MPs and ultimately defeated. Change, however, was only delayed. Despite the objections of the Volunteers, the Yeomanry and the Militia, Arnold-Forster's successor, Haldane, managed to create a new body, the Territorial Force, which came into existence in 1908.

The Territorial Force, 1908–14

In an ironic twist, the Boer War had vindicated the value of the amateur soldier – the Boers proved a formidable enemy, even if their successes were rather exaggerated. The public image of the British Volunteer too was enhanced, though the experts still had doubts. The returning Volunteers were greeted with a tumultuous welcome, but the reality of a war which ultimately required a force of nearly half a million men to defeat barely 50,000 Boers, was bound to call for some questioning among both the military and the politicians. For the auxiliary forces the next few years were a time of considerable anxiety, as official enquiries probed the experience of the war and politicians pondered the creation of a more reliable, more flexible force to replace the auxiliaries, possibly one raised by conscription on the continental model. But not until the arrival of R.B. Haldane as the new Liberal Secretary of State in 1906 was any substantial change actually brought about. In 1907 the auxiliary forces learned their fate and on 1 April 1908 a new Territorial Force came into being. The Yeomanry and the Volunteers were to form this new force, which would be further augmented by ancillary support units. At last the dream of a complete, self-contained Volunteer army was to become a reality, or so it appeared. The Militia, the 'old constitutional force', were not included. Its representatives having refused to join either the new Territorial Force or the regular army, the Militia were abolished and replaced by a new Special Reserve – much to the chagrin of the Militia's county supporters.

The new Territorial Force, however, was not all that its principal architect had wished for. In making it more palatable politically, compromises were made which blurred the force's intended role, later contributing to what the Territorials themselves saw as the mishandling of the force in its first test of war, in 1914. The Territorial Force was presented to the public as a purely domestic defence force, a ploy which concealed Haldane's ulterior design – that the force should act not only as a direct support for any continental expeditionary force, supplying additional divisions after a six month training period, but also serve as the principal means of expanding the army in the event of a major war. Only the so-called Imperial Service Obligation, to which the new Territorials could commit themselves individually, but only if they chose, hinted at the intention to use the Territorial Force as a second line to the regular army.

To administer the Territorial Force, each county was to create a Territorial Association, which would be responsible for the recruitment, equipping and maintenance of the county formations. Haldane's wider intention, that the county Associations act as an important link between the military and their respective local communities, promoting military virtues through rifle clubs and cadet corps, also fell victim to the compromises of political expediency. In the event there were no plans made by which the expansion of the army could be done through the county Associations.[91]

It had been expected that some 200,000 men of the old Volunteer Force and the Yeomanry would transfer to the new force, but only 183,000 actually did so. Nevertheless, recruiting for the Territorials was at first encouraging, benefitting in the early months of 1909 from fresh invasion fears kindled by Guy de Maurier's extremely popular play *An Englishman's Home*. Enthusiasm, however, soon waned. The full establishment of 302,199 proved unattainable – and this figure was only a third of what Haldane had originally proposed. By July 1914 the force had just over 268,000 men of whom only 18,683 had taken the Imperial Service Obligation. Haldane's energetic promotion of the force through extensive speaking tours, and the active support of Edward VII, failed to convince enough young men of the benefits to be had by joining up. In fact the terms of service being offered were not so attractive. The new Territorial Force demanded a greater personal commitment. There was an increased number of regular drills and attendance at an annual camp of fifteen days, yet the remuneration was no more generous than for the old Volunteers. The old Volunteers had enjoyed the privilege of being able to resign on fourteen days' notice, but the new Territorials were obliged to complete a four year engagement. Participation in all three of the pre-1908 auxiliary forces had run at about 3.6 per cent of the male population in 1903, but that in the Territorial Force, ten years later, registered only 0.63 per cent.[92]

The new Territorial Force was not simply the Volunteers under a new name. The force was to be better equipped, better trained and fully supported by all the ancillary units necessary for a modern army of the early twentieth century. Nevertheless the Territorials, as part-time amateurs, faced the same problem that had exercised the patience and ingenuity of the old Volunteers. Securing adequate funds for accommodation and training facilities, and especially for the remuneration of the men's expenses, was a familiar problem. Standing lower than the regular army in priority, the Territorials had still to make do with outdated equipment, while bearing the professional scorn of many regular officers, and public criticism of their unpreparedness for war. As ever, they needed the support of local employers in the ceaseless campaign for recruits, contending with an annual wastage of 12.5 per cent (compared to 7 per cent in the regular army) just to keep the numbers they already had.[93]

No critics of the Territorial Force became more vociferous than the advocates of conscription. Haldane had hailed the Territorials as a 'practical test of the voluntary system', but the very notion that adequate numbers of soldiers might be produced, and a nation taught military virtues on such a basis, was an anomaly by the military standards of the day. The far larger armies of continental Europe relied on short service conscription – a solution to military recruitment which not only ran contrary to the long cherished British ideal of volunteers, wherever possible, for all military service, but also appeared impractical, as any form of short service seemed unsuitable for the imperial duties which engrossed so much of the British regular soldier's time. All parliamentary attempts to introduce conscription before 1914 failed.

Only in 1916, after the voluntary system for general military recruitment had faltered in the midst of the Great War could conscription no longer be resisted. The voluntary system finally failed, but its eclipse was neither total nor permanent. The Territorials were soon submerged in Britain's armies, but at home, again responding to the challenge of possible invasion, the conflict of 1914–18 gave birth to a new force of Volunteers committed solely to defence. Once the war was over the new Volunteers disappeared, but the part-time Territorial again resumed his place in peacetime society.

CHAPTER FIVE

The World Wars, 1914–45

The Great War, 1914–18

However much the pre-war Territorials might have expected to be in the vanguard of the nation's military effort in a major war, such hopes were quickly dashed. On 7 August 1914, only two days after assuming office as Secretary of State for War, Lord Kitchener announced the creation of what were soon dubbed the 'New Armies'. The existence of the Territorial Force and its county Associations was ignored. By the end of September Kitchener's calls for recruits for his New Armies had produced some 500,000 men, organized in over 500 battalions and divided between 30 divisions. Territorial recruiting undoubtedly suffered, but by December 1915, when direct recruiting into the Territorial Force ceased, 725,842 men had been enlisted,[94] or approximately half the number recruited by then into the New Armies.

Kitchener's contempt for what he saw as 'a Town Clerk's Army' administered by 'mayors in their parlours' is a matter of record, but the precise reasons for his completely bypassing the Territorial Force and the county Associations as a principle means of expanding the army remain obscure. Home defence, the apparent *raison d'être* of the Territorial Force, worried the new Secretary of State. Nor could the force's smooth deployment overseas, with the flexibility required by war, simply be assumed. Haldane had left a flawed instrument. Although the vast majority of Territorials immediately offered to serve overseas, the response was variable from one unit to the next – individuals were under no obligation to go abroad. There was reluctance in some, and the extreme youthfulness of others, many being under 19 years of age, made them ineligible for foreign service. As in the South African War, there were also those found to be physically unfit for the rigours of active service.[95]

When war was declared the Territorial Force as a whole was certainly not ready for immediate active service. It had never been the stated intention that it should be, but as early as September 1914 some Territorials were sent to France. By the end of the year 23 Territorial infantry battalions, 7 Yeomanry regiments and 6 Territorial companies of Royal Engineers were with the British Expeditionary Force in France, while still other Territorials had been sent to relieve regulars in the Mediterranean and Indian garrisons. In March 1915 the first complete Territorial division (46th North Midland) arrived in France, soon followed by others. Although pushed aside in favour of Kitchener's New Armies, the Territorial Associations were soon ordered to raise second and third line formations. The ferocity of the war, with its unceasing hunger for young lives, eventually saw more than 5.7 million men don the army's khaki service dress. By the end of the war in 1918, 23 Territorial infantry divisions (out of a total of 29) and two out of the five mounted divisions had seen overseas service. A total of 692 Territorial battalions had existed, compared to 267 regular or reserve battalions and 557 New Army battalions. The New Armies had sent 404 battalions to serve abroad, the Territorials 318. Despite an inauspicious start, the Territorials had clearly made a major contribution to the war. Not only had they undertaken the burden of home defence, they had also served on all the principal fronts, and often with distinction, suffering a total of 577,016 casualties and winning 71 Victoria Crosses.[96]

The Territorials could claim to have inherited the tradition of the British Volunteer, but as so often in the past, war and the threat of invasion again prompted the spontaneous appearance of a new force of amateurs, part-time Volunteers in the same mould as those of 1803 and 1859. From the very start of the war there was anxiety over a possible German invasion of the east coast of England, a threat which in official eyes was not significantly reduced until December 1917; and in time-honoured fashion many unofficial town or civic 'guards' soon appeared, as they saw it, to take on the task of local defence. The government, however, though concerned over the threat of attack, was preoccupied with the enormous task of creating a large army destined for foreign service. There was little incentive to encourage local amateurs who would compete for both men and scarce resources. Nevertheless, in November 1914, as the rapid German advance towards the Channel coast produced an alarm, in which some 300,000 troops were deployed in case of invasion, a 'central association of Volunteer Training Corps' was given official sanction. The conditions of service imposed on the new VTC left little doubt over the government's view of such forces. All expenses were to be borne by the corps themselves. Men of military age were not to be enrolled unless they had genuine reasons for not enlisting in the forces, and even then eligible men were to undertake to enlist if required to. Neither conventional military ranks nor any uniform, apart from a brassard (an arm badge), were to be used. Should uniform be necessary, it was not to resemble that worn by the regular army.[97]

Government indifference towards the VTC left them without official recognition throughout 1915. Questions were raised over the legality of such corps actually bearing arms. Finally in May 1916 the VTC were made subject to the provisions of the Volunteer Act of 1863, which had remained on the statute book despite the creation of the Territorial Force in 1908. Uniforms and ranks were authorized, but neither arms nor financial compensation were offered. In July, regulation of the VTC was taken a step further when their central association became one of 'Volunteer Regiments'. In September, the administration of the Volunteers passed into the hands of the Territorial County Associations. By the end of 1916 Parliament completed the transformation of the VTC with the passing of a new Volunteer Act which required service for the duration of the war, provided for proper service uniforms of khaki, some arms, a grant of £2 per man and mandatory training. What had prompted this final stage in the regulation of the Volunteers was conscription. Men could seek exemption through local tribunals, but exemptions could be given only on condition that such men served in the Volunteers. The Volunteer Act of 1863 however permitted resignation on fourteen days' notice. To close this loophole, it became necessary to pass further legislation.[98]

Through the early months of 1917 the Volunteers were reorganized and members graded according to fitness and availability for service. The progressive centralization and regulation of the VTC reflected the government's growing concern over the problem of manpower. It was a question of finding sufficient men, not just for the armed forces, but also for sustaining war production and essential work on the domestic front. The VTC were criticized as a convenient means of avoiding real military service and their military value was castigated in no uncertain terms. Popular wit dubbed them 'Genuine Relics' and 'Grandpapa's Regiment' after the GR on their brassards. Lack of funds, equipment and arms prevented the Volunteers from becoming an effective defence force. Nonetheless they did perform a variety of important services. Apart from digging London's defences and guarding vulnerable points, they did munitions work and assisted in the harvest. In 1918 over 13,000 Volunteers did a three week tour of coastal duty to relieve regulars then needed in France. Had invasion come, they were to have provided garrisons and guards in order to release regulars for other duties, to have assisted in the evacuation of civilians, and where necessary to have taken part in actual resistance.[99]

As early as January 1918 the War Office was considering the disbandment of the Volunteers, but not until November was the Volunteer Act of 1916 suspended. The ultimate fate of the force continued in doubt until September 1919 when members received a final letter of thanks from the King. The force was disbanded – but not quite all of it. In a situation not so unlike that at the end of the Napoleonic Wars, the Motor Volunteer Corps, like the old Yeomanry regiments, were kept in being (until March 1921) for their potential use during a time of domestic disorder. The almost unnoticed demise of a force which had so often been at odds with the government was perhaps not so surprising. The brief history of the VTC had been much like that of so many of its Volunteer predecessors, and in its turn the VTC was the immediate precedent for the next war's display of local patriotism – the Home Guard of 1940.

Between the Wars

In December 1918 the disembodiment of the whole Territorial Force began; its reconstitution was by no means certain. Finding a justifiable role for a large force of part-time amateurs was difficult, the more so as the Territorials themselves made their acceptance of any liability for general service overseas conditional on promises to maintain the integrity of Territorial units. The preparation of a force for home defence or for the expansion of the army in the event of another European war seemed of little relevance. In the post-war world the regular army turned its attention to policing the empire – a duty for which the part-time Territorial was unsuitable. Re-establishment of the force took place only in 1920 after much delay and considerable opposition from the army's general staff. In the words of Winston Churchill, then Secretary of State for War, the purpose of the reconstituted 'Territorial Army' was to be 'Imperial Defence, including our obligations to France and Flanders'.[100] Such a commitment, however, was only agreed to after the War Office's acceptance of a set of conditions known collectively as the 'Pledge'. In the dispatch of troops overseas the integrity of individual Territorial units and larger formations was to be respected, and although there was now to be an acceptance of an overseas liability, it was conditional on the passage of certain legislation in the event of a crisis. The Pledge was intended to give the Territorials guarantees against the repetition of particular grievances from the war years, but the compromises agreed to succeeded only in assuring future friction between the Territorial Army, the War Office and the government, as the real purpose of the Territorials seemed hard to define. Only in April 1939 were the last vestiges of the Pledge abolished.[101]

A further obstacle to the reconstitution of the Territorials was the difficult issue of their availability as an aid to civil power, a disagreeable task which the amateur soldier had often performed in the past. Haldane, in creating the Territorial Force in 1908, had made it clear that the Territorials were not to be used in domestic disputes and this was written into the regulations of that force. It had been clear that his new Territorials, like the Rifle Volunteers before them, would have to rely on the recruitment of working men and he had no wish to alienate the labour force by having the Territorial Force appear as a tool for strike breaking. In the years immediately after 1918 this was again an issue of concern for both the government and the Territorials. The post-war years saw no relief from the social unrest which had preceded the war, while the successful example of the Russian Bolsheviks underlined government fears of a British revolution. The regular army voiced its long standing reluctance to be involved in domestic disputes, and in any case its much reduced peacetime strength was soon fully committed overseas. The Territorials seemed an obvious alternative, but in a nation where trade union membership had doubled from four to eight million between 1912 and 1919, the question of harming working class recruitment was if anything more serious than ever. Threatened by the miners' lock-out dispute in 1921 and the general strike of 1926, the government resorted to the awkward expedient of trying to use trained Territorial manpower by asking for volunteers to fill the ranks of temporary forces which it wished to present as entirely separate from the Territorial Army. In 1921 a special Defence Force was formed and in 1926 selected Territorial units were asked to volunteer en masse to be members of a Civil Constabulary Reserve. The Defence Force was by no means wholly made up of Territorials, but the legal veneer of it being an entirely separate force was too thin, when recruiting was carried out at Territorial drill halls and service counted towards fulfilling an engagement in the Territorial Army. Inevitably the Territorials became associated with strike breaking.[102]

To what extent recruiting for the Territorial Army was hurt by its involvement in the troubles of 1921 and 1926 is difficult to say. Although initially some of the county Associations felt that they had benefitted as new men came in from the Defence Force, later there were complaints over their quality. Adverse effects following the general strike of 1926 were less noticeable, but what is clear is that until almost the end of the 1930s the Territorials struggled against falling numbers. Some units, notably in the north of England and in south Wales, did well enough, but others, especially in London, did not. From the very start, in 1920, recruiting was slow, a result of war weariness and apathy (and later hostility), soon underscored by the government's own indifference. Financial cuts which curtailed personal allowances and prevented improvements to facilities, together with other economies such as the cancellation of the annual summer camps in 1926 and 1932, hurt the force, making it unattractive to recruits.[103] *The Times* proudly saw the Territorials as carrying on 'The voluntary principle . . . one deeply rooted in the social structure of the British nation', but was indignant at the prospect of those volunteering being 'financially handicapped' for their trouble.[104] Even if certain areas, and particular units (like those of the Yeomanry), did much better, overall the Territorial Army was sadly under establishment strength. As in the past, social activities played a vital role in keeping the force in being. From 1928 to 1932 the Territorial Army passed through its worst period, but as late as 1937 the county Associations were still preoccupied with recruiting troubles.[105]

While the Territorials were engrossed with the problem of keeping up even their under strength numbers, so often devoting their time to activities which had nothing to do with hard military training, discussions of their military role could seem rather academic. Yet the problem of recruitment and the Territorial Army's purpose were of course closely linked. For, as long as the Territorials seemed to have no real role, their irrelevance only served as a further bar to recruiting. Imminent danger, and the threat of foreign invasion had always been the clarion call for the British Volunteer in the past, and for the Territorials of the 1930s this again proved their salvation. The resurrection of a powerful and belligerent Germany, together with the threat of aerial bombardment, were suddenly to give the Territorial Army new meaning and purpose.

Germany's moves against Austria and Czechoslovakia in 1938 brought a dramatic change in the fortunes of the Territorial Army. The public awoke suddenly to the possibility of war and in particular to the dangers of aerial attack. The Territorials had been given a responsibility for anti-aircraft defence as early as 1923 but, with recruits hard to find and funds not forthcoming, little had been accomplished. Now, in the wake of German aggression, recruits clamoured to join. The Territorial Army's anti-aircraft units were soon filled, and by December 1938 the force was almost complete to a newly expanded establishment of just over 200,000 men. The purpose of the anti-aircraft units was clear enough and the call of home defence attracted an embarrassing number of recruits, but the role of other Territorial units remained less certain, being dependent on the government's commitment to another European Expeditionary Force.[106]

Although there had been revived interest since the mid 1930s in the long discarded idea of such an expeditionary force, it was not without opponents. To the War Office and the general staff, the Territorial Army was of great importance to such plans, but it took the twin crises of 1938 to secure the regular army's real acceptance of the Territorials as a true second line. The government too saw the Territorials with renewed interest, but in a different light: primarily for anti-aircraft defence. From the end of 1937 Chamberlain's Government adopted a policy of 'limited liability', eschewing any commitment to a continental strategy. Such a stance was not dropped until March 1939, when it was also announced that the Territorial Army was to be doubled in size. Plans were made for a Field Force of more than nineteen divisions, at least half of which were to be Territorial. In the months that remained before the outbreak of war that September the recruiting needs of the Territorial Army shifted from anti-aircraft defence to those of the new Field Force. The chronic recruiting problem vanished, but was immediately replaced by new ones: lack of instructors, deficient equipment and inadequate facilities – all of which were made worse by the government's spur of the moment decision to double the size of the force.[107]

The Second World War, 1939–45

Through the 1920s and 1930s the Territorials had kept alive the 'voluntary principle' of the amateur part-time soldier, and, despite criticism, had maintained a reservoir of military experience on which the nation might draw. In the spring and summer of 1939, in an atmosphere of impending doom, the Territorials were able to provide an element of stability in the rush towards mobilization. Following the government's decision to double the size of the Territorial Army, limited conscription was introduced and a parallel second line of 'militia' (as the conscripts were named) came into being. The new force presented a direct challenge to the Territorial Army's claim to be the sole means of expanding the nation's military forces. Was Kitchener's decision of 1914 to be repeated? Conflict was smoothed over by a certain amount of integration, but on the outbreak of war in September, one of the government's first measures was to create one vast National Army. Territorial status was suspended for the duration and distinctions between regulars, the Territorials and the newly created Militia, were done away with as much as possible – a policy which nonetheless took some time to implement.

The mixing of Territorial and regular units in larger formations began, and by the spring of 1940 was well advanced.[108]

The absorption of large numbers of recruits changed the character of the peacetime units and the war soon submerged the Territorials in an expanded army which was to grow to an enormous size. Despite harsh criticism of the Territorial Army's efficiency and the standard of its training, the notion that its units would undertake considerable training before embarking for overseas service was quickly dropped and some units were immediately sent to France. By early 1940 three Territorial divisions had arrived in France and had taken their places in the front line. Inexperience and insufficient practice were all too common, but when the German offensive in the west finally came, in May 1940, Territorial units showed a tenacity and fighting spirit which drew comment even from the enemy. Over the next five years of war Territorial units, even if such in name only, continued to distinguish themselves in battle in every European theatre of war, and their achievements won the highest praise.

Although the pre-war Territorials were soon lost in the ranks of one vast national army, the distinct tradition of the local Volunteer soldier was again revived in 1940. Under the threat of invasion a new body of part-time Volunteers, the Local Defence Volunteers, or LDV, soon named the Home Guard, sprang into being. Unlike its predecessors this new force of Volunteers could date its birth precisely, to the evening of 14 May 1940 when the new Secretary of State for War, Anthony Eden, made a radio appeal for Volunteers. Four days earlier, after months of 'phoney war' along the Franco-German frontier, the Germans had at last launched their western offensive. What especially worried the Secretary of State was the German use of airborne troops to secure strategic positions in advance of their main attack, and to counter this threat in particular he called the LDV into existence.

The history of the LDV, or Home Guard, over the next four and a half years followed a familiar pattern.[109] The force was subjected to mounting regulation, making it more uniform, more military and more responsive to central direction. In this there were certainly similarities with the VTC of the previous war, but there were also crucial differences. Unlike the emergence of the VTC, which had been unsolicited and largely unwanted by the government, the initiative for the Home Guard came directly from the government itself. The old VTC had appeared at a time when voluntary enlistment was the sole means of recruiting into the army and it had not been greeted with enthusiasm in government circles. The overriding concern had been to make certain that the VTC did not harm army recruitment. As the Great War had continued, eventually requiring full conscription by 1916, the VTC had had to be more closely regulated and its terms of service altered to fit into a national manpower scheme. The climate of 1940 was very different. With conscription for the armed forces already in place, the Home Guard was able to avoid many of the contentious problems which had strained the VTC's relationship with the government. Created at government request, the Home Guard were immediately given as much encouragement as possible. They were promised both uniforms and weapons, and were clearly stated to be a part of the armed forces. The King showed a personal interest in the Home Guard and was appointed their colonel-in-chief in 1942. Where the VTC, according to one claim, had passed a million men through its ranks, the Home Guard could claim perhaps three and a half times that number, its peak strength being 1,793,000 men, reached in March 1943.

Even within the first twenty-four hours some 250,000 men enrolled in the LDV at their local police stations. The government's appeal was directed to men aged 17 to 65 who for one reason or another (principally age or occupation) were not then in the armed forces. An earlier idea to confine the force to former servicemen was dropped and although ex-servicemen enlisted in large numbers, so too did many with no previous military experience. Throughout its existence the Home Guard was unpaid. Though eventually fully clothed and armed by the government, there was at first, of necessity, much improvisation. On 23 July 1940 the name 'Home Guard' was made official, and in August units received county titles, and more regulations. From November 1940, however, its transformation into a more military force began in earnest with the announcement that it was to be given a firmer and more permanent shape. A director-general for the whole force was appointed, while each battalion was to receive a full-time officer to act as adjutant and quartermaster. All officers were to be properly commissioned after passing a selection board. A year later, after a decline in numbers, it was announced that conscription would be used to maintain the strength of the Home Guard, even though at 1,530,000 it was three times as large as originally intended. From January 1942 the new conditions of service came into effect. Any male aged 18 to 51 could be ordered to join, and under threat of a month in jail or a £10 fine, was to attend for up to forty-eight hours each month for training or duty. Once in, a man could not leave until age 65. The 'directed men' of 1942 had their parallel in the 'tribunal men' of 1916, and the Home Guard, like the VTC, its Great War predecessor, became increasingly an army of well uniformed and armed conscripts, very different from its earliest days when volunteers might do duty with a shotgun or a homemade cosh, their uniform nothing more than a cloth armband.

Through the summer and autumn of 1940 the Home Guard had focussed its attention on 'dusk to dawn patrols'. To assuage the widespread fears of imminent invasion preceded by airborne attack and fifth columnists, the Home Guard's allotted role was to observe and report the landing of enemy parachutists and the presence of suspicious strangers. The LDV title, taken as 'Look, Duck and Vanish' by local wags, seemed not inappropriate. Subsequently the role of the Home Guard changed considerably in emphasis. 'Static Defence', a defence in depth everywhere, based on road blocks, tank traps and defended 'keeps', with fewer patrols and more training, came to dominate Home Guard activity from 1941. By 1943 the force was embarking on more ambitious ambush schemes, being eventually encouraged to form mobile reserves capable of some offensive action against an invader. From 1943 the real need for the Home Guard seemed to have passed, as the Germans were clearly on the defensive, and through 1944, though actively training in case of German suicide raids, the force began a long decline. Finally on 1 November 1944 units of the Home Guard began to stand down, and in December a final parade was held before the King in Hyde Park. A year later, in December 1945, the force was disbanded.

Unlike virtually all of Britain's previous part-time amateurs serving on the home front, the Home Guard not only engaged a foreign enemy but also suffered casualties – both a result of aerial warfare. The anti-aircraft units of the Home Guard and also its coastal defence batteries saw action and inflicted losses on the enemy. Together with civilians, the Home Guard suffered from enemy air raids and especially from flying bombs. Over 1,200 men were killed on duty, mostly by enemy action, but also in training accidents. If in the final year of the war the usefulness of taking so many men away part-time from their usual occupations might seem questionable, in the dark days of 1940, even if pathetically weak, the Home Guard through raising public morale made an important contribution to Britain's defence.

Postscript

The war with Nazi Germany had once again seen the amateur part-time soldier take his place in Britain's military forces. The pre-war Territorials served overseas with distinction, and at home a Volunteer army of unprecedented size was created, almost literally overnight. At the end of it all, both Territorials and Home Guard were disbanded, but the story of the British Volunteer soldier continues still. After an expression of doubt about its future, the Territorial Army was reconstituted once again in 1947. Its post-war history has been one of almost ceaseless change.

Numbers dwindled and many units disappeared through amalgamation. The late 1960s were an especially bleak period, and if subsequently the prospects for the amateur soldier revived, his future in the post-Cold War world of the 1990s must again appear to be one of uncertainty.

The part-time Volunteer has been a persistent phenomenon in Britain's history. In the past, previous Volunteer legislation has often remained on the statute books for many decades after its apparent usefulness had ceased – only to be revived for some fresh crisis. In the 1950s there was a short revival of the Home Guard. The Home Guard Act of 1951 still remains on the statute books.

PART TWO

The Volunteer Tradition in Leicestershire and Rutland

CHAPTER SIX

The Volunteers of Leicestershire and Rutland to 1816

Leicestershire to the Peace of Amiens

Leicestershire has been no stranger to the mustering of soldiers and their preparations for war. Within her borders, in the late fifteenth century, the kingdom's fate was decided on Bosworth Field, in the following century she made her contribution to the wars of the new Tudor age, and in the next herself suffered the wounds of civil war. Her citizens have often been soldiers, if not from choice, then from necessity. The Elizabethan lieutenancy established the Militia, an institution of the state in whose ranks service had always an element of compulsion. But as occasion arose, the men of Leicestershire have also come forward entirely of their own accord, as Volunteers. Over their long history the military pretensions of these local volunteer soldiers have been both praised and ridiculed. They have known good times and bad.

The first great age of the Volunteer, in Leicestershire as elsewhere, is associated with the era of the French Revolution and Napoleon, but the local Volunteers who appeared in the late 1790s were not the first. Their eagerness to take up arms was but a more military manifestation of the Georgian concept of community self-help. Volunteers had been known in Leicestershire before, though their conduct had not endeared them to posterity. In 1745, according to Throsby, Leicester's late eighteenth-century historian, certain of Leicester's citizens had been roused to action on account of the Jacobite Rebellion, which had made them 'warm and threatening partisans in the cause of their king'. They had 'appeared in arms at mock fights in the castle-yard', but at the crucial moment their nerve had failed them. When the Jacobite army reached Derby, only twenty miles away, 'they deserted the parade, and sneaked away with the aged, the women, and the children, to asylums under the humble roofs of neighbouring villages'.[1] Local resistance did not materialize: two men demanding quarters for the Jacobite army entered Leicester unopposed, and at Market Harborough the only preparations to meet the Highland army consisted of baking a large quantity of bread for their consumption – which, if hardly heroic, had at least been prudent.[2]

Subsequently, in 1757 during the Seven Years War, the government in London created a 'New Militia', ostensibly a remedy for such local failings as had been experienced during the previous rebellion. In 1759 and again in 1778, under threats of invasion, the New Militia of Leicestershire and of Rutland was embodied for service. The military ardour of the two counties, however, did not extend to a warm embrace for the concept of Volunteers. When in 1782, Lord Shelburne's plan 'for raising Volunteer Companies &c in the great Towns and Villages in the Kingdom' was proposed to a general meeting of the 'Noblemen, Gentlemen, Clergy and Freeholders' of Leicestershire, it was rejected. Though elsewhere, at Sheffield, Leeds, Hull, York and Chester, it was reported to have been received favourably, there seemed no compelling reason 'to form any Military Associations in the County of Leicester'. Various objections were made, Leicestershire's reaction being consistent with the consensus of opinion in the House of Lords, where Shelburne's Volunteer Corps Bill 'was allowed by almost every noble Lord to be imperfect'. The fall of Shelburne's ministry put an end to such plans – at least for the moment.[3]

Shelburne's Volunteer Plan of 1782 had found little favour in Leicestershire, but Britain's first great age of the Volunteer was near to hand, its scale foreshadowed by Ireland's experience during the American Revolutionary War. The outbreak of yet another conflict with France in 1793, and particularly the renewal of that conflict with Napoleon in 1803, produced in its wake a vast army of British Volunteers. Supporters claimed it was a 'new Military System'.

News of the war was prominent in Leicester's newspapers, and from 1793 the streets of Leicester were frequented by an assortment of recruiting parties, both military and naval. Public subscriptions for war widows and orphans, for supplying additional warm clothing for the British army in Flanders and extra shoes for the county Militia, were given enthusiastic support. Though some coastal counties had raised Volunteers within the very first weeks of war, it was not until 1794, when the allied campaign in Flanders was going seriously wrong, that public opinion in Leicester became alarmed over the possibility of a French invasion. The French revolutionaries, now in the midst of the Terror, seemed 'desperate and mad enough to attempt any apparent impossibility'. The men of Leicester were urged to step forward to show their 'Loyalty and Patriotism' and reminded that they were 'at War with our ancient enemy, an enemy who threatens to exterminate us and drive us into the midst of the sea'.[4]

Alarm over the plans of the French was not the only concern. Attention was also focused on the 'Demon at Home', those English Jacobins who it was feared would overthrow their own constitution and welcome the invaders. By the end of February 1794 the possibility of creating some sort of local defence organization was under public discussion in Leicester, and the following month a general meeting at Oakham took positive steps towards forming a Volunteer cavalry in the neighbouring county of Rutland. This and similar news from other counties was duly reported in Leicester and on 10 April 1794 a General Meeting of the County of Leicestershire assembled at the Three Crowns Inn in Leicester 'to carry into execution a Plan for the Internal Protection and Security of the County at this Crisis'. Among the resolutions carried was the decision to form a body of not less than 100 cavalry, agreeable to the fourth article of the Secretary of State's recommendations, dated 14 March 1794. A subscription was opened to support the meeting's resolutions, which included an addition of eighty-eight men to the Leicestershire Militia. The origin of the Leicestershire Yeomanry may be traced to this meeting, and the example soon produced another Volunteer corps, the Loyal Corps of Leicester Volunteer Infantry.[5]

On 28 April 1794 another meeting of the subscribers decided on the details of the county's new force, announced in the *Leicester Journal* as 'The Loyal Leicestershire Volunteer Yeomanry'. It was resolved to form six troops, each not less than fifty officers and other ranks – a considerably larger force than originally discussed. A further meeting on 6 May, again at the Three Crowns, began the process of enrolment and made arrangements for recruiting the force from every part of Leicestershire. Enrolment was carried on at various inns in the principal towns throughout the county, gentlemen representing the corps appearing on appointed days to enrol names and explain the nature of the service which would be required. Several local bankers were nominated to take subscriptions, the fund having reached £7,350.16s.0d. by early May. On 14 June the *Leicester Herald* reported that 'Major Sir W.S. Skeffington and

Capt. Curzon of the Leicestershire Independent Cavalry kissed the King's hand on Wednesday on having completed their complement of men'.[6]

Not to be left out, a number of gentlemen, among them the Mayor of Leicester, the banker John Mansfield, convened a meeting at the Town Exchange on 15 May to enable the residents of Leicester to cooperate with the county plan to raise six troops of cavalry for internal defence. It was suggested that the town itself raise a part of that force, which would assist the general plan and 'serve as a sufficient Protection of the Town'. Enrolments for a Leicester troop in the new Yeomanry force were begun; but a clamour also arose for a corps of Volunteer infantry to be formed in Leicester to accommodate those 'spirited Men of Reputation who have not Horses'. It was hoped to attract 'every respectable Inhabitant disposed to support the present constitution'. More than a month later government approval was received for an infantry company of 50 to 100 men.[7]

Within one week the Leicester troop was filled and by the middle of June the regiment needed only thirty men to complete its establishment. On 4 July 1794 the Loyal Leicestershire Volunteer Cavalry was mustered on the Leicester race ground and formed into six troops, Sir William Skeffington being presented as its colonel. At the end of August the corps made its second public appearance, 300 strong, to receive its standards, a 'royal banner' donated by Lady Charlotte Curzon, daughter of Lord Howe, and a 'provincial banner' made by Miss Mary Linwood, a local celebrity, noted not only in Leicester but also nationally for her artistic needlework. In October the whole regiment paraded again for its first review and attracted 'a large concourse of spectators'.[8]

The Loyal Leicester Volunteer Infantry was a less prestigious affair and its subscription funds were paltry compared to those of the Yeomanry Cavalry. In July 1794 it reached its maximum authorized establishment of 100 men, but as more men continued to come forward it was soon formed into two companies on an augmented establishment. Colours however were not received with any despatch: after a postponement, it was not until 19 October 1795 that the colours were finally presented. In the meantime the corps had been regularly at drill, made several church parades (its first in September 1794 being to pay 'a proper compliment' to the mayor) and a token appearance at the funeral of a marine sergeant. It had also had a taste of something akin to real service when in March 1795 it had made a forced march in support of the Yeomanry's suppression of rioting canal workers to the south of Leicester.[9]

Elsewhere in Leicestershire, Volunteer infantry corps were formed in Loughborough and in Melton Mowbray. Commissions in the Loyal

Loughborough Volunteer Infantry were dated from 22 August 1794 and a muster roll of that autumn recorded a total strength of seventy-one men, all ranks (including a 'President' listed with the staff), formed into one company. In January 1795 the Loughborough company, attended by a troop of the county's new Yeomanry, received their colours, the gift of Mr Boultbee, a local banker. In Melton Mowbray sixty of the 'most respectable inhabitants' had enrolled in a 'Melton Mowbray Company of Volunteer Infantry' by December 1794 and were expecting to double their numbers from the surrounding neighbourhood, if sanctioned by the government. Commissions in the Melton Volunteers were dated from 1 January 1795 but not until July 1796 did the corps receive colours, the work of Mrs Caldecott, the wife of Lieut Samuel Caldecott; and once again a troop of the Yeomanry was also in attendance.[10]

No further additions were made to the county's Volunteer forces until 1798 when the fear of invasion again assumed prominence, Britain's situation appearing all the more perilous because of the Irish Rebellion and recent mutinies in the navy. That summer a corps of Volunteer infantry was formed in Hinckley, while an Infantry Association and a Cavalry Association (one troop) were created at Ashby de la Zouch. In Leicester there was an abortive attempt to form an Armed Association, the services of which were to be restricted to within five miles of the town, the idea being to replace the Leicester Volunteer Infantry should they be marched elsewhere (for they had now undertaken to serve in any part of the country if needed). The plan failed but the Leicester Volunteers were augmented, adding another company to their establishment. At Lutterworth the efforts of Henry Otway brought into being a troop of Loyal Lutterworth Gentlemen and Yeomanry, and by this time also the new Provisional Cavalry (formed in Leicestershire in 1797), with the Duke of Rutland as its colonel, were in existence, raising further the number of local men in military uniform. To the *Leicester Journal* it already seemed by 1797 that there was no dress to be seen in the towns and villages of Leicestershire save that of the military.[11]

The end of the Irish Rebellion, Nelson's victory of the Nile and the formation of a new coalition against the French eased the military situation which had caused so much anxiety in 1798, and with the Peace of Amiens in 1802, the county's Volunteers were disbanded. It was intended that the Leicestershire Yeomanry be kept in being, but after nine years of war it proved impossible to find enough men willing to continue and this corps also was disbanded.[12] Otway's Lutterworth troop was dissolved, as was the Ashby de la Zouch Cavalry Association.

Defying Napoleon, 1803–16

The Peace of Amiens, however, proved only a brief respite. In May 1803 the war with France recommenced, its resumption hardly greeted with enthusiasm. The government's attempts to mobilize the nation's strength became increasingly urgent, and chaotic. Local officials were bombarded with a bewildering number of parliamentary Acts and government instructions. Leicestershire's response to the danger was slow, but as the summer progressed the sinister intentions of the enemy forces gathering at Boulogne raised the fear of imminent invasion to fever pitch. In July the town of Leicester made an offer to raise at least 600 Volunteers, but discouragingly received no immediate response from London.[13] Not until August were other offers made, if not induced solely by the fear of invasion, then prompted by growing consternation over the prospect of compulsory service, either through the government's latest Levy en Masse or by being balloted for the Militia forces or the new Army of Reserve. On 14 August George Anthony Legh Keck, of Stoughton Grange, offered the services of a new and larger 'Leicestershire Regiment of Yeomanry Cavalry'.[14] Apart from this, it was notably the residents of the county's principal market towns who came forward with offers, while elsewhere, for the moment, much of the countryside remained uncommitted. Melton Mowbray, Lutterworth, Market Harborough, Loughborough and Ashby de la Zouch all made offers, but to the west of Leicester canvassing for subscriptions was met with indifference, and 'with regard to Volunteering there is apathy'. That August in Bosworth and adjacent villages all was 'dullness and apathy'; no one seemed inclined to subscribe himself as a Volunteer unless there was 'some one of consequence to spur them on . . .'.[15]

To the north-east however, the county's Lord Lieutenant, the Duke of Rutland, gave volunteering a further push when he summoned all those living on his estates to meet him on the Statherine Hill, south of Belvoir Castle, to consider the idea of forming a Volunteer corps. On 25 August 'near one thousand' men assembled to hear the Duke denounce Bonaparte and his French armies. He reminded all Leicestershire men, 'all Ranks and Classes of Persons', that they would be equally victims of the enemy's murderous onslaught. Within 'half an hour from the time of the Proposal' 938 men enrolled themselves for the Duke's 'Belvoir Castle Volunteers'. His words were printed for public distribution and in September his deputy, Clement Winstanley, was able to forward to the government further offers from various of the county's smaller villages.[16] By 1 September a generous offer from Hinckley and its neighbouring parishes was on its way to London, but elsewhere in west Leicestershire there continued to be some hesitation. Not until October were offers sent on from Market Bosworth and Earl Shilton, and finally at the end of the month an offer to form the 'Kirkby Mallory, Peckleton, Thurlaston, Desford, Barwell and Stapleton Loyal Volunteers'. Perhaps ironically, it was west Leicestershire which in the end produced the largest of the county's Volunteer corps. At the end of October the Hinckley corps and the independent companies offered by Market Bosworth, Earl Shilton and Kirkby Mallory, came together under the leadership of Viscount Wentworth, as The West Leicestershire Regiment of Loyal Volunteers.[17]

In all, Leicestershire had raised about 3,500 rank and file (3,000 infantry and 500 cavalry) for her Volunteer forces by the end of 1803 – a figure still under the county's quota (set by government that August) of 3,858. There were four corps of infantry (a 'corps' to be at least three companies of sixty men each), of which the largest, the West Leicestershire Regiment, had an establishment of 512 rank and file, divided among eight companies. When finally accepted, the Loyal Leicester Volunteers had had to settle for an establishment of only 480. In addition there were twelve 'independent companies' of infantry and one small artillery detachment of two curricle guns, the 'Loddington Volunteer Artillery', raised entirely at the private expense of Major Morris, 'a gentleman resident at Loddington'.[18] The subsequent history of Leicestershire's Napoleonic Volunteers was various. Only one, the Leicestershire Regiment of Yeomanry Cavalry, was to endure, surviving not only the end of the great conflict with France, but continuing far beyond into the twentieth century.

The Melton Mowbray Volunteer Infantry, the very first of Leicestershire's Volunteers to receive official acceptance by the government, were also the first to gain notoriety – by being 'dismembered' (i.e. disbanded) in June 1804 for gross misconduct. Humiliated, the residents of Melton Mowbray very quickly re-established their Volunteers, but by the autumn of 1806 enthusiasm had waned to the point where they were again dissolved.[19] Even earlier, in 1805, the Allexton infantry had been disbanded. Finding officers in such a remote rural community had been a problem at their formation and by the spring of 1805 they seemed unable to muster more than thirty men out of a supposed establishment of 120.[20] Others however seemed to be flourishing. The Duke of Rutland's Belvoir Castle Volunteers soon established a high reputation, while the Loughborough and the Shepshed and Garendon companies expanded their numbers, both achieving the status of a corps in 1804. In 1805, 'when immediate danger was greatly apprehended', the major commandant of the Loughborough corps, James Boott, 'Prompted by a zealous desire to be useful to my King and Country', added a further company to his corps, bringing its establishment to 252 rank and file.[21]

While Boott's personal enthusiasm for part-time soldiering continued unabated, despite considerable personal expense (for which he soon requested assistance), that of others was beginning to fade. In September 1806 the Belvoir Castle Volunteers resolved 'to resign their Military Functions . . . as the dangers which . . . threatened the country appear to have subsided . . .'. In forwarding their resolution, the Duke of Rutland commented on what he considered to be 'the leading cause' of their wish to resign, namely 'the great extent of country over which they were scattered', which had 'rendered their assembling together, even for the common purposes of exercise, extremely difficult and inconvenient . . .'.[22] The Duke's Volunteers sought a convenient moment at which they could retire 'with honour & credit to themselves', and the occasion of their demise seems likely to have suggested a moment of opportunity to others. By the end of 1806, the Shepshed and Garendon corps, the Melton Mowbray company and the Donington Park corps had all resigned. Early in the following year the Lutterworth troop of Yeomanry too resigned their services.[23]

For the remaining Volunteers the year 1808 was one of great importance, as the county's lieutenancy went ahead with plans to implement the government's new scheme for a Local Militia, which it was hoped would ultimately replace the Volunteers. At the year's end only 923 other ranks were still serving as Volunteers, almost half of them in the county's Yeomanry. An almost equivalent number (915 other ranks) had enrolled for the Local Militia.[24] The county's Volunteers were canvassed and those who were willing to transfer were enrolled in one of four new battalions of Local Militia which finally emerged early the next year. The creation of the Local Militia reduced the county's infantry Volunteers to only four independent companies, who nonetheless seemed determined to carry on as before. Only one however, the Great Glen company, was to survive until the general disbandment of almost all of the nation's remaining Volunteer corps in March 1813. By March 1809 resignations and transfers had extinguished the Volunteers at Ashby de la Zouch and in May the Appleby company too was disbanded. By August 1809 the government's withdrawal of a clothing allowance had forced both the Ibstock company and those at Market Harborough to 'beg to decline further service, in consequence of the new regulations'.[25]

In February 1809 approval was received for a plan which divided Leicestershire into four districts, each of which was to raise and maintain a battalion of Local Militia. Battalion headquarters were established in Leicester, Hinckley, Loughborough and Melton Mowbray, and the battalions numbered one to four, known respectively as the Leicester, the West Leicestershire, the Loughborough and the Melton regiments. Where voluntary enlistment and transfers from the Volunteers did not make up the necessary numbers, balloting was used. Indeed it was the need to draw up new parish lists, to ensure 'an equitable apportionment' that had delayed Leicestershire's scheme for some months. By September 1808 new lists had become necessary on account of the ' . . . disbanding of several Volunteer corps, the change of servants from one part of the county to another and the Increased liability of young men, to serve, who . . . previously . . . had not attained the age of 18 years . . .'. The new force assembled for its first annual training period in May 1809, and continued to do so each year until finally disbanded in 1816.[26]

Rutland in the French Wars, 1793–1816

In Rutland there appears to be no trace of Volunteer activity prior to the outbreak of war with revolutionary France in 1793. In early March 1794 the county sent a proposal to the government for the creation of 'Volunteer Troops of Cavalry', and a week later, in letters from Whitehall dated 14 March, the government circulated its own ideas on raising auxiliary forces, including mounted corps of 'Gentlemen and Yeomanry'. In response, a meeting was held at Oakham Castle on 22 March, at which the original proposal was reconsidered, some alterations made and a subscription opened. Three troops, each of fifty men, officers included, were to be formed 'to serve during the War, to consist of gentlemen and yeomen, and such Persons as they shall bring forward, to be approved of by the Lord Lieutenant, under Authority from His Majesty'. The new proposal was accepted by the government and on 5 April 1794 the High Sheriff, with those local noblemen, gentlemen and yeomen who intended to form the new corps (some 154 men in all) met at Oakham to select their officers and conduct other pertinent business.[27] Commissions in the new force were dated 25 April, the Rutland Yeomanry claiming the distinction of being the first Yeomanry corps raised under Parliament's Act of April 1794 to encourage Volunteers. Their claim to have been 'the first body of British Volunteer Yeomanry' is not without rivals, but the regulations adopted by the Rutland corps were indeed those recommended by the government as a model for others to follow.[28]

Despite its small size, the Earl of Winchelsea, who was originally nominated as one of the three captains, soon assumed the command of the new corps as its colonel, a distinction allowed him in consideration of his being the county's Lord Lieutenant. The presentation of standards did not take place until 29 October 1795 at Uppingham, being delayed by the death of the donor, John Heathcote senior. The Earl of Winchelsea took the occasion to emphasize the importance of the corps' example to the whole country. Describing the Rutland Yeomanry as 'the leading corps of British Yeomanry' he referred to 'the obligations expressed by the neighbouring counties to the Yeomanry of Rutland for a plan and institution so beneficial to the kingdom'. The presentation, and the Earl's words, were reported nationally in the *Gentleman's Magazine*.[29]

Subsequently the troops were expanded in size (to seventy-three men each in 1797) and a fourth troop added in 1801. Unlike the Leicestershire Regiment of Yeomanry Cavalry, the Rutland corps did not disband at the Peace of Amiens in 1802, but renewed its services that summer. The corps continued, and in August 1803, after the renewal of war with France, its four troops could muster a total of 168 rank and file. That same month plans for the creation of an infantry Volunteer force in the county were also progressing, and the Earl of Winchelsea took the opportunity to raise a rifle company (95 rank and file) to be attached to his Yeomanry as 'Sharpshooters'. Together, the Yeomanry and the new company of dismounted riflemen were christened 'The Rutland Legion'. At the close of 1808 the Legion had on its register 307 men, 204 of whom were in the Yeomanry and 103 in the rifle company. Despite the government's withdrawal of the clothing allowance for Volunteer infantry in 1809, the rifle company continued its services and was not finally dissolved until the general disbandment of Volunteer infantry corps in 1813.[30] The Yeomanry however, as elsewhere, continued in being even after the general peace of 1815, their strength fluctuating between 160 and 190 men. In 1828 the Yeomanry too were disbanded, being included in the government's termination of the services of twenty-four regiments of Yeomanry which had 'very seldom or never' been called out in support of the civil power over the preceding ten years. From 1828 onwards the names of former Rutland Yeomanry officers appeared on the rolls of the Leicestershire Yeomanry, the Leicestershire corps in effect becoming the Volunteer cavalry of both counties.[31]

Infantry Volunteers were slower to form in Rutland, but in the summer of 1798 both a Rutland Volunteer Infantry and an Oakham Armed Association (of company strength, 'for the defence of the Town and Neighbourhood of Oakham') were created. It was intended that the Volunteer infantry should consist of five independent companies (324 all ranks), and four of those companies were duly raised. The fifth, however, was stillborn, perishing when its captain, Francis Wooton, and his son, the company's lieutenant, resigned immediately upon receiving their commissions. In November 1799 however, Gerard Noel Noel, the wealthy proprietor of Catmose Lodge, Oakham, proposed to raise a fifth company and to form the whole into a battalion under his own command. As Gerard Noel Edwards, he had previously served in the county Militia, and in 1794 had undertaken the expensive task of raising a regiment of cavalry (The Rutland Fencible Cavalry), for whom, and 'for the service of His Majesty', he built in 1794–5 a splendid riding house with a sixty-foot roof span, complete with stables and quarters, opposite his mansion in Oakham. He became a colonel in the process – but by the end of 1799 his regiment was facing disbandment. In Winchelsea's opinion Noel's standing in the county (as a member of the Earl of Gainsborough's family of Exton) made him 'a very proper person' to command a Volunteer corps, and Noel was shortly gazetted as Lieutenant Colonel Commandant of the Rutland Volunteer Infantry, his appointment dated 11 January 1800.[32]

The episode of the fifth company underscored the difficulty of finding suitable gentlemen in such a small and scattered rural community as Rutland to serve as officers. As it was, one of the company captains was a clergyman. The raising of the Yeomanry and the need to supply Militia officers strained the county's resources, and following the end of the Peace of Amiens, the acuteness of the situation forced Winchelsea, as Lord Lieutenant, to resort again to the nomination of local clergymen to fill two of the vacant commissions in his county's Volunteer forces. They were appointments which were approved only on the grounds of necessity.[33]

At the Peace of Amiens, in 1802, both the Armed Association and the Volunteer Infantry were disbanded, Lt-Col Noel retaining a large number of the arms. When war was resumed in 1803 Rutland's infantry Volunteers were formed afresh. Putting aside a first plan to create three independent companies, the whole came together once again under the command of Gerard Noel Noel. The new corps of Rutland Volunteer Infantry (consisting of three companies of 80 rank and file each) was accepted by the government on 22 August 1803 with Noel as major commandant, a loss in rank which he was unable to reverse despite pleading his former services in raising the Rutland Fencible Cavalry. The men in Major Noel's corps came from every part of Rutland and being 'dispersed in many Villages which are distant from Each other . . . it is extremely difficult for him to have them trained & exercised as they ought to be'. Nonetheless the corps maintained its strength, returning 270 men at its inspection in April 1809. But the loss of the government

clothing allowance that year put the future of the corps in doubt. By the
end of 1809 it had been decided to continue if clothing could be provided
from a fresh county subscription, but otherwise they would go on 'only
as long as their present Clothing will last'. At their assembly for training
in June 1810, the officers and men of the Rutland Volunteer Infantry gave
in their resignations.[34]

Following the demise of Major Noel's corps, plans were made to
replace the Volunteers with a new corps of Local Militia, to be filled by
ballot if necessary, as had been done elsewhere. Neither Major Noel, nor
any of his officers were willing to take appointments in the new force,
and their refusal prevented any general transfer of service into the
proposed corps. Arranging a ballot and finding new officers took time
and only after unavoidable delays did the new Rutland Local Militia
come into being during the first months of 1811. The Earl of Winchelsea
took the command himself and was confirmed as lieutenant-colonel
commandant, despite the corps' very small size – three companies,
totalling only 207 rank and file. It was of course the very rank which
Noel had been denied. Superior connections, the county's lieutenancy
and an earl's coronet doubtless had their privileges. In 1814 however,
following the disbandment of Winchelsea's Rutland Legion riflemen, the
rank and file of the Local Militia was increased to 310. The Rutland Local
Militia continued in being, training each May at its headquarters in
Oakham, until 1816 when the ballot was suspended and the corps'
clothing and arms returned to stores in London.[35]

'Hearts of Oak'

In 1794 the menace of a French invasion had sparked off the creation of
Volunteer corps in Leicestershire, but fear of the French was not
necessarily uppermost in the thoughts of those who first subscribed their
money and their time to the Volunteers. Many believed that an
insurrection would be simultaneous with an invasion – which was in fact
what the would-be invaders intended – and saw the Volunteers primarily
as an 'internal defence'. Not surprisingly it was the 'respectable Inhabitants' in Leicester, Melton Mowbray and elsewhere, who came forward
to support the new Volunteers. The Yeomanry in particular attracted the
county elite, both noble and gentry, and where substitutes were taken in
place of 'Gentlemen and Yeomen', they were to have 'an Interest in Land
. . . or . . . be substantial Householders, whether Farmers, Graziers, or
Tradesmen'. Most emphatically Yeomanry substitutes could 'not be
Persons whose Situation makes it at all probable that they would enlist in
the Army, Navy, or Militia'.[36]

Raising a subscription fund was an integral part of forming a new corps, and a controlling committee, typically including the greatest benefactors, was appointed to administer it. The Leicestershire Yeomanry's committee was restricted to those men who contributed £20 or more. The committee of the Harborough Volunteers of 1803 had a slightly more democratic tone, as it included not only all subscribers who gave five guineas or more, and all those who were selected as officers, but also four privates.[37] It was however clearly the subscribers who were intended to exercise real authority: the committee quorum was five members, specified as three subscribers, one officer and one private. The funds collected defrayed a variety of expenses. The Loyal Leicester Volunteer Infantry decided to accept arms and accoutrements (or an equivalent allowance) from the government, but required that each member furnish his own uniform. Their subscription fund was to cover the cost of drummers, fifers, drill sergeants, ammunition and other incidentals. Both the Loughborough Volunteers and those from Melton Mowbray had similar funds. Among the expenses defrayed by the 'County Subscription', which for the most part was used to support the much more prestigious Yeomanry, were those for saddlery and for 'Uniform coats, Waistcoats, Breeches, Boots and Hats', though individuals were free to pay for their own if they so chose. By the end of June 1794 the county fund totalled £8,116.13s.6d., but even this did not seem sufficient. In August, with some subscribers still not actually paying, it was resolved that subscribers must pay a further 25 per cent on their respective subscriptions. A general meeting of the subscribers in October inspected the Yeomanry's accounts, and discovered that they had been overcharged by the London tradesmen who had supplied them. By November a balance of only £2,400 remained and that was still dependent on all of the subscribers honouring their commitments.[38] Such a sum, however, still dwarfed any of those collected by the county's infantry Volunteers, who counted their funds by hundreds only.

The exact terms of service in the early corps varied enormously, but for those formed later, in 1803, there were uniform conditions laid down by the government. The Leicestershire Yeomanry of 1794, following the example of Rutland, agreed to accept no pay unless actually embodied, and further decided that any pay received for service was to be divided equally among all ranks. By contrast, their humble comrades serving on foot were more inclined to accept pay, if it should be allowed them. A private of the Rutland Riflemen who attended his exercise and firing practice in 1804 received one shilling per day, and all of those who qualified as 'best shots' (a not inconsiderable number) were further rewarded, usually with another shilling. Being part of the 'best company', when at firing practice, could bring a further shilling, or even two shillings.[39] Service in the Yeomanry meant a liability to serve anywhere in the kingdom in the event of an invasion, but those who served in the Loyal Leicester Volunteer Infantry, raised in 1794 'for the Protection of the Borough of Leicester, and its precincts', were intended 'solely for the Defence of the Town'. In March 1798, however, the Loyal Leicesters agreed to extend their service, if needed, to include the whole kingdom. In 1803 such unlimited service within Great Britain 'in case of Invasion or the Appearance of an Enemy in force upon the coast or for the purpose of quelling any Rebellion or Insurrection . . . or in consequence of any Summons from the Lord Lieutenant of the county or general Signals of Alarm . . .', was agreed to by all of Leicestershire's Volunteers at their formation.[40]

The early Volunteers' insistence on extremely parochial boundaries in their terms of service stemmed directly from fears of serious domestic strife and open insurrection. When, in 1798, the Loyal Leicester Volunteer Infantry agreed to extend their service to the whole of the kingdom, an attempt was made in Leicester to create a new Armed Association, confined to service within five miles of the town, to replace the Volunteers should they be called away. The attempt failed but a similar proposal was made again in Leicester in 1803 and in Hinckley two years after that.[41] The resolutions adopted by the Loughborough Volunteer Infantry in October 1794 were most specific as to the purpose of the corps. They saw it as their duty to 'assist the Executive Government, in protecting our Laws and Constitution', a duty they intended to carry out by taking up arms 'to defend our Town and Parish, and by a prompt assistance to the Magistracy, ensure due obedience to the Laws, and preserve the Peace of the same'.[42] The Yeomanry in particular were seen as having a specific role in policing not only their own neighbourhood, but also in assisting the Volunteers in any adjoining county in the suppression of disorder. Some insisted that this was 'the most important Part of their Duty'. The 'Gentlemen, and some of the better sort of Farmers' who in 1803 tried unsuccessfully to re-form a troop of cavalry in Ashby de la Zouch, did so expressly 'for the purpose of checking the Colliers, cotton weavers, etc, in that neighbourhood, when the interior parts of the country may be unfurnished of Troops'.[43]

The ideals of equality and the universal rights of man, as espoused by the French Revolution, and taken up by radicals in Britain in their opposition to privilege and property, added a new ideological challenge to traditional Anglo-French enmity. In Leicester there was an atmosphere of almost paranoid suspicion. The Volunteers declared themselves to be enemies not only to the French, but particularly to those of their countrymen who held to 'Jacobin ideas', an accusation which was freely thrown at anyone who seemed to threaten the domestic peace. Under such circumstances, action by the local Volunteers in support of the magistrates was only too likely to cause resentment, the more so as the Volunteers drew much of their support from society's more affluent members, by whom they were financed, officered and directed. By the time the Loyal Leicester Volunteer Infantry received its colours, in October 1795, they had already acquired a number of enemies, 'malignant accusers', who they claimed had 'misrepresented and vilified' their intentions.[44] In March of that year the Loyal Leicester Volunteers and the Yeomanry Cavalry had suppressed rioting workers on the Union canal. The following month the Yeomanry ended a food riot in Hinckley. But a growing anxiety over food shortages that summer was not to be so easily put to rest. Worry over the violent behaviour of the poor led to a public subscription in Leicester to relieve their distress. In July the *Leicester Journal*, referring to the fund's subscribers, asked the poor to believe in the good intentions of 'that patriotic band, equally prompt to relieve the distress of their fellow-citizens with their purses, and to repel the enemy with their swords . . .'.[45] Unmistakably the benefactors of the poor were also among those who served in the Volunteers. Such an image of Charity, fully armed, was not perhaps especially reassuring.

What trust there was between the Volunteers and the common people was shattered on 6 August 1795 when Leicester's own troop of Yeomanry was called out to rescue a load of corn which had been seized by a mob of food rioters at Barrow-on-Soar. The Riot Act was read, and eventually the Yeomanry opened fire, killing three of the rioters and wounding eight. It was claimed that the Yeomanry showed great restraint for some time, but the incident was long remembered by radicals and by working people as 'the Barrow Butchery'.[46]

In the summer of 1803, when the cry for Volunteers was again raised, much greater emphasis was put on resisting the renewed threat of invasion, though the need to guard against 'the evil designs of all the Enemies of our most excellent Constitution' was still held to be good reason for gathering subscribers together. Both 'Rich and Poor' were urged to recognize a common danger, and 'every inhabitant who is capable of bearing Arms' was pressed to enrol in a local corps.[47] The nation as a whole was more united than ever before in its opposition to the French, now personified by the insatiable Bonaparte, but volunteering seemed at first to meet with apathy. From July 1803 onwards however, invasion fever grew, becoming rampant on both sides of the Channel, and in the end the scale of the French preparations (quite unlike those of the 1790s) produced an unparalleled number of Volunteer corps. The need for Volunteers was more generally accepted and men came forward in every corner of Leicestershire and Rutland. The intensity of the response was not be be equalled again until the summer of 1940.

'Loyalty, Discipline and Good Conduct'

On Sunday 6 May 1804 the Melton Mowbray Volunteers were at their usual exercise in the town square. All went well enough until the thirty or forty of their number who had muskets were ordered to go through the platoon firing exercise. Lieut Samuel Caldecott, who was in command, could not remember the correct words and soon threw his men into confusion, to the delight of onlookers who laughed and made fun of the Volunteers. The men 'became exceedingly out of temper' and as the exercise continued their officers were unable to keep them silent. When finally ordered to fall out for a short rest the men collected in small groups and talked loudly of going home. Reassembling them to continue the exercise proved extremely difficult, and refractory individuals refused to fall in unless they were all to be ordered home. Lieut Caldecott tried to continue with the exercise but another incorrect order prompted more grumbling and more confusion, with some men pressing the whole company to march off the parade. Caldecott managed to form the men into a circle to inquire into their behaviour, but faced a torrent of complaint. The men declared they 'would not be so Commanded' and 'set up a very general cry of wrong, wrong, wrong'. The situation was beyond Caldecott's control and, thinking it 'necessary to leave them', he and the other officers left the parade, to cries of 'no Caldecott', and the men 'continued hooting & hollowing' while the officers remained in sight. Only one officer, Lieut William Hill, seemed to find favour with the company. He was dragged back, raised shoulder high and implored to lead them in the rest of their exercise. He refused, and instead marched the remaining men into the market place, where he dismissed them.[48]

The behaviour of the Melton men was hardly inspiring. It may have amused their fellow citizens, but it worried the government. Although the question of actual disloyalty was quickly dismissed, there was complete agreement in London with the Duke of Rutland's view that the incident was 'a crime of too dangerous a tendency to pass unnoticed'. An inquiry was made, the evidence considered, and the Melton company disbanded.[49]

In the eyes of authority the Melton Mowbray Volunteer Infantry had exhibited 'a total want of Discipline and of Subordination, the Noncommissioned [officers] and privates not having any Confidence in their

Officers & rather holding them in Contempt, and the officers themselves conscious of not possessing Authority to enforce obedience . . .'.[50] For a nation momentarily expecting an invasion this was hardly reassuring, but given the nature of the Volunteer service it was not so surprising. The Volunteers, quite unlike any of the nation's other military forces, if not actually on service, were perfectly entitled to resign. In 1803, while the Loyal Leicester Volunteers had waited in vain for an acceptance of their offer of service, many men had drifted away, having taken the idea that 'from their Services not being accepted they were not wanted . . .'. By October further 'anxiety' over the long delay in confirming the appointment of officers, and frustration over the non-arrival of arms, had manifested itself in a certain 'impatience'. There was 'a little inattention' when the corps paraded for exercise and a further loss of members was expected daily. The very same circumstances had by then already caused 'a great decrease' in the membership of the Great Glen and Stretton company.[51]

The trouble was that discipline in the Volunteers jostled uncomfortably with an insistence on a certain degree of freedom and democratic choice. These were not full-time regular soldiers, but strictly amateurs who spent but a small part of their time in uniform. Indeed it was remarkable, and quite without precedent, to find so many of the male population, of all ages and occupations, drilling together as soldiers, and this even in the most remote rural villages. How much could reasonably be expected of a 'village infantry'?

Military discipline in a body like the Loyal Loughborough Volunteers of 1794, which saw itself as based on 'Friendship and Mutual Assistance',[52] had perforce to be gentle. The authority of officers and non-commissioned officers, who might also be social acquaintances and neighbours, could be strictly limited and rendered tenuous indeed where those in the ranks were also the local electors. Wealth and social standing might secure a commission, but there was often an assumption that there would be a certain degree of equality. The Lutterworth company's resolutions of 1803 called for a subscription to provide arms, accoutrements and clothing for those who could not afford them, but it was also stipulated that 'the Uniform of every Volunteer of whatever rank be in all respects the same . . .'.[53] To achieve that unanimity and perfect confidence in each other which the Loughborough Volunteers deemed 'absolutely essential to the existence, and prosperity of the Corps', it was resolved among them that any of the members could propose another for expulsion, the final decision to rest on a ballot of the whole corps. In common with the rules adopted by other Volunteers, the Loughborough resolutions made mention of certain fines to be levied against disobedient members – 6d. for an absence from parade or disruptive talking during exercise, one shilling for appearing drunk or for swearing – but stipulated that 'all Fines be determined, by the Eight Gentlemen nearest the offender, when at his Post'. In the Hinckley corps men who refused to obey the lawful commands of their officers could only be fined five shillings.[54] In the last resort an offender could be expelled, but commonly such action was not to be solely at the discretion of the officers, but also required a majority vote from the whole membership. The disgrace might be made worse by being published in the newspapers or otherwise prominently advertised in the local parishes – the threat of such humiliation very likely being a stronger deterrent than the prospect of fines. Resignations in such a closed and club-like atmosphere, if 'without assigning some good and substantial reason' to be approved of by a majority of members, could be resented. Such members ran the risk of being 'deemed a Coward and voted to Coventry'.[55]

Leicestershire's corps, and especially her independent companies, were first and foremost local institutions, and as such could hardly avoid the intrusion of personal animosities, and town or village politics. In October 1795, at the presentation of their colours, the Reverend Thomas Robinson cautioned the Loyal Leicester Volunteer Infantry to 'Beware of everything which may tend to excite jealousies and animosities among you. For the division of your Corps would be worse than the rending of your Colours . . .'.[56] Such internal dissension was something the Volunteers themselves were quite prepared for, and within weeks of Robinson's address the Corps was holding a general meeting to consider the conduct of one of its members, John Mann, 'in consequence of his having made use of some very invidious Language against the Corps'. Mann refused to come to the meeting or to explain himself, and was expelled. Within days, one Charles Mann announced his own departure from the Corps with a sarcastic farewell to the 'Gentlemen' of such an 'honourable' body.[57] In a climate charged with apprehension over the threat of invasion and of insurrection, such clashes between members could quickly become attacks on the loyalty of individuals. When dismissed from the county's newly formed Yeomanry, William Peake, of Twyford, hotly resented his departure being termed a mere 'Dismission for bad conduct' and publicly protested his adherence to 'loyal Principles'. He too had been called upon to resign by his colonel, 'in conjunction with the whole Corps'.[58]

Far more grave than the dismissal of difficult colleagues was the prospect of local feelings and personalities spawning serious disunion between neighbouring corps and companies. In the summer of 1805 an unseemly quarrel between the Shepshed and Garendon Volunteers and those of Loughborough came to a head. The cause of their disagreement, which the Duke of Rutland insisted was singular among the Leicestershire Volunteers, had implications which in military terms were just as unsettling as the scant regard which the Melton men had shown for their own officers the previous year. The true origins of the dispute are not clear, but Benjamin Fleetwood Churchill, commandant of the Shepshed and Garendon Volunteers, described his own and the Loughborough corps, as 'rivals in discipline'.[59] In this context it is probably significant that it was the Shepshed and Garendon Volunteers and those of Loughborough who, alone of all the Leicestershire Volunteers, added new companies in 1804, each thus acquiring the status of a proper corps, their respective captains commandant receiving the rank of major commandant. Nor would it seem mere coincidence that the more public eruption of their rivalry in the summer of 1805 occurred at the very time when Major Commandant James Boott was raising yet another company for his Loughborough corps, the success of which took him to the rank of lieutenant colonel commandant, one step beyond his Shepshed rival. Boott's success was achieved only at great personal expense, and was beyond the resources of Fleetwood Churchill and his Shepshed men to emulate, the residents of Shepshed being 'Loyal, but not affluent'.[60] Two thirds of the Shepshed corps were described as 'mechanics'.

The dispute, as it landed on Lord Hawkesbury's desk in London, centred on the outright refusal of the Shepshed and Garendon men to be inspected with the Loughborough men, though they had been positively ordered to do so by the regular General Officer commanding the brigade to which they had been assigned. Even a personal interview with the Duke of Rutland would not move Fleetwood Churchill and his officers from their chosen stance. The Duke's urging that they maintain a reputation for 'Loyalty, discipline and good Conduct' had little effect. They were not disposed 'to be treated with disrespect' by the brigadier who had instructed them to parade with the Loughborough men. Major Commandant Fleetwood Churchill found the brigadier to be an unpleasant man and in retort to his commands informed the brigadier that the Shepshed corps were 'equally firm with yourself in our determination never to be *Inspected* with the Loughborough Corps'. The Shepshed and Garendon men claimed it was perfectly immaterial to them with whom they might be brigaded in the event of actual service, but until that moment arrived they were 'sorry to observe that for us to meet the Loughbro Corps would be so mutually unpleasant that we are necessitated entirely to decline the thought of it'.[61]

Military considerations were completely subordinated to local animosities. The affair revealed not only the intense parochial character of the 'village infantry', but also the uncertainty over the exact status of the Volunteers, the limits of control over them, and their relationship with the regular forces. Fleetwood Churchill saw 'the comfort, and convenience' of the Volunteers as paramount, and no less than their due from government as they had so generously offered their services 'at the risque of their lives and property'. The Secretary of State and the Duke of Rutland did not agree. Parochial feelings could not be allowed to undo the government's arrangements, regardless of how much it might be wished to reward local Volunteers for their patriotism. The Duke of Rutland saw 'no solid grounds' for Fleetwood Churchill's objections and pointed out the military necessity of corps which were brigaded together actually exercising together *before* going on active service.

A resolution of the affair was not straightforward. If to later generations Fleetwood Churchill's position might appear short-sighted and amateurish, it was not without contemporary supporters, for Lt-Gen Pigot, who commanded the North Inland District, largely endorsed it. Though Pigot noted the desirability of corps acting together, he concurred in Fleetwood Churchill's view that the wishes of the Volunteers be respected – and this is what he told his brigadier. Although the Duke of Rutland hinted at stern measures being taken, there were no disbandments. As for the chief protagonists, Fleetwood Churchill had tired of soldiering by the autumn of 1806 and his resignation caused an immediate collapse of his corps, as no other officer was willing to take the command.[62] James Boott however soldiered on, and at the creation of the Local Militia in 1808–9, took command of the new and very much larger Loughborough battalion, as lieutenant colonel commandant. It was indeed hoped that the creation of the Local Militia might rectify many of the troubles which had afflicted the Volunteers, but in this there was certainly some disappointment. Incidents of insubordination and indiscipline continued to appear, much as they had in the Volunteers.

The behaviour of the Melton Mowbray Volunteers in 1804 and of the Shepshed and Garendon men the following year did little for the reputation of the Volunteers, but such failings must not be attributed to all. Keck took the Leicestershire Yeomanry firmly in hand and the Duke of Rutland's Belvoir Castle Volunteers were soon brought up to a standard which an Inspecting Field Officer who saw them could only describe as 'astonishing'. The success of the Duke's corps had much to do with the status, personal authority, experience and attention of the Duke. The ties of personal loyalty in his corps were manifest in a unique request. The Belvoir corps expressed a 'universal and strong desire', should they be marched out of the county, 'to join their Fellow Countrymen serving in the Leicestershire Regiment of Militia' – the other corps commanded by the Duke of Rutland. The Duke's Belvoir corps was greatly oversubscribed: 938 enrolled, but little over half of that number were selected, taken from the 'young unmarried men from the 1st Class [i.e. under thirty with no living child under ten years].' Those living on the Duke's estates in Framland Hundred joined his Belvoir Castle Volunteers; almost no one in the hundred joined the county Yeomanry.[63]

Success, such as that achieved by the Belvoir Castle Volunteers, was gained only by surmounting considerable difficulties. Gentlemen who were willing to serve as officers were not always to be found and their scarcity affected the efficiency of both the county's Volunteers and their successors the Local Militia. The Belvoir corps was officered by gentlemen selected from the Duke of Rutland's tenants, who 'have not therefore any previous knowledge of military matters . . .'.[64] This made the acquisition of a qualified sergeant-major an absolute necessity, but suitable non-commissioned officers were no easier to find than commissioned ones.

The success of Volunteer training relied heavily on the presence of competent adjutants and non-commissioned officers, but government allowances for permanent instructors did not suffice. Subscription funds were used to provide additional drill sergeants and corporals, and in the case of the Melton Mowbray Volunteers some payments, at least, had to be made from parish funds. Instructors with experience in the regular army were in short supply. Almost all of the eight drill sergeants appointed to the Loyal Leicester Volunteers in 1804 had acquired their experience in the auxiliary forces: four had served in the Leicestershire Militia and two in the Loyal Leicester Volunteers of the 1790s. All had been non-commissioned officers before, the most experienced having seen over twenty-five years in the Leicestershire Militia, almost all of it as a sergeant.[65]

The physical problems of assembling and training a concentrated urban corps like the Loyal Leicester Volunteers might be overcome with relative ease, but the wide dispersal of many rural corps, including the Yeomanry, was a serious obstacle. Far more elaborate schemes were necessary to train a large and scattered rural corps such as the Duke of Rutland's Belvoir Castle Volunteers. The Duke's corps was organized as four companies, each with an establishment of 107 other ranks, and was drawn from over twenty-six different villages and towns in the north-eastern corner of Leicestershire. In order to drill them, it was necessary to break the whole corps down into eight separate parts, each based on a group of villages and towns, each group having an appointed meeting place which was more or less central. Four sergeants, each with an assisting corporal, were assigned to instruct the groups, each sergeant being responsible for two groups, each of which he and his corporal would drill on three days every week. For those who did not live at the meeting places, the journey to them was usually not more than one to two miles. Under these circumstances it was indeed in a 'most astonishing manner' that Robert Cox, the man chosen by the Duke to train his corps, had by June 1804 'perfected the Regiment in the whole of the 18 Manoeuvres, the Manual and Platoon Exercise – in every part of which they are now the equal of any Regiment of the Line'.[66] The exertions required of such rural volunteers on training days were recalled by the 'old Volunteer' (who had lived in west Leicestershire) in J.T. Burgess's *Life Scenes and Social Sketches*:

> Yes, I used to get up at five in the morning and milk my cows, then put on my uniform and walk a mile and a half to parade and drill. I then walked home and worked till the afternoon, when I had to walk the same distance to parade and drill again, then home again and milk my cows and attend to my family.[67]

The annual stints of Permanent Duty which the Leicestershire corps began in 1804 offered an opportunity for more continuous training, which lasted over a two to three week period, while billeted in a nearby market town. The months of May and June were the preferred time, and the duty was done locally. In 1804 the Market Harborough infantry loaded its baggage into wagons and marched to Melton Mowbray for fourteen days of duty. The following year they marched south the same distance, about twenty miles, to Daventry. The other corps made similar marches. The Belvoir Castle Volunteers did Permanent Duty in Leicester in 1804, and the Corps of Donington Park United Volunteers were in the town the following year, Leicester's own Volunteers having gone to do their duty that year at Derby. The financial cost of sending the Volunteers on Permanent Duty was not inconsiderable. The Belvoir Castle Volunteers' twenty-one days at Leicester in the spring of 1804 was estimated to cost £713.6s.8d., which included their pay, the carriage of their baggage, an allowance to the innkeepers who had to billet them, medicines, and their 'Beer Money'.[68]

In the end the Volunteers did not fight Napoleon. Their pretensions, their foibles and their failings subjected them to much ridicule, but if the obstinate refusal of a man such as Benjamin Fleetwood Churchill to parade his corps with the Loughborough men seemed petty and irresponsible, it was also the defiant spirit of John Bull. Whatever anyone else thought, his Shepshed and Garendon men were convinced that their 'exertions and diligence have not been surpassed in any village in England'.[69] They declared their unshakable affection for the King, and their wish 'to partake of the glory of defending our Country'. But the Volunteers waited in vain, and inevitably the waiting produced frustration. By March 1813 the last of Leicestershire's infantry Volunteers had been disbanded, leaving only the Yeomanry. Perhaps the final word can be given to Francis Hoyland of Burton Overy who that November wrote to Viscount Sidmouth, the Home Secretary, on behalf of himself 'and Brother Soldiers' (the spelling and capitalization is his own):

> . . . I am a private in the Leicester Yeomanry and have been Since (nearly) . . . Their first Establishment, a few of us have met to consult about our future operations, we rejoice at the late Glorious news, we have made Sacrefices and are ready to a man to make any Sacrefice for our Beloved King and Country, Glad Should we be to be calld upon to perform any duty required by Govement either in or out of the Kingdom Headed by our much Respected Colonel G.A.L. Keck Esqr M.P., . . . we are anxious to Attain to as high a State of Discipline as possible . . . we have no other wish but to render the most essential Services to our Country – We are persuaded My Lord that the long wished for moment is arrived, and that now is the time to use every Effort to rid the universe of the most execreble tyrant ever lived in it. we hope to see every disposable force Sent to that Quarter likely to effect the downfall of our Inveterate Foe. we are ready My Lord to do the duty of any Regiment So Sent as Horse or Foot Soldiers . . . we Shall rejoice My Lord to see (Formally) an offer of our Whole Regiment for any Service which we presume is the ardent wish of our Regiment to a man . . . [70]

CHAPTER SEVEN

Yeoman Service:
The Leicestershire
Yeomanry, 1815–99

Keeping the Peace

In the summer of 1815 over twenty years of near-continuous war with France came to an end. Napoleon's defeat at Waterloo was a cause for celebration, and a great relief, but peace abroad did not bring tranquillity at home. For many of the common people life in post-war Leicestershire was simply a continuation of hard times. The depression which had overtaken the local hosiery trade in 1811 did not improve, and the malaise of poor wages and unemployment was joined by a renewal of radical agitation for political reform. In 1816 a vengeful attack on a Loughborough lace factory again raised the spectre of Luddite violence.

Respectable society viewed the scene with growing trepidation. The unemployed worker, the political radical and the machine-breaking Luddite were merged in a single sinister image: that of the Jacobin-tainted revolutionary. Nor was a remedy for society's ills to be found easily. For the next thirty years the tranquillity of many Leicestershire towns was periodically ruptured by disorder and violence. It was a situation which ensured the continuation of the county's Yeomanry when those in many other counties, as in neighbouring Rutland, were disbanded.

The attack on the Heathcoat and Boden lace factory at Loughborough in June 1816 quickly rekindled fears of insurrection, convincing George Anthony Legh Keck, one of the county's Tory Members of Parliament and lieutenant-colonel commandant of the Leicestershire Yeomanry, that a bloody confrontation with local radicals was inevitable, unless their activities were checked in time. The next few years were witness to much agitation and even greater apprehension. In the spring of 1817 near hysteria was provoked when, following the public execution of several Luddites, there was official warning from the government to be prepared for a general uprising that June. The aftermath of the 'Peterloo Massacre' of 1819 put Leicester magistrates on tenterhooks when a mass meeting was called in November to discuss the events of the 'Massacre'. As one of the more effective arms of local law and order, the Yeomanry were not only held in readiness, but on several occasions called into the streets, as much in the hope of preventing serious trouble as to suppress it. Fortunately violent confrontations were mercifully few and bloodshed was minimal.[71]

The Yeomanry's role in such parlous times, pervaded as they were by a deep-rooted fear of revolution from below, is well illustrated by the events of October 1831, the year of passage of the great Reform Bill. Leicestershire remained largely free of the violence seen elsewhere in the country, but when 'Riots and proceedings' erupted that month in Loughborough, as they had in nearby Nottingham and Derby, magistrates requested the assistance of the Leicestershire Yeomanry. The two troops in the immediate vicinity of Loughborough were called out and were soon joined by two more, commanded in person by Lt-Col Keck. In all, four of the regiment's ten troops assisted in restoring order, in the course of which two of them were called away to a more pressing situation in Derby. The magistrate who led them found it '. . . impossible to say too much in praise of the Yeomanry Cavalry whether alluding to the zeal & alacrity with which they assembled or to their sobriety and steadiness during their stay at Loughborough and Derby, or to their obedience to orders & forbearance towards the Mob who pelted & annoyed them wherever a narrow Lane or low wall afforded an opportunity so to do with a prospect of impunity.'[72] His description of their assembly is a graphic one:

> . . . At the time the Cavalry were called out the greater part of them (being farmers) were at the great cheese fair of the year at Leicester. On the serj.[ts] arriving to give notice of their being ordered to assemble the men left their cheese pitched on the pavement in the Hands of any body they could find & returned immediately Home for their accoutrements & instantly proceeded to Loughborough & from thence to Derby without dismounting.[73]

At first, the magistrate who directed the Yeomanry '. . . made an attempt to collect a constabulary force to attack the Riot with, but as is usual with that species of force the danger was over before many of them made their appearance.' Fortunately the Yeomanry saved the day, for '. . . a report prevailing that the Yeomanry were closely following me caused the Mob to disburse [sic] . . .'. The arrival of Lt-Col Keck enabled two troops to be despatched to Derby, but the 'appearance of tumult & attempts at plunder' kept the other two in Loughborough, where their '. . . patrolling most of the night prevented serious Mischief.'[74] All told, the Yeomanry were on duty the best part of a week, but even after the formal dismissal of the troops involved, sixteen Yeomen who resided near Loughborough continued to assemble at sunset in order to pass the night in town.

Throughout the 1830s the wretchedness of the county's impoverished workers led to sporadic rioting, while elections were a further source of regular disturbances. At the end of the decade Chartist agitation was causing so much unrest in the industrial villages of Leicestershire that the wealthier residents of Loughborough, so often a scene of trouble, pressed the Home Secretary for permission to form an Armed Association for their self-defence. After being refused, they sent a delegation to London to urge a permanent military presence in their town. The cause of their consternation, as was pointed out by the magistrates in Hinckley, was the absence of a police force. Apart from the occasional appearance of regular soldiers, the only method of keeping the peace was said to be by intimidation through the ostentatious use of the Yeomanry and the Militia staff.[75]

As was evident from the proceedings at Loughborough in October 1831, the Yeomanry could be invaluable to the magistrate on the spot, but the decision to involve them, according to Thomas Burbidge, the Leicester Town Clerk, had been based on necessity, not preference. The absence of any accessible regular troops had made a call for the Yeomanry unavoidable, but what the borough magistrates really wanted were regular soldiers, stationed in Leicester itself, to *prevent* disturbances.[76] There had been 'for many reasons' a wish to avoid the use of any domestic military force. The fears of well-to-do property holders were not shared by their less prosperous neighbours. While the mustering of the Yeomanry and the other local forces of order might comfort some, it appeared to others only as a provocative and partisan act of repression. The Home Office too had a decided preference for using regular soldiers whenever possible, avoiding local forces which might themselves appear as interested parties in the disputes they were asked to police.

In Leicestershire the leadership of the Yeomanry was clearly Tory, and appearing as it did to represent only one side of politics, the Yeomanry were never without critics. Nor were matters helped by the ill-considered hooliganism of some of the Yeomanry's wealthy young officers when drunk, during the annual Race Week in Leicester.[77] Towards the end of the 1830s it was rumoured that the Leicestershire Yeomanry was to be disbanded, a prospect which local radicals welcomed. The *Leicestershire Mercury* feigned its 'inconceivable dismay' at 'such a calamity':

> It appears . . . that there is considerable danger of the disbandment of the Yeomanry Cavalry! We need hardly say that we contemplate the remotest possibility of such a calamity with inconceivable dismay. To say nothing of the guinea per day, which the leaders of these brave men occasionally receive for their perilous functions; to say nothing of the rich patronage thus vested in the hands of our county gentry; what would the schoolboys and loungers of the town, for instance, do for amusement when they are deprived of the annual evolutions of the cavalry? What supplementary fun which the borough magistrates could devise, could compensate for the kicking up of the horses, the tumbles of the men, and the glorious wounds received by men and horses owing to the extreme difficulty of drawing and sheathing the sword?[78]

The Yeomanry's involvement in county politics, as a Tory instrument of repression (as the radicals saw it), faded with the coming of better times and a professional police force. Nevertheless for as long as the names of the great landed families of the county were synonymous with those of its political masters, the Yeomanry (whose ranks always included officers from those families) had a distinctly political flavour. Only in the late nineteenth century, when the political dominance of these prominent families was at last overtaken by the rise of political parties and semi-professional politicians, did the Yeomanry's political edge grow duller, though the social élitism of its officers lost none of its lustre.

The 1840s brought little relief to Leicester's downtrodden poor. For thousands of framework knitters, 1842 was a year of little or no work, grinding poverty and disillusionment. That August northern England experienced mass strikes, and the unrest soon spread into Leicestershire. Leicester itself was convulsed by a week of riot and turmoil. Strikers paraded in the streets while a detachment of dragoons was held in readiness, special constables sworn in, and the Yeomanry given quarters in the inns around the market place. Violence soon followed. The Riot Act was read and the market place cleared by the police. A procession returning from a meeting on the new Welford Road Recreation Ground was broken up by the Yeomanry and the special constables. The next day, 19 August, there occurred the 'Battle of Mowmaker Hill'. Another procession of strikers, hundreds strong, having attended an inflammatory meeting in Humberstone Gate, proceeded along Belgrave Gate towards Loughborough, once again the scene of rioting. Being pursued by a force of constables and Yeomanry, they turned off the road at Mowmacre Hill, some taking refuge behind the hedges. Here they were charged by the Yeomanry, whose most agile members, inured to the perils of fox-hunting, cleared the obstacles in easy style. The strikers fled at once and the 'Battle' passed into local folk history.[79]

The bloodless 'Battle of Mowmaker Hill' seems to have been decisive in ending the immediate unrest and along with the 'Barrow Butchery' of 1795 has always been associated with the Leicestershire Yeomanry's role as guardians of public order. But six years later, in 1848, there occurred far more serious rioting in the streets of Leicester. For three days and nights there was continual alarm as mobs battled with the police, the special constables and the military pensioners. The Yeomanry too were brought into the fray, but the worst which seems to have happened was that one unfortunate Yeoman by the name of Davis, 'an old landlord of the Black Lion', was roughly handled and pulled from his horse when he tried to enter the yard of the Bell Hotel by way of Humberstone Gate. Davis was saved by his comrades, the police and the pensioners, but the clashes continued, especially in Gallowtree Gate, and were not finally suppressed until a company of the 87th Regiment of Foot arrived.[80]

The riots of 1848, christened the 'Bastille Riots' after the popular nickname of the local workhouse, marked the end of an era. Though there were still hard times ahead for Leicester's poor, the town was entering an age of increasing prosperity, fuller employment and rapid growth. The public order duties with which the Yeomanry had long been associated became a thing of the past. Despite much criticism of the Yeomanry, local confrontations between Yeoman and citizen had seen very little bloodshed. The only Yeomanry casualty of 1848 occurred in September during the annual training week, long after the rioting was over. Sergeant Goodfellow died and his fellow Yeomen took the opportunity to bury him with full military honours.[81]

Leicester had been fortunate in having a police force at the beginning of the 1840s, but owing to middle-class sympathy for the grievances of working people, Leicester was also a difficult place in which to recruit the additional Special Constables needed to deal with large crowds and possible rioting. This made the Yeomanry's role more important than it might otherwise have been, the more so when regular soldiers were not immediately available.

The Yeomanry in 1850

At mid-century an officer of the Leicestershire Yeomanry in full dress cut an imposing figure. His black beaver shako was adorned with silver lace, gold 'lines' and drooping white feathers, his scarlet double-breasted jacket ornamented with silver lace and bullion-fringed epaulettes. Collar, cuffs and turnbacked skirts were distinguished by 'Royal Blue', a colour repeated for his trousers. Of particular interest were the buttons and appointments which now bore a new title, 'Prince Albert's Own', acquired in 1844 as a result of escort duty performed during a visit by Queen Victoria and Prince Albert to Leicestershire in December 1843. The young Queen and the Prince Consort had been impressed by the 'very soldier-like appearance' of the Yeomanry and 'the orderly and efficient manner in which they performed the voluntary duty undertaken by them'. In two hours they escorted the royal couple from the Duke of Rutland's seat at Belvoir Castle to Leicester, a distance of twenty-eight miles. It became a matter of tradition in the regiment that the journey had effectually cured all of their kicking horses. Nor were the Queen and Prince Albert the first royal visitors to have been impressed by the Leicestershire Yeomanry. The Dowager Queen Adelaide had remarked very favourably on them during an earlier visit in 1839.[82]

In 1850 the Leicestershire Yeomanry was one of the more substantial regiments of Yeomanry cavalry, having a total effective strength of 641 officers and men, divided among ten separate troops. Apart from occasional vacancies among its most junior commissioned officers, the cornets, the regiment was kept up to, and even over, its establishment of 519 privates. Robert Read, a local Rifle Volunteer enthusiast, referred to the Leicestershire Yeomanry as a 'stalwart rural cavalry', a description endorsed by the *Royal Militia and Yeomanry Cavalry Army List* of 1850 which described the rank and file of Britain's Yeomanry regiments as being drawn from 'the Yeomen in their counties . . . selected from an unexceptional class of agriculturists'.[83] However, both descriptions were somewhat misleading, for the Leicestershire Yeomanry did not draw its recruits exclusively from rural parishes. Almost one quarter of the regiment's other ranks, at the beginning of 1849, came from within the borough of Leicester itself. Captain Hartopp's troop was one of two troops which drew nearly three fifths of their men from Leicester, and two more troops drew a third each. The stronger troops, however, were those which drew most particularly on rural parishes. Viscount Curzon's was the strongest of these, mustering sixty-nine other ranks, all of whom were enrolled from the immediate vicinity of his family's country seat at Gopsal Hall; it included only one man, a sergeant, from the borough of

Leicester. Different again was Captain Palmer's, which took a third of its fifty-seven men from Leicester and nearly as many from the county borders, particularly from Rutland and Northamptonshire.[84] Men from outside Leicestershire, most of whom were in this troop, accounted for only 4 per cent of the regiment's manpower.

The officers were mostly from Leicestershire, with a few from neighbouring counties. Among their number were three Members of Parliament and eleven Justices of the Peace. As in other regiments of Yeomanry, 'The local influence possessed by the officers . . . is . . . great, as those Corps are generally commanded by noblemen and gentlemen, of large fortune and estates . . .'. Lt-Col Keck, still in command, had himself previously served as one of the county's MPs for thirty-two years. Of the nine captains, at least five had country seats. The regiment's other lieutenant-colonel was the Earl Howe of Gopsal Hall. His son, Viscount Curzon, served as a captain, while the Hon Henry Dugdale Curzon held the commission of a lieutenant and his brother William Henry that of a cornet. Viscount Campden of Exton Park, in Rutland, held a lieutenancy and Henry St John Halford, future commanding officer of the Leicestershire Rifle Volunteers, was serving as a cornet.[85]

The Yeomanry's leadership was unmistakably Tory. Keck, who commanded the regiment throughout the first half of the nineteenth century, was a die-hard Tory, an 'old independent true-blue'. He was followed in the command by Lord Howe, also a Tory. Keck's long career as an MP had ended during the Reform Bill controversy, but the active involvement of the Yeomanry's officers in politics remained strong. In 1850 two of the county's four MPs (all of whom were Tories) were officers in the Yeomanry. Major C.W. Packe, Member for south Leicestershire, had first been elected in 1837, as had Capt E.B. Farnham. When Farnham retired from politics in 1859 his brother-in-law, E.B. Hartopp of Little Dalby, an extreme Anglican who had previously been a Yeomanry officer for over twenty years, was nominated in his place.[86]

Apart from turning out in aid of the civil power, a frequent event prior to 1850, and occasional special duties and parades, the regiment assembled once a year in Leicester for training. Yeomanry regulations made a distinction between training which was an 'Assembly for Exercise' and that which was an 'Assembly for Permanent Duty'. The latter put a regiment under the articles of war and made it subject to the same regulations as the regulars, but it could not exceed six consecutive days, besides the days of marching to and from the assembly. By contrast, an 'Assembly for Exercise' left a regiment under its own rules of discipline, and while it could not be less than five consecutive days at one time, it could be for as many as fourteen days in a year. Both forms of assembly required the prior approval of the Home Secretary, but the pay for Exercise was only 2s. for each man and 1s. 4d. for each horse, while that for Permanent Duty was 7s. per man, to cover 'every other Charge whatsoever'. The Leicestershire Yeomanry generally assembled for a week of exercise each September during Race Week, the social zenith of each year when the important and fashionable of the county converged on Leicester. From 1859 however the week's training was changed to May. Assembly for Permanent Duty was exceptional – the regiment assembled for Permanent Duty in September 1845, but did not do so again until 1853.[87]

At its annual inspections the regiment seems to have made a good impression. In the 1850s it was reported to be 'in a good state of discipline and a most useful body of men', able to form 'a very efficient Corps' if called out. For the inspection of 1854 only fifty-six of its more than 600 horses were 'borrowed', i.e. belonged to someone other than the rider himself, one of his relatives, or his employer. The men were generally 'young and active' except for 'a few old Men who joined many of them with their Colonel'. The officers appeared very knowledgeable of their duties and 'both Officers and men . . . well acquainted with their Drill'. They 'worked with great steadiness & precision & officers & men are well practised in the Sword Exercise'. As in other Yeomanry regiments, discipline, except when on Permanent Duty, was enforced only by fines or dismissal, but attendance at the regiment's annual muster was said to be 'Rigidly enforced and very good'. It was a well-dressed and well-mounted corps, though Colonel Doherty of the 13th Light Dragoons, who saw them in 1853, noted that many items of their equipment were by then at least fifty years old, having been issued in 1803. In fact they were of the same vintage as the commanding officer, Lt–Col Keck, who had commanded the regiment since November 1803. In 1854, after fifty-one years of command, he was reported to be 'still wonderfully well able to perform his duties'. He continued with his regiment until his death in 1860, a remarkable command of fifty-seven years.[88]

The attainment of an acceptable level of discipline and efficiency depended principally on the activity and competence of the regiment's adjutant, sergeant-major and sergeants: among these it was most important to have men of previous service in the regulars. Few, however, of the officers and men of the Leicestershire Yeomanry had been professional soldiers. Apart from brief service in the 10th Light Dragoons as a young man, Keck had no military experience beyond that with his own

Yeomanry, and of his captains only one had been a regular soldier, in an infantry regiment. None of the lieutenants and only one of the cornets could claim any regular military experience. To remedy such problems adjutants were 'invariably selected from the Line' and care taken that at least an adequate proportion of the non-commissioned officers had once been regulars. From 1834 until his retirement in 1863, the adjutancy of the Leicestershire Yeomanry was held by Frederick Jackson, a former lieutenant and adjutant from the 3rd or King's Own Light Dragoons. Each troop had a staff sergeant of previous regular experience, and the regiment benefitted further from the presence of other former soldiers in the ranks. There was however one difficulty. Despite the regiment's numbers, and the obvious importance of a regimental sergeant-major, the government would not pay an allowance for one. Finding it impossible to carry on without an RSM, especially as the ten troops were so widely scattered, the regiment employed James Hurran (formerly of the 4th Dragoon Guards) in that important post, and was obliged to pay him from regimental funds.[89]

An Established Institution

In the second half of the nineteenth century the Yeomanry settled down to a quieter life, without the repeated calls to be ready in case of civil strife. Their register of officers continued to be a roll call of the county's most privileged families. They were a well-established part of county life, the activities of their annual musters always having drawn crowds of onlookers, even in dismal weather. 'Wet day. Yeomanry races – capital sport – if it had been fine almost all the world would have been there', scribbled Benjamin Goodman Chamberlain in his diary for 26 September 1834.[90] Chamberlain also went to see the military reviews, which for many spectators were the best part of every muster. Mrs Carey Franklin recalled her childhood memories of such reviews in the Leicester of the 1850s and 1860s thus:

> The old racecourse, now Victoria Park, was full of interest once at least every year. I do not mean the races held upon it, but the Review of Soldiers. The Yeomanry and Militia had each a week's drilling. The Yeomanry was of special interest. Lords Howe and Curzon used to come, and a good band, and it was all very gay, and we children used to be allowed to go and see the gaiety and enjoy the sight of the horses. The Militia faded into insignificance, I am afraid, after the prancing horses.[91]

Beginning in the 1870s with the localization and territorialization schemes of the Cardwell era, the auxiliary forces were brought into closer association with the regular army. Authority over the Yeomanry passed from the Lords Lieutenant and the Home Office to the War Office. The squadron had become the standard tactical unit of formation instead of the troop, and Permanent Duty was undertaken each year. In line with the training of the Rifle Volunteers, a minimum number of squad and mounted drills, to be worked on throughout the year, was introduced, and became increasingly more stringent. In 1888 the Yeomanry became liable for service anywhere in the country in the event of an invasion, and both they and other Volunteers were finally put into brigades. The emergence of the Rifle Volunteer movement encouraged shooting skills among the Yeomanry, and both the Militia and the Yeomanry in Leicester made regular use of the new ranges established by the local Rifle Volunteers. By the last years of the century rifle shooting and dismounted actions had been steadily gaining ground on the traditional skills of sword-cutting and the close order charge.[92]

As the violent confrontations of Keck's generation had become ever more remote, it was said that the Leicestershire Yeomanry were now 'more ornamental than useful', their annual inspections 'merely good excuses for the gentry and yeomen of the County to enjoy an urban holiday'.[93] Supporters insisted that in the event of an invasion, the services of the Yeomanry would be 'invaluable', but not until the very end of the century were the Yeomanry themselves able to answer their critics with deeds, rather than words. Ironically the opportunity came not as the result of invasion, but from the mounting embarrassments of a remote colonial conflict in southern Africa.

CHAPTER EIGHT

'Defence, Not Defiance': The Rifle Volunteers of Leicestershire, 1859–99

Riflemen, Form!

For much of the nineteenth century, the Yeomanry alone were Leicestershire's Volunteer force, but in the wave of patriotic enthusiasm which swept through Britain in 1859 and 1860 as a result of the third 'panic' over French military and naval plans, the county raised ten separate corps of Rifle Volunteers. Leicester itself claimed to be among the first to form a rifle corps, and her Volunteers were constituted as the 31st Regiment of Volunteers accepted by the War Office. For this early appearance in the new Rifle Volunteer Movement the mayor, William Biggs, must take some of the credit, for he seems to have played a decisive role in the formation of the first corps. His sober observation that members of a mere rifle club, should they use their arms with fatal effect, would be hanged without ceremony if caught by an enemy, is claimed to have turned enthusiasts away from the idea of a club to that of a uniformed rifle corps.[94] Mayor Biggs was again present on 3 November 1859 at the Old Cricket Ground in Leicester, when members of this '1st Leicestershire Rifle Corps' took an oath of allegiance, swearing to 'honestly and faithfully defend Her Majesty, her heirs and successors, in person, crown and dignity, against all enemies . . .'.[95]

Leicester's first rifle corps dated its official creation from the end of August 1859, but other corps in the county were much slower in forming. Only as the Volunteer Movement gained momentum nationally during the ensuing winter and spring were other Leicestershire corps formed. By the end of 1860 Leicester had raised four 'Town Companies' and another six were to be found scattered throughout the county, principally in the main market towns but including the Duke of Rutland's own corps of 'Belvoir Rifles'. The combined strength of all corps soon numbered some 600 men. By 1863, after a number of resignations, Leicestershire's Rifle Volunteers claimed 825 members, and, still growing, reached over 950 by 1870.[96] Success, however, was hardly uniform. While Loughborough and Ashby de la Zouch had very soon produced strong corps, that in Lutterworth (where the town population was in decline) had to struggle with dwindling numbers, and in 1873 was finally disbanded.[97] Market Harborough was not to join the Volunteer Movement until 1880, and in Rutland participation was limited to individual enrolments for even longer. Only in 1908, after the reorganization of the Volunteers as part of the new Territorial Force, did Rutland acquire two companies of its own – although previously there had been an Oakham detachment of the Melton Mowbray Volunteers, and from 1889 there was a rifle corps at Uppingham School, also attached to the Leicestershire Volunteers.

In Leicestershire as elsewhere in Britain the impetus for the creation of the Rifle Volunteers came principally from the middle classes, but this did not result in perfect social homogeneity. Although the claim of one early Leicester participant, Robert Read, that '. . . high and low and rich and poor came eagerly forward to enrol their names and learn the duties of citizen soldiers', cannot be taken literally, his anecdote concerning 'the swells' of the 9th Leicestershire corps (one of the Leicester town companies) does point to social differences, and to the potential for dissension. Read recalled that the Leicester Volunteers had made their way to Warwick to take part in a field day and a review by the Duke of Cambridge, and like good soldiers each carried his own food in his own haversack – except for 'provident No. 9' which 'had brought a caterer along with them, to supply them with an elegant spread at the contract price of half-a-crown per head'. The commanding officer, Lt-Col Turner, who prided himself on a 'strictness of discipline', seeing this 'dainty dejeuner', announced to the humbler Volunteers that there was but a quarter of an hour 'to fill your bellies'. A moment later new orders arrived, and Turner immediately ordered his men to fall in at once. What ensued was 'an indescribable scramble for the toothsome viands of Number 9, which found their way into many an illegitimate haversack'. Grumbling, the companies made their way to the reviewing ground, but the incident was not forgotten by the men of the 9th. They resigned en masse, and the corps had to be rebuilt.[98]

The 'swells' of the 9th had resigned in pique, but the resignations from two of the other town companies stemmed from a very different problem: the considerable expense of becoming a Volunteer. The 4th and 5th corps were chiefly composed of artisans, many of whom simply could not afford uniforms if it meant paying all of the cost at once. To purchase a full dress tunic, trousers and shako in the 5th corps required an outlay of £2 17s. 6d., a forage cap and undress tunic another 16s. 9d. Many found such costs prohibitive and were forced to withdraw, and 'many others who are anxious to join have been prevented doing so by the difficulty of obtaining their outfit without great delay and inconvenience'. From the very start many in the Volunteer Movement wished to encourage the enrolment of willing artisans, and to assist those in Leicester a 'Guarantee Fund', enabling men to purchase uniforms on credit, was soon established by those 'gentlemen who are well wishers to the Volunteer Force . . .'. Many of the fund's subscribers were themselves Volunteer officers, and when the scheme appears later to have faltered, they took on personal responsibility for guaranteeing payments.[99]

From Autonomy to Integration

Although Leicester's early rifle enthusiasts may have been dissuaded from forming a rifle club, the club-like atmosphere of the early rifle corps was unmistakable. An entrance fee of 10s. 6d. was demanded by both the 1st Leicester corps and the 8th or Ashby de la Zouch corps, with continuing annual subscriptions of one guinea and of half a guinea respectively. Each year officers in the 10th or Hinckley corps were expected to part with five guineas if a captain, or three if a subaltern. Members could be either 'Enrolled Members' or 'Honorary Members', the latter 'contributing to the funds of the Corps, but not being enrolled for service'. Candidates for membership needed both the sponsorship of current 'Gentlemen members' and the approval of the Commanding Officer. The sound management of financial matters, crucial to the survival of every corps, was left in the hands of a small committee, whose members were elected by the corps annually, and whose accounts were regularly presented for the scrutiny of their colleagues. In the Hinckley corps any extraordinary expenses required a special general meeting and the approval of two-thirds of those present. Both discipline at the weekly drills and proper conduct at the rifle practice ground were enforced by fines or the threat of dismissal. Certain powers of punishment were invested in the Commanding Officer, but others might be reserved for the exercise of an appointed committee.[100] As family, friends and neighbours could serve in the same squad, what was disliked on the parade might be further discussed in the parlour or at the shop.

The early rifle corps were both club-like in their constitution and intensely local in their outlook. Major Wollaston touched a responsive chord when he told the Hinckley Volunteers, in October 1860, that the formation of their rifle corps was a singular event in the evolution of their town, elevating Hinckley to 'a level with other towns, which have been more fortunate and more prosperous'.[101] In the market towns in particular a considerable amount of civic pride was invested in the creation of each corps – and their autonomy was carefully guarded. When in 1860, the War Office urged the merging of corps to create larger battalions, it was necessary to smooth any ruffled feathers. As explained in a memorandum of 4 September 1860, the creation of the new 'administrative battalion', particularly suitable for scattered rural corps, was solely intended 'to unite the different corps composing it under one common head, to secure uniformity of drill among them, and to afford them the advantage of the instruction and assistance of an adjutant'. It was 'not intended to interfere with the financial arrangements of the separate corps, or with the operation of the respective rules, or to compel them to meet together for battalion drill in ordinary times, except with their own consent'.[102] In July 1860 all of the Leicestershire corps were brought together as the '1st Administrative Battalion Leicestershire Rifle Volunteers', with headquarters in Leicester. That November, when the redoubtable Lt-Col Turner of the Leicester town companies attended the official inauguration of the Melton Mowbray Volunteers he felt constrained to explain the purpose of the new arrangements to the Melton men, for, he said, 'they were apt to forget they were parts of a whole, and that they were joined to ten other companies for administrative purposes . . . .'.[103]

As the men of Leicestershire met to drill, to shoot for prizes, and to discuss the finances of their corps, it was only too easy to see these things as an end in themselves. The Volunteers were certain they had taken up arms to be ready if needed to defend their country from 'the lawless hand of the foreigner', but exactly how their drilling and rifle shooting was to be translated into effective military action was quite another matter. It was a question which Turner was anxious they should all consider. He reminded them that it was only 'when the whole were joined together they formed an imposing mass . . . they must oftener meet as a regiment for battalion drill'.[104] Major Wollaston gave the Hinckley men a similar message. Drilling and sharp-shooting were not sufficient. After acquiring a proper discipline they must learn to act in larger bodies, 'for unless you comprehend this you would only create confusion when you get into brigade'.[105]

That much was clear enough, but beyond the need to join with other corps for instruction lay the deeper problem of defining a real role for the Volunteers within the nation's military organization. The emergence of the Rifle Volunteers had been a wonder to many, but its persistence was perhaps an even greater surprise. Where the government had at first been disinterested, it had soon had to take notice of and eventually to face the problem of assimilating the Volunteers with the regular army and the existing auxiliary forces, the Militia and the Yeomanry.

Over the next half century the autonomous grey clad rifle corps of Leicestershire were to grow much closer to the regular forces, becoming part of the county regiment, the Leicestershire Regiment. In 1877 the Leicestershire rifle corps put aside their sombre shade of dark grey and put on the scarlet of the regular army, which, as predicted, caused some resignations.[106] In February 1880 the 1st Administrative Battalion Leicestershire Rifle Volunteers was consolidated as the '1st Leicestershire Rifle Volunteers', comprising eleven separate companies. The individual corps lost their financial independence and their distinctive titles, acquiring instead company letters. Later that year the regular army established a permanent presence in Leicester when the new military centre at Glen Parva Barracks was finally occupied by the 27th Brigade Depot, comprising the Nottinghamshire Regiment together with the two battalions of the Leicestershire Regiment. The Rifle Volunteers of both Leicestershire and Nottinghamshire had already been attached to the 27th sub-district brigade since 1873, as were the Militias of the two counties and the Leicestershire Yeomanry.[107] In 1881 plans for the full territorialization of the Volunteer Force were announced, each of Britain's 215 Volunteer battalions becoming a 'volunteer battalion' to a specific regiment of the line. The change in designation was carried out over a period of time, and in 1883 the 1st Leicestershire Rifle Volunteers changed their title again, to become the '1st Volunteer Battalion, The Leicestershire Regiment'. The new battalion consisted of twelve companies, Market Harborough having formed a complete company from the detachment first raised there in 1880. In 1884 the total strength of the battalion was reported as 1,080 all ranks, a figure which was little changed ten years later. Not until 1900, during the Boer War, was there a sizable increase in strength. Four new companies were then added, making a 'double battalion' of sixteen companies.[108]

The Volunteer Life

The progressively closer association with the regular army brought more than simply changes of name, though the essentials of Volunteer life were little altered. Drill, target shooting and field instruction were mixed with a full calendar of social activities, with fellow members and with the public, the latter for the serious purpose of raising funds.

The early Volunteers threw themselves into drill and musketry practice with a remarkable enthusiasm. At its formation in 1860 the Ashby de la Zouch corps proposed to conduct an hour of recruit and squad drill twice a day, three days in the week, with a general drill for all members once every two weeks. To remain 'effective', members were to continue to attend at least eight drills every four months. The Hinckley corps were still more ardent, requiring every member to drill twice each week for the first year and once a week, every week thereafter. Drills were held both morning and evening, some of the first Leicester corps being said to be 'so anxious after proficiency that they would parade on the Abbey Meadow by 6 a.m. on a Monday morning and before the next "Day of Rest" came round, would place sixteen drills to their credit within a single week'.[109] All of this was quite in excess of the minimum annual requirement set by the government, which until 1899 only required Volunteers to attend six company drills, three battalion drills, and the annual inspection of the corps. Recruits were to attend a minimum of thirty drills within their first eighteen months, but from 1881 this was increased to sixty drills in two years. By contrast, the enthusiastic Robert Read, in his first year (1862–3) with the 9th Leicester corps, presented himself for drill no less than 102 times.

The Volunteer year began in the late autumn and most drills were usually completed in time for the annual inspection. In April 1872, having just finished the examination and appointment of the year's new non-commissioned officers, Captain Smith's 5th Leicestershire Corps was holding a squad drill every evening, except Saturdays, at the Leicester Corn Exchange. Members had to attend three such drills before receiving their rifles and progressing to the company drills, which were held only once a week. That May musketry practice began for the third class shots, with firing taking place every morning at six and every evening at five, Saturdays excepted when there was a practice from mid-afternoon only. May also saw the beginning of full dress battalion drills in the Market Place, in addition to the squad and company drills, and by June the battalion drills were being held once a week in preparation for the annual inspection that July.[110]

On occasion the usual fare of drilling and musketry was supplemented by special parades, reviews and field days. From 1872, one brigade level drill a year become compulsory for all Volunteer corps, but such larger scale exercises had been undertaken even in the Volunteer Movement's earliest days. In 1861 the Leicestershire corps had attended a field day and review in Warwick, and two years later they travelled to Oxford for another field day. Both events, to Robert Read's mind, were remembered especially for the difficulty of getting a good meal – or if so lucky, of having time to eat it! Civic functions and royal events provided still other opportunities to parade before the local populace, or, as in the case of the special review by the Prince of Wales in Hyde Park in 1876, to set off by train for a day in London.[111] The Queen's Jubilee Review of the Army, held at Aldershot in July 1886, was another occasion long remembered by those Leicestershire Volunteers who attended it. For many, such excursions were exciting forays to almost foreign parts.

Camp was another break with the usual routine of office, shop or workshop – a chance to taste a bit of military life 'in the field'. By the mid 1860s regular annual camps were held locally in most parts of the country – but not in Leicestershire. Lt-Col Turner had urged the setting up of a summer 'camp of instruction' near Leicester as early as 1860, but his vision of the 'self-denial' necessary for this undertaking (which included drilling at 5 a.m., followed by a day's business in town and a return to camp in the evening), did not find enough supporters.[112] It was not until the summer of 1879, when Sir Henry St John Halford had assumed command of the Leicestershire Volunteers for the second time, that regular annual camps finally began.

The camp's blend of military, social and athletic activities epitomized Volunteer life. Those who went to camp returned from the vigorous outdoor life as 'better men both morally and physically, and above all, decidedly better soldiers'.[113] This was the hope which even critics of the camp's 'pomp and circumstance of mimic war' could share. At their first camp of 1879, Captain Adcock, 'the jolly Melton brewer', Quarter-Master Sergeant Tewley, 'the Hinckley butcher', and Sergeant Bowley, 'the Melton jeweller', together with their fellow Volunteers had, for a full week, the opportunity not only of greatly improving their drill and practising the movements of larger formations, but also of learning something of camp routine and of keeping kit and arms in good order while 'in the field'. For one week in the year it was all a novelty, and the men seemed to 'thoroughly enjoy their camp life':

The French Wars, 1793–1815

His Grace the 5th Duke of Rutland, as Colonel of the Leicestershire Provisional Cavalry (1797–1800). As Lord Lieutenant of Leicestershire he was accountable to the government for his county's auxiliary forces: the Militia, of which he was also the colonel, the infantry Volunteers and the Yeomanry cavalry.

Sir William Skeffington. As a former officer of the 1st Foot Guards, a member of a then prominent Leicestershire family and as a principal subscriber to the County Fund from which the Leicestershire Yeomanry were created in 1794, he became that corps' first commanding officer.

Henry Holland, Esq., Captain Commandant of the Loyal and Independant Loughborough Volunteer Infantry, 1800. The Volunteer Force drew in many men who would not otherwise have acted in any military capacity. Captain Holland was described in contemporary directories as a 'Coach-Master'. (*Anne S.K. Brown Collection, Rhode Island.*)

Sir Gerard Noel Noel, of the Gainsborough family of Exton. His attempts to cut a prominent military figure in local affairs involved him in heavy expense and personal disappointment. After the disbandment of his Rutland Fencible Cavalry in 1800, he put his energy into the Volunteers, but without achieving the recognition he thought appropriate.

Volunteers drilling outside the Reverend Moore's house at Little Appleby, Leicestershire, *c.* 1804–9. The Revd Moore's elder brother, George Moore, was Captain Commandant of the Appleby Volunteer Infantry, one of rural Leicestershire's independent companies of 'Village Infantry'. Such companies faced considerable difficulties in training. In 1805 the Appleby men did ten additional days of duty 'in order to make them more perfect in the use of arms'. (*Detail, plate LXVI, vol. IV, Nichols'* History and Antiquities of the County of Leicester.)

Inspection of the Leicestershire Regiment of Yeomanry, 30 September 1813, near Belgrave. The regiment usually trained together for ten days in May and four days in September. On this occasion Lieutenant-Colonel Keck was presented with a 'superb piece of plate' to mark his first ten years as commanding officer. (*Detail from a contemporary watercolour by J. Marshal.*)

'. . . a Speciman of a New Troop of Leicestershire Light Horse'. In 1806 when Daniel Lambert, a Leicester man renowned for his immense size (52 stone 11 lb), visited London he immediately became the subject of popular prints depicting him as an English champion, in this case wearing the light dragoon dress of the Leicestershire Yeomanry. The caricature captures well the defiant sense of local pride and national spirit with which Britons faced the threat of Napoleonic invasion.

The Yeomanry, 1815–99

Keeping the peace. Quartermaster J. Kirk of the Leicestershire Yeomanry, 1841. He had served in the regiment for forty-six years.

On parade in Victoria Park, Leicester, c. 1890. Throughout the nineteenth century the Yeomanry's musters were a great local attraction, especially the mounted band.

Officers of 'Prince Albert's Own' Leicestershire Regiment of Yeomanry Cavalry, 1861. Among them were the elite of county society. The Earl Howe, who succeeded G.A.L. Keck as lieutenant-colonel commandant in 1860 is seated in the centre, with him are Lt-Col the Viscount Curzon and the Hon. Charles Powys.

A 'stalwart rural cavalry'. Even if not an accurate description of all of the Leicestershire Yeomanry's ten troops, local farmers and their sons did provide a substantial part of the manpower. William Cuffling, a farmer from Mountsorrel, and later from Swithland, served in the Yeomanry from 1848 until his death in 1876, rising to the rank of sergeant. Four of his sons followed him, joining the Yeomanry in the 1860s and early 1870s. All served in Captain Story's 'C' troop. William appears in civilian attire, with two of his sons in uniform. (*D.H. Stanley*.)

The end of an era. Two mounted Yeomen in full dress at Oakham Castle, Rutland, c. 1890–5. The creation of the Imperial Yeomanry in 1901 and the introduction of khaki clothing was soon to change the Yeomanry's image, though the full hussar dress was to persist for more special occasions.

The Rifle Volunteers, 1859–99

Officers of the Leicestershire Rifle Volunteers, c. 1879–83. By the early 1880s the days of the highly independent rifle companies were fast fading and the growing assimilation to the regular army and the Militia was becoming unmistakable. The Leicestershire companies had adopted scarlet in 1877 and the spiked helmet in 1879, the year of their first annual camp. The changes were not to everyone's liking.

Cleaning and polishing at the annual camp of the 1st Leicestershire Rifle Volunteers, *c.* 1880–3. The Volunteers got only one chance a year to practise the soldier's craft 'in the field'.

Colonel Sir Henry St John Halford, Leicestershire's 'grand old man of shooting'. He was twice commanding officer of the county's Rifle Volunteers (1862–8 and 1878–91) and for thirty years his name was synonymous with the Volunteer movement in Leicestershire. In 1886 he was made a Companion of the Bath, in recognition of both his local and national service.

Band members, 1st Volunteer Battalion, The Leicestershire Regiment, 1883. Although the government did not deem bands to be worthy of its support, the Volunteers themselves considered them to be important, and Volunteer bands helped to encourage the spread of amateur brass bands throughout the country.

Maxim gun detachment, 1st Volunteer Battalion, The Leicestershire Regiment, c. 1888. On the occasion of Colonel Sir Henry St John Halford's sixtieth birthday, the officers of the battalion subscribed to give him a maxim gun, which he in turn presented to the battalion.

Men from the recently formed 'M' or Market Harborough company of the 1st Volunteer Battalion, The Leicestershire Regiment, winners of the Burnaby Shield in 1888. The many prizes to be won in shooting competitions were a powerful attraction for recruits, but encouraged critics to scoff at the Volunteers as mere 'pot hunters'.

Target shooting, c. 1900, possibly the Burnaby Shield competition. The recreational enjoyment offered by target shooting was central to the continued existence of the Rifle Volunteers, and the rifle 'club' atmosphere persisted into the twentieth century.

Into the Twentieth Century, 1899–1914

A reply to the critics. Men from the 1st Volunteer Battalion, The Leicestershire Regiment bound for South Africa.

On active service in South Africa. Lieutenant Evans-Freke (with pipe), Sergeant-Major Ewart (with glasses) and two men of the 7th (Leicestershire) Company, Imperial Yeomanry, reconnoitre the ground ahead from the 'Tiger's Kloof', a vantage point between Bethlehem and Harrismith. (*Private collection.*)

Camp of the 7th (Leicestershire) Company, Imperial Yeomanry. The service in South Africa was hard and often in barren surroundings. The few pleasures of camp life included a mess wagon and the antics of 'Adonse', the company's monkey mascot, just visible on the barrel. (*Private collection.*)

Men of the 1st Volunteer Battalion, The Leicestershire Regiment, in their new slouch hats, a short-lived style given popularity by the Boer War. The war brought more than simply changes in fashion, it also raised new questions about the military role intended for the Volunteer Force.

The new Yeomanry. The Boer War gave the Yeomanry in Britain a new image and a new title. Corporal A. Chamberlain, 'Prince Albert's Own' Leicestershire Imperial Yeomanry, in drill order, c. 1906.

Gunner Albert Carpenter, Leicestershire Royal Horse Artillery, c. 1908–14. Both Albert and his brother George joined the new horse artillery battery, one of several local units raised in 1908 to support the Territorial Force. Both were to see active service, Albert dying in 1916 in Salonika, after being bitten by a rabied dog.

Communications in modern war. Men of the Leicestershire Yeomanry with their new wireless equipment, *c.* 1908–14. (*Author.*)

Men from 'C' squadron, Leicestershire Yeomanry, in camp at Melton Mowbray, 1912. Training was taking on a graver aspect: the lastest modern rifles and, in 1913, practice at 'mobilization orders'.

The Great War, 1914–18

Lieutenant-Colonel the Hon. P.C. Evans-Freke, commanding officer of the Leicestershire Yeomanry, 1913–15. A Rutland man, son of the 8th Baron Carbery, and a veteran of the Boer War, his leadership and personal courage inspired the Yeomanry's stand at Frezenberg, 13 May 1915.

Officers and senior NCOs of 'A' squadron, Leicestershire Yeomanry, c. 1912–14. With friends and relatives in the ranks, many pre-war Territorial NCOs were accustomed to giving orders more in the manner of friendly advice rather than as sharp commands. If detrimental to discipline, such intimacy was also indicative of the strongest personal ties. At Frezenberg the men of 'A' squadron fought together with exceptional courage.

Territorial recruit, Robert Eric Pochin of Wentworth Road, Leicester, lance corporal, 4th Leicestershire Regiment (later 1/4th), *c.* 1914–15. The type of man then enlisting in the Territorials was described as 'wonderful', ensuring 'an un-failing supply' of officers. Pochin enlisted on 10 August 1914 and was commissioned into the 2/4th Leicesters in June 1915, subsequently serving in Ireland and in France. He described his civil profession as 'engineer and iron founder'.

Pochin with 'tin hat', trench waterproofs and a subaltern's commission, possibly in spring 1916. He received training as a 'Bombing Officer' and himself became a bombing instructor. In 1940 he again took up arms in the LDV and the Home Guard.

Not the war they had expected. Men of the Leicesters on patrol, from a snapshot in Pochin's album, Dublin, Easter, 1916. The 2/4th and 2/5th Leicesters arrived in Ireland on 28 April and were deployed in Kingstown and at Ballsbridge. At the latter there was much sniping and houses were searched for hidden arms and ammunition.

Men of the 2/1st Leicestershire Royal Horse Artillery, 1915, with the Imperial Service obligation badge displayed prominently on the right breast. The war quickly created a need for 'second' and 'third' line formations. Intended initially to replace those of the first line who volunteered for overseas service, most of the Leicestershire's second line also saw active service. The 2/1st Leicestershire Royal Horse Artillery left for France in June 1916.

Men of the 1/4th Leicesters firing at German snipers and machine gunners on the edge of the Bois de Riqureval, near Bohain, 10 October 1918. The Leicestershire battalions in the 46th Division, having played their part in finally breaking through the German trench lines, saw the fighting revert to the open countryside in the last weeks of the war. (*Trustees of the Imperial War Museum.*)

Recruiting for the Junior Training Corps, Leicester, October 1914. The Volunteer spirit in Leicester produced 'Training Corps' for both those over the age of enlistment and for those under age, the latter started by Mr T.H. Crumbie, a local businessman, whose enthusiasm soon involved him in great personal expense.

Twentieth-century Volunteers. Leicester's Motor Volunteers emerged in the first days of the war. Originally an armed motor-cycle unit, it ended the war as motor transport. When photographed in February 1915 the sixty members were expecting uniforms in a few days. Obtaining petrol was their most difficult problem.

Officers of the Rutland Volunteer Battalion, with Lord Ranksborough, the Lord Lieutenant of Rutland, December, 1918. The battalion had endured all the problems of its Napoleonic predecessors, including that of finding suitable officers. None the less it had persevered, and claimed to have had the highest proportion of efficients in England.

Between the Wars, 1920–39

Reconstruction – the band of the Leicestershire Yeomanry at the second annual camp, September 1921. The previous year the band of the 5th Leicesters had been loaned to the Yeomanry, but in early 1921 the Yeomanry reformed its own. Music marked many of the camp's activities and the reconstituted band proved 'a great success'.

'Arab Tent Pegging', Leicestershire Yeomanry. The annual camp ended on Whit Monday with a display of 'Yeomanry Sports', a traditional public event going back well into the nineteenth century, at which the regiment hoped to augment its funds from the gate money. The 'Arab' display is first noted in the regiment's inter-war diary in 1924 and 1925.

Annual training, Leicestershire Yeomanry at Stoughton Park, May 1929. The regiment was one of the fourteen Yeomanry regiments to continue as cavalry after 1920. Armed with sabre and rifle, their expected role was that of reconnaissance.

The 'C' Squadron Ball, Leicestershire Yeomanry, Loughborough, 1933. Social events were an important bond for all Territorial units, especially over the winter months.

The 'Saturday night soldiers', signallers of the 5th Leicesters, *c.* 1930. Youthful recruits and a rapid turnover characterized the Territorial battalions between the wars. The public did not take them seriously. (*Leicester Mercury.*)

Drummers of the 4th Leicesters preparing to beat retreat, *c.* 1930. Martial music was of no small importance in attracting recruits, a difficult and unrelenting problem, especially for the 4th or City battalion. Public parades and special ceremonials were all tried to encourage new men to join. (*Leicester Mercury.*)

Ceremonial inspection of the 44th (The Leicestershire Regiment, Anti-Aircraft Battalion, RE (TA), Victoria Park, July 1938. The customs of the old 4th Leicesters were continued, as was their regimental cap badge. (*Leicester Mercury*.)

The Second World War, 1939–45

Signals exercise, 1/5th Leicesters, Carrickfergus, 30 July 1941. Decimated in Norway in April 1940, the battalion saw no further active service and was eventually given a training role. (*Trustees of the Imperial War Museum.*)

The 2/5th Leicesters training in Scotland, 5 December 1940. Like the 1/5th Leicesters the battalion had been shattered before the war was a year old, but after rebuilding it was to see hard service in North Africa and in Italy. (*Trustees of the Imperial War Museum.*)

Men of the 154th (Leicestershire Yeomanry) Field Regiment, RA, manhandling one of their 65 cwt, 25-pounder guns, during mountain warfare training in Lebanon, 7 June 1943. After El Alamein, in October 1942, the 154th did not see battle again until April 1944, in Italy. (*Trustees of the Imperial War Museum.*)

Leicester Home Guards receiving instruction on the Lewis gun, October 1940. The Local Defence Volunteers of May 1940 were quickly transformed by the government into a uniformed force, dubbed the Home Guard in July, and in August allowed county titles. The arrival of uniforms was greeted with relief by all, even if initially they were only army denims. (*Leicester Mercury*.)

Home Guards from Melton Mowbray district practising with 'Molotov Cocktails', under the eye of Lieutenant-General Sir Ronald Adams, commanding Northern Command, 2 October 1940. The home-made 'cocktails', a bottled pint of inflammable liquid with a suitable fuse, were intended for 'tank hunting'. (*Trustees of the Imperial War Museum*.)

The volunteer spirit. Colonel J.E. Sarson, as County Commandant of the Leicestershire Volunteer Corps, May 1919. Sarson, a Leicester man, had become a Rifle Volunteer in 1860, retiring as Colonel Commandant of the 1st Volunteer Battalion, The Leicestershire Regiment, in 1903. In World War I he served as Commandant of the 3/4th Leicesters and, from 1917, as County Commandant of the Leicestershire Volunteer Corps. He was a member of the County Territorial Association and, from 1925 to 1937, honorary Colonel of the 4th Leicesters. He died in April 1940, aged ninety-five having in his lifetime not only seen the city's Rifle Volunteers of 1859 evolve into the AA troops of 1936, but also having himself been an active participant the whole of that time – nearly eighty years.

Home Guard training soon became more ambitious, progressing from mere observation, through static defence to aggressive counter-attack. Here 'enemy' paratroops, provided by the 8th or Market Bosworth battalion of the Leicestershire Home Guard, await a 'British' counter-attack during a large scale civil–military exercise in March 1943. (*Leicester Mercury.*)

Men of the 11th or Ashby de la Zouch battalion, Leicestershire Home Guard, await the 'enemy' at the Coalville War Memorial. Local knowledge was expected to give the Home Guard an advantage, making up for deficiences in training and equipment. In the end the idea was never put to the test. (*Leicester Mercury.*)

The daily routine of a military camp is interesting to those who have to experience it once a year, and then only for one week. Reveille is sounded at half-past five in the morning, when the men have to turn out and wash the 'bishop' from their eyes. The walls of the tents are then neatly rolled up if the weather is fine, the bedding rolled into small compass, and the tents made tidy, the non-commissioned officers in charge being called to account if everything is not clean and respectable. At half-past six o'clock they have to be on parade, and woe be to any fellow who is then found gaping, or drowsy. At 7.30 the canteen is opened, and at eight o'clock breakfast is served, and at half-past ten there is another parade, which gives an appetite for dinner which is partaken of at one o'clock. An hour or an hour and a half is allowed for digestion, and at three o'clock there is another parade, and tea at five. The day guard and piquet mount at 9 a.m., but piquets fall in with their respective corps on all parades. At half-past eight o'clock in the evening the night guard march out, and half an hour later tattoo is sounded. At half-past nine the subaltern of the day collects the reports on the parade ground, the canteen having closed at 9.15 and at ten o'clock, on a prolonged G being blown on the bugle, lights are put out. . . . Strict silence is enforced in camp between lights out and reveille, not the least noise being allowed. This order was well observed in our Leicestershire camp each night.[114]

Military training and camp routine were by no means the sole activities. A 'Programme of Athletic Sports' – races, hammer throwing, high jumping, all for cash prizes – was included regularly, the grand finale being a tug of war. In the evenings there were concerts, both music from the bands and songs by the officers and men. For the price of six pence the public could attend a performance of Lieut Brindley's 'Battle March of Delhi', 'The Village Blacksmith' by Lieut Pickering and Cpl Elliot's rendition of 'The Rifles of England'.[115]

However gently, both officers and men were introduced to the discipline of ordered communal living and, to some extent, to the privations of military life. For the Leicestershire men, that very first night under the stars in 1879, at Willesley Park near Ashby de la Zouch, proved an extremely wet one. A torrential downpour soaked both bedding and clothing, for, being 'green at the business of camping out', none had taken the precaution of trenching round their tents to drain off the rain. As morning dawned the camp took on the appearance of an extensive laundry, but through the good graces of the Earl of Loudoun, the men were allowed to dry their sodden bedding by a fire in his lordship's hall, and to fill it afresh with straw.[116] Even if critics did poke fun at such not-so-terrible 'privations', Volunteers of all ranks did get a taste of soldiering that was different from that of the drill hall and rifle range. Officers gained some appreciation of the logistics involved in assembling, moving and sustaining their men, even if only locally and only for one week a year. The early camps were held within the county, but in time they became more ambitious affairs, involving much more travelling, and participation with other battalions in brigade camps. The final camp held by the Leicestershire Volunteers as part of the original Volunteer Force was at Towyn in north Wales in 1907.

The Volunteer Movement of 1859 had sprung up around an almost cult-like interest in the rifle, and rifle shooting perhaps more than anything else sustained the Volunteer Movement. Acquiring and maintaining a rifle range was a most important item of Volunteer business and the earliest regulations of many corps, like those of the 8th or Hastings Company of Ashby de la Zouch, devoted more attention to the use of its practice range and the behaviour of members while there, than they did to military discipline while on duty. Competition in this 'interesting, healthful and manly exercise' was encouraged by a National Rifle Association as well as by similar associations at county level. Rifle shooting in Leicestershire was given further stimulus by Sir Henry St John Halford, twice commanding officer and finally Honorary Colonel of the Leicestershire Volunteers. Halford, as 'the grand old man of shooting', was celebrated nationally as an outstanding marksman and was a prominent figure in the promotion of rifle shooting, not only competing at home but also leading Volunteer teams abroad as far as Canada and the United States. For almost thirty years Sir Henry's name was synonymous with that of the Leicestershire Volunteers.[117]

Competitiveness was encouraged at every opportunity. In Ashby de la Zouch, one evening a week was deliberately set aside for members of the corps to 'compare their skill' with each other.[118] All companies organized their own formal competitions for prizes and were supported in their endeavours by the generosity of local patrons, town corporations and wealthier members. In 1887, one officer and thirty-six different non-commissioned officers and men, or almost one man in three, of the Market Harborough company, won prizes in the company's jubilee year programme of rifle competitions.[119] There were also regimental competitions, and from 1879 the culmination of the shooting year in Leicestershire was the annual competition for the Burnaby Challenge Shield, a much admired trophy presented by Maj-Gen A.E. Burnaby upon his appointment as Honorary Colonel of the Leicestershire Volunteers.[120] Beyond the county boundaries the Leicestershire men shot an annual return match with the neighbouring Robin Hood Rifles of

Nottingham, and travelling further afield sent a contingent each year to the National Rifle Association meet at Wimbledon. There were also foreign competitions. In 1864 Ensign Biggs returned with a gold medal from a shoot in Belgium and four years later Quarter-Master Sergeant Tustin distinguished himself, again in Belgium, at the 'Tir National'.[121] The shooting matches were themselves social events, attracting crowds and providing opportunities for a public dinner at the local town hall. The residents of Market Harborough followed closely the fortunes of their own local champions from M Company – ten times winners of the Burnaby Shield between 1888 and 1907. When word was received (by telegraph) of victory in the annual competition with the other Leicestershire corps, the crowds would turn out to greet the winners as they arrived at the local railway station.[122]

The rifle competitions, the band concerts, dinners and balls were all popular local events, but as soldiers the local Volunteers had still to endure the scepticism, or worse, of those who saw them only as 'pot hunters' or 'butterfly shooters', interested only in silver cups, cash prizes and socializing while in uniform. In 1899, however, in far distant South Africa, a war started which was at last to give the Volunteer riflemen, like the Yeomanry, an opportunity to prove their critics wrong.

CHAPTER NINE

Into the Twentieth Century: A Distant Colonial War and a New Image, 1899–1914

South Africa

In September 1899 the tension between the Boer republics and the British colonies in South Africa flared into open conflict. The Boers soon proved resourceful adversaries, quite able to inflict defeat on Her Majesty's army. Even before hostilities started, there were offers of assistance from the Volunteers and the Yeomanry, but not until December, after the disasters of 'Black Week', did the government reconsider its initial refusal and accept them. As it was illegal for both the Volunteers and the Yeomanry to serve overseas, special legislation was needed to allow the creation of units for the South African War.

On 2 January 1900 special Service Companies, to be attached to the regular infantry battalions, were authorized. The men were to be aged 20 to 35, first class shots, physically fit, of good character, efficient for the last two years and preferably unmarried or childless widowers. They were to enlist for one year or the duration. In Leicestershire 116 men from the 1st Volunteer Battalion of the Leicestershire Regiment were soon found to fill the establishment of one such Service Company, and still others enlisted elsewhere. Local enthusiasm ensured each Volunteer a rousing send off, and in February the company embarked for South Africa, eventually joining the 1st (Regular) Battalion, The Leicestershire Regiment, in General Buller's 4th Division. At later dates two further drafts, each of twenty men, were sent to join them.

Although the main Boer army had been defeated before their arrival, the Volunteers did take part in the fighting at Laing's Nek and Belfont, and in the operations around Lyndenberg, being included in General Buller's commendation of the Leicestershire Regiment's action against the Boers in the Crocodile Valley on 4 September 1900. The company suffered eight casualties, four of which were deaths.[123] In 1901, despite the fact that the war was not over, men from the Service Company arrived back in Leicestershire after little more than a year's absence – and were accorded a euphoric reception. Those who had gone to South Africa were welcomed home as heroes. They had experienced the privations and dangers of real service, and could justifiably feel themselves to have fully answered the sceptics at home. Fortunately for family and friends few had been lost. At the next call to arms, very few indeed were to be so lucky.

The Yeomanry at War

The image of the war which most caught the public imagination was that of the mounted soldier, with slouch hat and rifle, and it was the mounted man who was soon in demand. In response to General Buller's pleas from Natal for 8,000 'Irregular Mounted Infantry', an Imperial Yeomanry Committee was established, and just before Christmas 1899 an appeal was made for volunteers from the Yeomanry regiments. Buller had requested that the force be formed into companies, and each Yeomanry regiment was given an opportunity to raise the nucleus of such a company, every four being formed into a battalion. True to their cavalry origins, however, the 'companies' were more often referred to as 'squadrons' – and true to other traditions of the past, the new force was only partly supported by a government capitation allowance, the shortfall being made up by private subscription. Saddlery, uniform, and even the cost of sea passage had to be found from non-government sources, and practically every man in the Leicestershire Yeomanry's initial contribution, the 7th Company Imperial Yeomanry, produced his own horse.

The journey to South Africa was itself an adventure. After brief preliminary training in Leicester and on the Syston range, the 7th Company sailed on 7 February 1900 on board the SS *Kent*. Both men and horses were very seasick in the Bay of Biscay, and by 20 February thirty-two horses had died. Bottles of Bass beer, sports and more training afforded some relief from the tedium of a lengthy voyage, but by March the company was in South Africa, becoming part of the 4th Battalion I.Y. Over the coming year, the Leicestershire men were to serve alongside those from the Derbyshire, Gloucestershire, Hampshire, Middlesex and Staffordshire Yeomanries. The company was soon actively employed and, as part of Sir Leslie Rundle's command, saw its first real service in support of Lord Roberts' advance to Pretoria. On 5 May it came under fire for the first time, and by the end of the month had suffered its first casualties in an engagement with the Boers at Big Kopje. The actions were notable for being the very first time in the already long history of the Leicestershire Yeomanry that men from the regiment had come under enemy fire. Pte Richard Harrison, the son of a grazier from Newton Harcourt, made a terse record of the action at Big Kopje on 28 May in the diary he kept throughout his South African service.[124] 'All went well for 4 miles when suddenly fired on from behind hill – took horses under cover then advanced & had a very hot 2 hrs – J. Dawkins wounded & 1 Hants [Hampshire Yeomanry] & 2 horses killed – had to be Colonels orderly.' The next day Pte Berry of the 7th Company was killed, but such losses were light indeed compared to what others suffered. According to Lord Carbery's son, Lieut the Hon P.C. Evans-Freke, of Glaston, Rutland, another diarist of the 7th Company, the Grenadier Guards had been 'very much cut up' in the same action, with 160 casualties of whom thirty were killed.[125]

The war dragged on far longer than was expected, involving ever greater numbers of British troops. The 7th Company passed the rest of 1900 in making 'demonstrations' against the Boers, in escorting convoys, doing piquet duty, and in foraging: 'D. Ward shot a blesbox & hare – MacCormac bayoneted a pig', noted Harrison on 30 June. The monotony was punctuated by occasional successes such as the surrender of the Ladybrand commando at the end of July with about 3,000 men, and in September Harrison took part in a night attack which bagged forty-two prisoners, nineteen wagons and 'a lot of loot'. Only days later, as a member of a party under Evans-Freke, he helped to carry despatches through the enemy lines, the party taking five Boer prisoners in their passage. Boer farms were pillaged and burnt in retaliation for attacks by their commandos, but there were moments too of respite from the war's horrors – time for football matches with the Derbyshire men and for the antics of Adonse, a monkey mascot taken from the Boers. Casualties were usually light, but in November Harrison himself was wounded in an action in which two of his friends were killed, and as a result was 'marked for home' along with other Yeomanry casualties. He spent Christmas at sea on the voyage home, arriving at Southampton on 17 January. In Newton Harcourt he was greeted as a hero: 'the villagers met us & took the horse out [of the carriage] & drew us down round the village then back home which I was very pleased to get to.' By the close of 1900 the 7th Company had been involved in endless 'drives' to round up the remaining Boer commandos still at large. The major battles of the war were over, but the Yeomanry saw arduous service in continual patrols, escorts and running fights. Harrison was glad to be back home: 'sincerely hoping I shall get my discharge as 12 months is quite long enough & as much as we bargained for.'[126]

For Harrison's comrades still in South Africa there were several more months of service, but finally, in June 1901, although the war was still not ended, the 7th Company was withdrawn and sent home. Of its original strength (5 officers and 132 men), 4 men had been killed and 5 wounded. Five had died of disease, and 1 officer and 30 men were sent home sick. The casualty rate was not significantly different from that of the other squadrons in the 4th Battalion, which overall lost 10 men killed, 3 officers and 29 men wounded, 1 taken prisoner, 26 men fatally ill, and 10 officers and 144 men sent home sick.[127] Diseases such as enteric fever proved more dangerous than the enemy.

As no drafting organization had been set up, a second force of Imperial Yeomanry was raised in March 1900. Among the new companies was another created largely from the Leicestershire Yeomanry, the 65th Company I.Y. Before embarking, the men were billeted among the hotels of Leicester for a mere five weeks' training which consisted 'principally of foot drill on the parade-ground at the Headquarters of the 1st Vol Battn Leicestershire Regiment'. Mounted drill was also practised daily by alternate troops 'in a large field adjacent to the town', under the instruction of non-commissioned officers from the 17th Lancers and the company's own officers, four of whom were from the Yeomanry.[128] The company left England as part of the 17th Battalion I.Y. in the Rhodesian Field Force under the command of Lt-Gen Sir F. Carrington. After service in Rhodesia, the company was sent in November 1900 into the main theatre of war. It was constantly split up, the Yeomanry leading a hard life which often involved fatiguing marches in pursuit of an all too elusive foe.

Among the men of the 65th Company was Sharrad H. Gilbert, a Hinckley man, a former Volunteer who before leaving for South Africa had arranged 'to contribute to the press' his impressions of the war. His vivid description of one especially 'stern' and exhausting 'chase' after a Boer commando under Hertzog encapsulates much of what was experienced during the final 'guerilla' stage of the war:

The modern chase begins at dawn and proceeds at three miles an hour till dark. Then, after a few hours' sleep – with every second or third night passed on watch against swift surprise – the chase again begins with another dawn. And so day by day, till the quarry is run to earth or your horse is killed. And the latter case is ten times more frequent than the first. . . .

Yet another day's weary marching, and last night we encamped within eight miles of Britztown. It was the Eve of Christmas and as we ate our fare of bully beef we wondered if the rules of the Geneva Convention provided for a rest on the morrow – for time to cook a meal, and eat it, and think on the fare and the good things they are having at home. . . .

Several times during the day did we of the rearguard have to dismount and sit awhile on the veldt to allow the convoy a little more start, for our horses could not walk slow enough, and if not checked would soon outpace the wagons we should be in the rear of. Should we catch this guerilla great credit will be ours – the augmented credit of the heavily handicapped. For we have four miles of transport, of mule wagons and ambulance wagons, of Cape carts and Scotch carts and water carts. . . .

Six days' chase and no end in sight. Most of the morning was passed in getting the transport across a swamp. The whole of the narrow valley lay one vast sheet of glittering water. It was not two feet in depth, but hid a sea of treacherous mud in which each wagon stuck in turn. Each load was fetched through by double teams; twenty plunging mules goaded to frenzy by the long cutting lashes. . . . A hell of waist-deep screaming Kaffirs, of straining mules with piteous appealing eyes, of cracking whips, and long heavy wagons; the whole churning through a sea of semi-liquid mire – of evil smelling, evil looking, nauseating mire. . . .

Seven days. And we rode into Vosberg – a half-looted village. Telegraph wires trailing across the streets; outside the granaries huge heaps of forage; the sidewalks littered with piles of clothing, with broken boxes of stores and barrels of 'dop' with the heads staved in. . . .

Each day passing two, or mayhap three lonely farms with their dam, their one or two irrigated fields, their garden and their stolid Dutch inmates, not knowing the English tongue, though living in a British colony, and subjects of a British Queen. Then across the veldt, mile upon mile of sand, thinly dotted with sun-dried colourless bush. The most barren part of the Karroo. Hour after hour with no relief from the sand which burns the eyes with its glare, no shade from the scorch of the sun. Oh! for a change, a farm, a fall, an accident, anything; most of all, oh! for a fight . . . [On the ninth day Gilbert's wish for a fight seemed about to be granted, but after the brief excitement of a 'false alarm', the march continued.] . . . And the column again goes forward at three miles an hour, one foot before the other, on on the mechanical monotonous march. . . .

Ten days, and the horses are tired soon after they start in the morning. Poor brutes! They are on half rations as well as their riders. . . .

Eleven days, and the horses want pushing, and at night the light of the camp fires shine red on blood stained spurs. The shots at the rear of the column becomes more frequent during the day. Men ride in with the tail of the transport, an hour after their squadron has encamped; other men come in not riding at all. Their saddles are on the wagons, their horses lie miles behind, done to death on the veldt. . . .

Twelve days, and the sacrifice of the animals becomes piteous. . . . A dozen times a day the transport is pulled up with a jerk. A mule has dropped in its traces. In a moment the black drivers are down and the body is freed of its harness and dragged to the side of the road. . . .

Fourteen days – and equine nature can keep it up no longer. The column encamped and an inspection of horses and mules took place. Per chance there might remain enough fit ones to mount several squadrons to continue the chase. . . .

I can only speak on the veterinary's report on the troop to which I belonged, but it may be taken as fairly representative of the whole. We are twenty-one of the Leicesters, and we brought out twenty-one horses. We have lost three, obtained two remounts, and out of the twenty horses we brought into camp today, *four* were passed for further work. On the fifteenth day we turned our heads for Victoria West – to refit.[129]

The actions were little more than skirmishes, but entailed 'as much wearying work . . . with equal danger to the soldier as the "battles" of

the earlier stages of the campaign'. Gilbert recorded his own experience of
one such 'fight', writing it up later from rough notes 'made in the failing
light when the last echoes of the guns had not long died in the hills'.[130] He
and others in an advance guard had suddenly been fired upon from a ridge
'lined with a hundred Boer rifles'. In the ensuing chaos he found himself
knocked to the ground:

> . . . a second horse sprang over me, and they had gone, my horse with
> them, and I was left alone in an exposed place on the open road with the
> whistling bullets for company. Springing up, I seized my rifle, and ran
> as well as I could – for the fall had taken most of my breath – to some
> small boulders which had been piled in a little foot-high ridge by the
> roadside, and, lying behind this, I began to look around where the
> firing was coming from. I was in a good position, and lay there firing
> on any spot where I thought an enemy lay. I had nearly emptied my
> bandolier before the day was over. The guns were soon in action; and
> from this time the fight became a duel of rifle and (one-sided) artillery
> fire. I looked around. I was on a high spot and had a good view. There
> was not a man visible on either side. No smoke to be seen except from
> the bursting shells or from one or two old Martini-Henris the enemy
> had. *They* were soon silenced. Nothing but the incessant crack of rifles,
> the whistling and 'phitting' of bullets, or the occasional crash of a big
> gun. Near by were several Kaffir huts, and I could hear the laughter of
> children and the shrill scolding of women inside, as though nothing out
> of the common was taking place. Hens walked deliberately round the
> huts searching for food in their every-day manner. A little terrier
> sniffed round from hut to hut. Nothing more in the shape of life was to
> be seen. But the air was full of invisible death. The firing commenced
> at three hours past noon, and the sun had dropped behind the hills some
> time when the Boers were pushed back into the hill-road between the
> kopjes, and the firing ceased, and a strange silence fell over the valley.
> Then men came out to search for the wounded and the lost horses. I
> lifted my water-bottle from my side for a much-needed drink, and felt
> it strangely light. There was no water in it. But two neat bullet holes
> instead.[131]

Letters sent back home were no doubt welcome, but not always
reassuring. On 20 October 1900 another trooper in the 65th Company
wrote of a recent experience:[132]

> . . . a pretty lively time we had of it I can tell you they had entrenched
> themselves in a fine position for we did not know there were Boers

anywhere near us so well had they hid themselves but when our advance guard was about thirty yards of the kope [sic] they were on they opened a Hellish fire upon them and soon emptied Half a dozen saddles then the fight commenced in earnest the 65 Leicester's were escort to the Artillery the day. of course we had to gallop into action with the guns and didn't the bullets hum and whistle around us . . . our little maxims were Blazing away for the world sounds like a Boston lasting machine however after four hours we drove them all over the show. . . . Tell Mother not to talk about fish and chips also Ham and eggs for I have forgot the taste of them. . . .

The same writer also expressed what probably became a common sentiment, as he advised those back home:

. . . tell [Frank] . . . if he [h]as any idea of coming out here in any of the mounted Police tell him to take my tip and leave South Africa severly [sic] alone I have seen the police corps and I can assure him their treatment is not of the best if he wants to soldier tell him to stick in the Volunteers for home service I myself would not go through another winter out here on the Velt for £1 a day . . .

In June 1901 the 65th Company, like its sister company the 7th, left for home. In military circles the part played by the Imperial Yeomanry during the war was controversial, not all being impressed by their performance, but any such doubts were not shared by those family, friends and neighbours who welcomed their 'heroes' home with grand dinners and illuminated testimonials of their service. Nor did they doubt but that the two Leicestershire companies had fully earned their regiment's first battle honour, 'South Africa 1900–2', soon to be incorporated into the regimental badge.

A New Image

The sharp crack of rifle fire across the South African veldt ushered in a new era in the history of both the Yeomanry and the Volunteers. The companies of Imperial Yeomanry which had gone overseas had been formed to act as mounted infantrymen, and in 1901 the whole of the Yeomanry force in Britain was re–equipped for the same role. New khaki clothing, modern rifles and a new emphasis on scouting and rapid open order movement were accompanied by a new title, the entire force becoming the 'Imperial Yeomanry'. The old dress uniforms were retained for ceremonial occasions, but the force took on a new, graver image. The annual training period was extended from ten to eighteen days, of which fourteen days were compulsory. All regiments were to adopt a uniform establishment of four squadrons and a machine gun detachment.[133]

The war also stimulated interest in the Volunteers and four new companies were created, two in Leicester, one at Wigston and one at Mountsorrel, bringing the 1st Volunteer Battalion up to a strength of sixteen companies. A Cyclist Company appeared and a new medical support unit, the Leicester and Lincoln Volunteer Brigade Bearer Company, was also added to the local Volunteer forces. The war introduced the use of khaki coloured clothing to the Volunteers, and in 1906 a new 'kharki' service dress was taken into wear by the 1st Volunteer Battalion, their cyclists having by then already made use of the dull hues of modern war for some time.[134]

Participation in the South African War also pointed to a new level of military involvement for the part-time Volunteer. His future became a topic of public debate which led ultimately, in 1908, to the abolition of the Volunteer Force and its replacement by Haldane's new Territorial Force, whose nucleus was drawn from the old Volunteers and the Imperial Yeomanry. The existing Volunteer and Yeomanry regiments were to be reorganized into divisions and brigades, and new artillery, army service corps, engineer and medical units raised to support them. In Leicestershire this meant the creation from scratch of four completely new units. To raise, equip and maintain the new force, Territorial Associations were set up in each county. From their very inception those in Leicestershire and Rutland worked together as the Joint Territorial Associations of Leicestershire and Rutland.[135]

Nationally the new Territorial Force was to consist of fourteen cavalry brigades and fourteen infantry divisions, each division complete in infantry, artillery and ancillary formations. Leicestershire and Rutland were to contribute to the creation of a North Midland Division, which would also include units from Lincolnshire, Nottinghamshire, Derbyshire and Staffordshire. In addition the Joint Associations would also provide units for a North Midland Mounted Brigade.

The 1st Volunteer Battalion, The Leicestershire Regiment, already a 'double battalion' since 1900, was split in two, the Leicester companies and the Wigston one becoming the 4th Battalion, and those from the county becoming the 5th Battalion, The Leicestershire Regiment. In the reorganization, the old Belvoir company was disbanded, one of the Leicester companies was absorbed by its fellows and two new companies were created in Rutland, one at Oakham and the other at Uppingham.

The new 4th or 'City Battalion' took up headquarters in Leicester, while the 5th or 'County Battalion' soon established its battalion headquarters in Loughborough. Together the two battalions formed half of the North Midland Division's Lincolnshire and Leicestershire Brigade. The Bearer Company of the old Leicester and Lincoln Volunteer Brigade was expanded to become the 2nd North Midland Field Ambulance, RAMC, and a new Army Service Corps unit, the Lincoln and Leicester Brigade Company, ASC, was now formed. In addition a 5th Northern General Hospital was created and two new units, the Leicestershire Royal Horse Artillery and the North Midland Mounted Brigade Company, ASC, were raised to join the Leicestershire Yeomanry as the Joint Associations' contribution to the formation of a North Midland Mounted Brigade. In total, the establishment under the Joint Associations was to comprise 111 officers and 3,090 other ranks, spread among eight different units. The task of filling that establishment began officially on 1 April 1908.[136]

Recruitment for the Territorials did not run a smooth course. There was concern over the amount of freedom which would be enjoyed by those who joined – whether it would be the same as in the old Volunteer Force. Although stated to be for home service only, an imperial service option was left open to individuals who wished to take it. According to the Mayor of Leicester there was an impression that the new Territorials might be used 'in buccaneering expeditions abroad'. The mayor, himself a former Volunteer, wanted 'to bring home . . . that the territorial force was for home defence, and that it was a continuation of the old Volunteer Force'.[137] Attracting recruits, however, was only part of the battle; keeping them was equally troublesome. Resignation on fourteen days' notice, as in the old Volunteers, was no longer allowed and men signed on for four years, but at the termination of that time many left and did not return. To this 'wastage' was added those who obtained a free discharge to proceed abroad (principally to Canada and Australia), or to join the police, and especially to enlist in the regular army. By November 1913 the Joint Associations were facing an annual rate of loss of one third of their total establishment.[138]

Overall however, the Joint Associations felt that the Territorial Force in Leicestershire and Rutland fared better than in many other areas of the country.[139] The one truly weak spot was in finding sufficient officers, a problem experienced from the very start. At the end of their first year of recruitment, the Joint Associations had only 69 per cent of the necessary number, and one of its units, the North Midland Mounted Brigade, T & S Column, had not a single commissioned officer. By the end of 1910 the full establishment of commissioned officers had still not been achieved. That June it had been 86 per cent complete, but by October it was 20 per cent below the full establishment. In actual numbers there were only eleven more officers than in April 1909. Recruiting the rank and file was more successful, though finding the required specialists, bakers, butchers, saddlers, etc., especially for the Army Service Corps units, was always difficult. In June 1910 the Joint Associations had over 95 per cent of the required other ranks, although they were enlisting on average only about 1.1 per cent of the area's population. In Leicestershire recruits were easiest to procure in the county, where they enlisted 1.9 per cent of the local population at Ashby de la Zouch and 1.4 per cent at Market Harborough. The employers of labour in Leicester itself had been invited to assist in recruitment from the very beginning but in 1910 only 0.6 per cent of the city's population (then comprising almost half of the entire county) were in the Territorials.[140] In fact, it was the 4th or City Battalion which was one of the most difficult units to fill. Nonetheless, in 1913 when there was grave anxiety over Territorials elsewhere in the country, the Joint Associations' president, the Duke of Rutland, felt confident in saying that Leicestershire and Rutland were 'keeping their end up'.[141]

To fulfil his obligations, the Territorial infantryman was to complete in his first year a minimum of forty drills, a musketry course and at least eight days of a fifteen day camp. The training syllabus for recruits required that ten hours be spent on squad drill and rifle exercises, another ten on skirmishing and twenty hours on musketry instruction. In subsequent years the minimum number of drills was reduced to only ten, with his musketry and annual camp still included.[142] Officially, such training was not intended to make a man immediately fit for service on the outbreak of war – it was imagined there would be a period of six months' grace, after hostilities began, to do that.

For the Yeomanry, integration into Haldane's new force meant losing the title 'Imperial Yeomanry', but it also meant the end of the old requirement to act in aid of civil power. Even before becoming part of the new Territorial Force, the Leicestershire Imperial Yeomanry had adopted a khaki field uniform and had taken up a new programme of instruction. The annual training camps laid emphasis on the duties of the outpost, on reconnaissance, patrolling and the protection of convoys.[143] Becoming Territorials made little material difference. There were day-long manoeuvres, marches and dismounted actions in the surrounding countryside – all very different from the glittering reviews of the old annual musters on the Leicester racecourse. The squadrons now practised with the regiment's new maxim gun. Scouts were selected and 'each day receive tuition in the art of taking cover, advancing towards the enemy, and also receive special instruction in reading maps, being also taught how to sketch maps and plans so as to bring definite and accurate information back to their officers'.[144] All this had the serious intent of preparing the Yeomanry for modern war as it then was. But volunteer soldiering has never been without its lighter side, and a sports programme was usually included, along with the musical fare of an evening 'smoking concert'. There were prizes for the best turned-out man and horse, shooting and riding competitions, tent-pegging and horse-racing, 'several well-known chasers and racehorses' ridden by the Yeomanry during the training of 1909 being the focus of 'great interest.' A visit from the Quorn Hounds, with their two new whips, was an occasion of some excitement.[145] Camp could be hard work, but it was also an enjoyable time and for many the unique opportunity of a holiday with pay! Despite the South African War and the many changes which had followed in its wake, the smiling faces in camp hardly contemplated the grim realities of war, yet the nature of war and the Yeomanry's likelihood of involvement in it had changed greatly. In the summer of 1913 there were many things to learn and to practise: among them was something quite new called 'mobilization orders'.

The Territorial Force did attract new men, but it took its character from those who had done long service in the old Volunteer Force. The annual camp programme of 'Regimental Sports' in the 4th and 5th Battalions, The Leicestershire Regiment, always included a special 'Long Service Race' open only to men with sixteen or more years' service. Even six years after their creation, the Leicestershire Territorials had within their ranks men who had seen over thirty years of part-time military service. Some had served in South Africa.[146] At the beginning of 1914 it seemed unlikely they would ever see active service again.

CHAPTER TEN

The Great War, 1914–18

August 1914

The annual camp for Leicestershire's Volunteers, and then for her Territorials, had always been in August. That for 1914 was to be at Bridlington, on the Yorkshire coast, but it never really happened, being cancelled almost before it had begun. It was, however, to be more memorable than any camp that the oldest Volunteer veteran could remember. On Sunday 2 August the various companies of the 4th and 5th Battalions, The Leicestershire Regiment, set off by train for Bridlington; within forty-eight hours they were back home. Talk of war had been current for at least two weeks, and on 4 August the worst finally came true. Britain was at war with Germany. On the same day, two telegrams arrived at each company headquarters. The second contained only one word: 'mobilize'.

A quite ordinary bank holiday week was suddenly charged with excitement. All across Leicestershire and Rutland the Territorials were getting ready to depart for their 'war stations'. In Leicester, at the old Magazine in the Newarke, men in khaki field dress came and went throughout the day. The Magazine was headquarters for the 4th Battalion, The Leicestershire Regiment, and in an upper room, hung with pictures and photographs of the early Volunteer days, the battalion's secret mobilization orders were now out on the table. The eight companies of the battalion were gathering, each at a different school in the city.[147] Beyond the borough limits, the scattered companies of the county battalion, the 5th Leicesters, began to assemble in the principal market towns. When Aubrey Moore, a fresh twenty-year-old subaltern, only recently commissioned in the 5th Leicesters, arrived at Hinckley to join his company on Wednesday 5 August, he found a town which 'seemed to have gone mad. By midday the pubs were running short and men were crowding into the drill hall to sign on for enlistment with us, being quite prepared to take on the whole German army single handed.'[148] The following day, the Oakham company left Rutland to a rousing send-off, making their way to Loughborough for the 5th Leicesters' battalion mobilization. The next day the Hinckley company too began its march for the Loughborough headquarters, pursued by a 'contingent of ladies . . . on cycles', and with a number of men who insisted on going although they were still in civilian dress.

From Loughborough the 5th Battalion went by train to Belper, north of Derby, to join with other units of the Lincoln and Leicester Brigade, including their sister battalion, the 4th Leicesters. Being Territorials, they were under no obligation to serve abroad, but on 13 August the men of the 5th were asked if they were willing to undertake such service and 'a rough estimate was made that at least 70 per cent would consent gladly without further thought'.[149] Two days before, on the Magazine square in Leicester, Col Harrison had formed the 4th Leicesters in a hollow square and in dramatic fashion asked all those willing to go to step one pace forward – practically the whole had done so, though the exact numbers had to be counted later. Soon after arriving at Belper, the Lincoln and Leicester Brigade proceeded south by train to Luton, to assemble with the other territorial units which made up the North Midland Division. On 17 August the men of the 5th Battalion were asked more definitely about their commitment to serve abroad, and the proportion willing was estimated at 90 per cent.

To meet the demands of mobilization, the Joint Territorial Associations of Leicestershire and Rutland created an Emergency Committee. At first the committee dealt with purely Territorial matters, concentrating its energy primarily on the clothing and equipping of the two infantry battalions, the regiment of Yeomanry, the battery of horse artillery and the supporting troops which came under their care. Once mobilized, these units were to have been clothed and equipped for service by the army's Ordnance Department, but this proved impossible. The Ordnance Department was unable to find all the supplies needed, and the Territorial Associations were asked to step in, under guarantee of repayment by the War Office. The work of the Joint Associations was greatly increased, as they had not only to supply a second clothing issue and additional equipment for their own units, but were also soon asked to assist in the housing, feeding, clothing and training of the new Kitchener battalions of the regular army.[150] The output of local suppliers, however, was simply not equal to the demand, and the War

Office itself made the work of the Joint Associations even more difficult. What particularly annoyed the Associations was the fact that the 'Military Authorities' had asked them to equip the Territorials for service, and then 'threatened Manufacturers with various pains and penalties if they dealt with other than the War Office'.[151] Makeshift steps had to be taken to fill the gaps. Wagons and bakers' carts were requisitioned to carry ammunition. An appeal for donors was necessary to supply the Leicestershire battalions with field glasses – each case carefully marked with the donor's name that they might be returned 'at some future time'.

At the beginning of August 1914 the Joint Associations were administering eight different units, with a total strength of about 2,700 men. By the end of March 1915 there were almost thirty units, and 8,700 officers and men. After one year of war the number of men had more than quadrupled.[152] All of the original units volunteered for foreign service, and the Joint Associations were then asked to duplicate them, creating a 'second line' of Home Service, or Reserve, units. The original 4th Battalion became the 1/4th Leicestershire and its new second line duplicate was christened the 2/4th Leicestershire, and so on through all the units under the care of the Joint Associations, except for the 5th Northern General Hospital. The second line units were to replace those going overseas and were to provide drafts for the first line when required, but eventually some of these units too were to find their way overseas. In 1915 third lines were added as draft finding units.

Little difficulty was experienced in obtaining recruits for the local Territorial forces. The class of man enlisting was described as 'wonderful'. There was 'an unfailing supply' of applicants for junior commissions. The war establishments were quickly filled and the second line units easily completed with 'an extremely good stamp of recruits'. The problem was finding instructors and, to some extent, men qualified to fill the higher ranks. The Territorials were well regarded in Leicestershire and Rutland, and took a far more prominent place in local recruitment than was true elsewhere in No. 6 North Midland District. Up to December 1914, 40 per cent of all those enlisting in Leicestershire and Rutland (and 39 per cent of those in Lincolnshire) went into the Territorials, against 28 per cent in Nottingham and Derby, and only 25 per cent in Staffordshire.[153]

The Joint Territorial Associations of Leicestershire and Rutland were pleased with their own success, but there was soon concern that, overall, Leicester and Leicestershire were not giving their share of men to the military forces. The first flush of enthusiasm, in which recruits seemed so plentiful, soon gave way to criticism of the city of Leicester's failure to realize 'a sense of its responsibility'.[154] At their meeting on 10 December the Joint Associations were told that Leicestershire and Rutland had produced some 9,105 recruits for the regular army and the Territorials – but this amounted to only 1.83 per cent of their population of 496,000. The goal was to recruit 4.5 per cent of the total population. They were 13,255 men short. This was disappointing, but what made matters seem worse was the news of losses at the front. The Leicestershire Yeomanry had left England at the beginning of November and had gone practically straight up to the front. The Joint Associations' members listened with pride as they were told that their Yeomanry had been mentioned in dispatches by Sir John French – but there was also the saddening news that they had suffered their first casualties.[155]

'They can't call us Tin Soldiers, now, eh!'

When war was declared the Leicestershire Yeomanry mobilized as three squadrons and a regimental headquarters, the men of D, or Lutterworth, squadron, being distributed among the others. After concentrating at Grantham as part of the North Midland Mounted Brigade, they marched by road to Diss in Norfolk, where they were incorporated into the First Mounted Division. When asked to volunteer for foreign service, 94 per cent gave their consent and those who could not were returned to form the nucleus of the second line, or reserve, unit.[156]

After a long train journey from Diss, the regiment embarked at Southampton and on the night of 2 November left for an unknown destination. It was to be the greatest adventure of their lives. The night was dark, but the Solent was brilliantly lit by searchlight. Some few, like Lt-Col the Hon P.C. Evans-Freke, now their commanding officer, had seen service in the South African War, but for most, active service and travel to foreign lands were complete novelties. In the morning they arrived at Le Havre, and the next day were again packed on to a train, once more destination not known. After a journey of twenty-four hours they arrived at St Omer in the small hours of the morning. The next day all were in the saddle marching eastwards.[157]

Upon reaching the village of Esquerdes, firing was heard for the first time, but the ensuing week passed uneventfully. Then suddenly the regiment was ordered to turn out for a 25-mile march to Ecque. It rained all the time and was 'so dark that you could not see a hand before you'. Ecque 'was full of trenches all sorts, Algerians &c' – and mud, ankle deep and sometimes knee deep. The next day the march continued, even worse than the day before. By nightfall they were approaching Ypres:

Night came with rain, hail and wind. Guide led us wrong. Gun fire quite near looked wicked. Regular Inferno! At last we found our way and marched or rather galloped through Ypres, which the Germans were shelling. Houses in ruins and on fire, Cathedral just crumbling. No people about. No lights except from burning houses and flashes from guns. Horribly weird! Passed through Ypres towards the front. Shells whistling overhead and bursting close by. Guns deafening.[158]

The shelling continued as they camped for the night, but all were too tired to take much notice. The next day, however, they were obliged to seek refuge in a nearby wood, where they encountered a regiment of French zouaves in dugouts. That night, after leaving their horses behind, the Yeomanry went forward into the reserve trenches (actually dugouts) on the front line, and waited. Their 'first baptism of bullets' was soon upon them:

> It was fairly quiet during the night except for two or three sharp bursts of rapid fire, in which we joined, when we got warning that the Germans were moving. We quite expected to be attacked at dawn, but they did not come out that day, although they were on the move in the wood where their trenches were situated. With the daylight, however, the cannonade began again. The earth fairly shook, and I realized that which I heard before, that it was hell in the trenches. The trench I was in was rather out of the worst of the shell fire. Hundreds of shells went over us and to the side, but none struck just near, and we did not know until afterwards what had been happening on each side of us. Within three feet of our trench a poor chap was lying with his head blown off; in the next trench, five yards away, were three dead men. All the time it was freezing very hard and we had the greatest difficulty in keeping ourselves warm, especially our hands and feet. We thought our relief would never come, but, at last, at 9 p.m., they arrived, and we filed away across the frozen ground, totally indifferent to the snipers, whose bullets were continually whizzing over our heads.[159]

The Yeomanry were not impressed by the marksmanship of the German infantry. When the Germans advanced, they fired from the hip: 'All high thank goodness. Weird whistling tho'.' It was the enemy's artillery that they feared most. Indeed it seemed that it was the artillery that had decided everything. The magnificent shooting of the French gunners had saved them, 'their quick-firing guns simply mowed down the German lines'.[160]

The Leicestershire Yeomanry had tasted real soldiering and real battle. It was nothing like the annual training camps. They were quite unprepared for their first encounter with the awesome power of modern artillery, but they had at least been fortunate. Their time in the Ypres salient towards the end of the first great battle for that city had been cold, wet, and uncomfortable, and the artillery bombardments terrifying, but the casualties were light. It was not the war they had expected. They had been 'foot sloggers all the time at Ypres. Rifle and Bayonet.' At Ypres they became part of the 3rd Cavalry Division, being brigaded with the 1st and 2nd Life Guards in the 7th Cavalry Brigade. They were 'doing just the same work as regulars' and were proud of it: 'They can't call us Tin Soldiers, now, eh!'[161]

'Hold hard, Leicester Yeomanry'

Over the winter of 1914–15 the Yeomanry were in billets near Haazebrouck. Despite their recent experience as 'foot sloggers' their spirit was undiminished. To enliven a dull routine, the officers arranged for two and a half couple of hounds to be brought over from England to hunt hares and a drag. By April the regiment still mustered twenty-eight officers and 500 rank and file. Unlike the Life Guards they had had 'splendidly good luck' and for some time it continued, earning them a new, if unofficial, title: 'God's Own'. But that same month the second great battle for Ypres began, with a new horror – chlorine gas.

The Leicestershire Yeomanry, as part of the 7th Cavalry Brigade, were moved into a reserve position behind Ypres, but were then withdrawn. On 9 May 1915, however, a trench party from the Yeomanry went forward and took up billets in huts about a mile west of Ypres, near Brielen. On the evening of 12 May, having first checked and 'doped' their respirators (goggles and a wad of material soaked in urine, to be tied over the face), a party of fourteen officers and 247 men set off for a section of trench east of Ypres, and north of the Ypres–Menin road, near Frezenberg. About midnight they went into the lines, and finding the trenches to be very poor, affording little protection from shell fire, they began digging.

Sometime before 4 a.m., as it grew light, their work was suddenly interrupted by a most terrific enemy bombardment of shrapnel and high explosive shells. The shelling continued intermittently most of the day, obliterating whole sections of trench. A trumpeter in the front line watched as 'Those who did not get blown up were buried either alive or dead under the parapet of the trenches blown in, and all the time they kept up a perfect hail of shrapnel'. About 5.30 a.m., the men of A squadron, holding the supporting trenches on the Yeomanry's extreme left flank, began a retirement, but Lt–Col Evans–Freke, emerging from his dugout, met them, and shouting 'Hold hard, Leicester Yeomanry' brought them to a halt. The men were ordered back to their positions, and held them throughout the day in the face of a major assault by the enemy's infantry, which began about quarter past six that morning.

At 8 a.m. the men of A squadron were informed that they were the only troops holding the ground originally occupied by the 7th Brigade. The Life Guards, on their left, had evacuated their trenches before 6 a.m., and the German infantry, advancing along these trenches, gradually forced back the men of B and C squadrons, who were clinging to what remained of the front line trenches. Under sniper fire, and without trench bombs and grenades to answer those of the enemy, B and C squadrons fought a desperate battle as they fell back from traverse to traverse, the survivors eventually reaching the positions of the 3rd Dragoon Guards on their right flank. Still in their support trenches, A squadron continued to hold out, checking any further advance by the enemy towards Ypres until, in the afternoon, a counter attack was launched by fresh troops coming up from the rear. The forty survivors in the A squadron trenches joined in the attack and 'cheering like madmen' drove the enemy back in a bayonet charge.

The action of 13 May 1915, for which the battle honour 'Frezenberg' was awarded, was an episode of exceptional bravery. The men of the Leicestershire Yeomanry did their duty in the face of great odds. For the Yeomanry which so many had known from long before the war, Frezenberg was the moment of its greatest glory, and inescapably, a tragedy. That day each man had stood loyally by friends and neighbours, and the losses were mourned throughout Leicestershire and Rutland. Seven officers, including Evans–Freke, were killed, and another five wounded. Eighty-seven men were dead or missing and a further eighty-eight wounded. No longer were they 'God's Own'.[162]

The Unremitting Struggle

The war continued for another three and a half years. For the Yeomanry, dismounted duty in the trenches alternated with time spent in training as cavalry, ever in anticipation of an opportunity to exploit a gap in the German trench line. Several times the Yeomanry's brigade assembled with other cavalry formations, waiting while a fresh offensive attempted to force such a breakthrough, but none came. By 1918 the shortage of infantry on the western front had become critical and in March the regiment was told that they were to lose their horses in order to become a machine gun battalion. The conversion, however, never took place. The last great German offensive of the war, Operation Michael, created a desperate situation, and on 4 April the Leicestershire Yeomanry were split up and distributed as reinforcements to the regular regiments forming the 3rd Cavalry Brigade. In their new brigade they took part in the Battle of Amiens, the piercing of the Hindenberg Line and the general advance towards Mons. In its closing stages the fighting at last broke free of the trenches, and the Yeomanry were finally able to act as cavalry on the battlefield, which was at least some compensation for the chagrin felt at being broken up as a regiment.[163]

The Leicestershire Yeomanry had been the first of the Leicestershire and Rutland Territorials to venture overseas and to see action. The pre-war infantry battalions, the 4th and 5th Leicesters, with supporting medical and Army Service Corps units from Leicestershire, followed suit in 1915 as part of the North Midland Division (soon the 46th Division), the first complete Territorial division to go into France. Like the Yeomanry they spent the entire war on the Western Front, and like so many other units suffered such grievous casualties that by the end of the war they were the same battalions 'in name and spirit only'.[164] Having acquired many battle honours they were disbanded in 1919.

The Leicestershire Royal Horse Artillery was more fortunate. After serving as part of the 1st Mounted Division on home defence duties, it embarked in 1916 for the eastern Mediterranean, and saw service in Egypt and Palestine. At the beginning of 1918 nearly all the men of the battery were still those who had started with it in 1914, plus a draft from the second line battery. Practically all of them had been raised in Leicestershire, a fact they were reported to be extremely proud of. Still with them too were a number of the original horses mobilized at the outbreak of war.[165]

Most of the second line units raised by the Leicestershire and Rutland Joint Associations during the war also saw active service. The 2/4th and 2/5th Leicesters, serving in the 2/North Midland Division (59th Division), after a period of home duty were sent to Ireland in April 1916, and early the following year landed in France. In December 1917, at the reorganization of infantry brigades into three instead of four battalions, the 2/5th was disbanded. It had recently suffered so many officer casualties as to leave the command of the battalion in the hands of a captain.[166] Its reduction was deeply felt, but only four months later the 2/4th Leicesters, after the heavy fighting of March and April 1918 during the great German offensive, were reduced to a training cadre which was ultimately absorbed by the 14th Leicestershire, formed at Aldeburgh in June 1918. The 2/1st Leicestershire RHA was sent to France in June 1916 in the 63rd (Royal Naval) Division as A Battery, 223rd Brigade, and served there until the end of the war.[167] The Yeomanry's second line (2/1st Leicestershire Yeomanry), however, passed the war in Britain as part of the Home Defence Force, a role which was made difficult as it was also called upon to provide drafts (both men and horses) for front line units. Maintaining the unit under such circumstances was often a demoralizing business, and was made that much worse by its conversion into cyclists in 1916, followed by remounting as cavalry later that year, and finally a return to cycles in August 1917.[168]

By the end of the war Leicestershire and Rutland Territorials had fought in many of the great battles in France and Flanders, and had served as far afield as Ireland and the Sinai. Too many friends and comrades had been lost, but their record of service was one which survivors would always remember with pride.

Volunteers on the Home Front

In Leicester the reaction to the outbreak of war was not one of universal enthusiasm for enlisting with the colours. After the first rush of eager recruits, there was a growing anxiety that rather too many of Leicester's males were reticent about enlisting. Britain's unique 'voluntary system' of recruitment continued with ups and downs in Leicester throughout 1915, giving way finally to full conscription in 1916. Nonetheless, although the war failed to produce an unreservedly patriotic response in all of Leicester's citizens, it did not fail to create a new force of Volunteers devoted to home defence and a host of supporting civilian organizations as well. The possibility of an enemy attack on a county which, in the Duke of Rutland's words, 'marched with the coast County of Lincoln for a distance of some fifteen miles, and was in some places within 30 to 35 miles of the Coast itself'[169] looked real enough. If the excitement of a major European war was not sufficient cause, stories of German atrocities and the early appearance of Belgian refugees in Leicestershire and Rutland soon seemed convincing reasons to take up arms in self-defence. In Rutland, the catastrophe of war was brought home to people with particular force by the arrival, in mid-October, of two special trains with a most unusual cargo – the whole of the horses, state carriages, liveries, harness and motor cars belonging to the King of the Belgians – which had been evacuated at considerable risk from Brussels. The 5th Earl of Lonsdale had offered to take everything into his stables at Barleythorpe on the edge of Oakham. Later, some thirty carriages were stored in the old Rutland Fencibles' riding school and in the Poultry Hall in Oakham.[170]

Within days of the declaration of war, an armed and motorized 'flying column', the Leicester Motor Corps, was formed, at first from motor cyclists only, although later it included motor cars as well. Others, over the military age limit, came together in a Citizens' Training Corps, while more than 1,000 boys aged between 16 and 19, who were too young to enlist, were formed into a Junior Training Corps by T.H. Crumbie, a local businessman whose patriotic zeal for recruiting was ultimately to cause him personal financial distress. By February 1915 Leicester's assortment of Civic Defence Corps included about 3,000 men. In Rutland a meeting in Oakham in September 1914 took the first steps to organize a Home Defence Corps to be recruited at Oakham, Uppingham and Ketton. Lord Ranksborough, the Lord Lieutenant, appointed its officers, and during the first six months its strength reached nearly 200 men.[171]

Not everyone however, least of all the government, was appreciative of the new Volunteers. Until the introduction of full conscription in 1916, and to some extent even after that, the Volunteers were suspected of harbouring men who ought to have enlisted for active service. What notice was taken of the Volunteers by the government was hardly encouraging. Material assistance of any sort was refused, while the terms of the government's belated acknowledgment of the force, in November 1914, seemed to be designed more to stifle than to promote it. Many Volunteers refused to accept such terms. In Leicestershire the Duke of Rutland was dismayed at the general lack of preparations to counter a sudden attack from the sea, but was even more worried by those of the county's Volunteers who had no arms and no uniforms, and existed without any official sanction. Their hostility against an invader in a guerilla style 'Franc Tireur warfare' might, he thought, 'result in the wholesale Shooting of the peaceful inhabitants'. He urged the government to take more positive steps.[172]

Not surprisingly, Volunteer enthusiasm began to fade and numbers declined. With few arms, and often no uniforms, the Volunteers did not cut an imposing figure. In Rutland old soldiers and Territorials gave instruction in the larger communities, but elsewhere the Volunteers were on their own, and during the harvest, exercise was suspended all together. Men quit through 'the want of encouragement by the Government' and many others left to answer a conflicting call for Special Constables.[173]

Not until the spring of 1916 was there any real indication that the official attitude to the Volunteers was changing. In May it was decided to apply the Volunteer Act of 1863 to the new force, and at the same time new regulations were published by the War Office. The Leicestershire

Territorial Association met to discuss these new regulations, and also a government request that they assume responsibility for the administration of the local Volunteers. Direct recruiting for the Territorials had been ended in December 1915, and the local Territorial Associations were to have their powers further pruned in coming months, but even so there was little enthusiasm for taking charge of the Volunteers. The state of Leicestershire's Volunteers was depressing. Mr Hull, of the Leicester Volunteers, spoke of 'a laxity' in the movement. Where twelve months before it had been possible to parade a company, now only a platoon could be mustered. Falling numbers were blamed on the raising of the military age limit, which took men away, while those who were left, being subject to longer hours and greater pressure at work, were less inclined to become Volunteers. There was also a general feeling of disappointment that the efforts of the Volunteers were neither appreciated nor felt to be useful. Although Major Rolleston assured the Association that the Volunteers were now organized enough to be of use in relieving the army's burden in the event of an invasion, it was not reassuring to hear that the Leicester men were so ill armed that 'it is not worth talking about', that little more than half the force had uniforms of any kind, and no one a proper overcoat. Nor were there any figures on the number of Volunteers in the county. Some units were 'rather sparse'. An 'optimistic' estimate put the county's total at about 3,000, but it was thought safe to expect that less than half that number would enrol under the new regulations, which still did not offer any assistance in the provision of uniforms, equipment, arms or ammunition. The future of 'the whole movement hangs upon the question of finance' said Rolleston, and no one disagreed.

Supporting the Volunteers through voluntary contributions alone, however, as the government still insisted, appeared quite unrealistic, especially when assistance to the Volunteers did 'not touch so much the points of the war which are now going on'. The Association agreed to help, but were reluctant to proceed unless the government 'will furnish the necessary arms, and undertake by way of capitation grant or otherwise the ultimate responsibility for clothing and equipment and providing funds for administration'.[174] Providing adequate finance for the Volunteers was to bedevil their development until their final disappearance in 1919. To the bitter end the question of who was to pay was still being discussed.

In June 1916, after assurances from the War Office that the Territorial Associations would not incur any financial liability for the Volunteers, the Duke of Rutland, following a meeting of the Leicestershire Association's Emergency Committee, on his own initiative committed the

Association to providing three Leicestershire Volunteer bat alions for service. The problem of financing the Volunteers' need. remained unresolved. While saying there would be no liability on the part of the Associations, the government itself made no move to provide funds and ruled out the possibility of issuing any arms – yet the Leicestershire Association already believed that a government grant was essential as it would be impossible to raise any further funds by voluntary contribution. The Duke of Rutland assured his Association that they had only to let the Volunteer Force 'find its own feet', but this was not to be. Two years later, in July 1918, he had to admit that the Volunteers remained an extremely 'complex question' which still 'appeared to defeat the best intentions of the War Office'.[175]

The Leicestershire Association assumed an administrative responsibility for the Volunteers under what some saw as pressure from 'the big guns in London'. Typically, the War Office had scoffed at the Volunteers, then discovered that they needed them, but remained unwilling to pay for them. The Leicestershire Association saw their task as that of 'Squeezing the War Office' for the necessary resources, keeping the War Office's nose 'close to the grindstone until we get what we want to equip these men'. The many hard fights with the War Office over equipping the Territorials were too freshly remembered.[176] Starting in an atmosphere of uncertainty, with the crucial question of finance unresolved, the process of preparing the new Leicestershire Volunteers for service proved a slow business which was only just approaching completion when the war came to an end.

The Duke of Rutland made his submission to the War Office in June 1916, and in September of that year the administration of the local Volunteers was devolved upon the Territorial Associations generally. The structure of the new force, together with terms and conditions of service, however, were still not sorted out and it was not until the early months of 1917 that any discernible progress was made in Leicestershire in providing modern equipment, arms and uniforms. The War Office finally promised rifles and equipment, and from January 1917 uniforms were to be provided through a capitation grant of £2 for every 'efficient' Volunteer, part of the grant going to cover administration.

The provision of khaki uniforms, however, made but painfully slow progress. For more than a year the whole process was strangled by regulations which required a man to pass as efficient before the Association could receive the grant necessary to provide him with a uniform. This had a clear precedent in the old Victorian Volunteer Force and would have been straightforward enough, save for the fact that the new Volunteers were rapidly becoming a force composed largely of 'exempted men' – B category according to classifications applied to the force in 1917. These exempted men were coming into the force via the local tribunals which were set up in 1916 to arbitrate cases for exemption under the new conscription laws. They were of military age and soon outnumbered those who were too old (A category) or too young (C category) for military service. The tribunals were exempting men on the proviso that they drilled with the Volunteers, and by February 1918, Col J.E. Sarson, County Commandant for Leicestershire, was worried over the large number of exempted men already in the county's Volunteers. He was anxious to enrol more older men. The 1st, or Leicester, Battalion, had grown so large that Sarson wanted it split into two battalions, one to be composed entirely of exempted men. By July 1917 83.3 per cent of the Volunteer Force in Leicestershire and Rutland were B category men. Quite apart from the fact that such men were not free agents, not true Volunteers, there was the virtual impossibility of their being able to pass as efficient and thus qualify for the capitation grant.[177]

Leicestershire tribunals were granting exemptions of only three months or slightly less (though they might be renewable on expiry), but in order to qualify for a grant a Volunteer had both to pass as efficient (which in Leicestershire was held up by a lack of adequate range facilities on which the men might qualify) and to have at least three months remaining of his exemption. Complying with both these requirements was nearly impossible, and clothing any appreciable number of men in Leicestershire stuck fast on this problem until the beginning of 1918. It was only relieved by the War Office decision that spring to put aside the efficiency requirement and cloth all A, B and C category men, up to a certain number, upon their enrolment.[178]

While the conundrum of the clothing continued to defy solution, the Association had also to bring order and discipline to their new charges, and to provide them with adequate training. Here too they faced an array of difficulties. Before anything could be done, willing and capable officers had to be appointed, but for some time it was not possible to complete the complement, especially the more senior ranks. The post of County Commandant was not adequately filled until February 1917 when Col Sarson, former commander of the old pre-South African War Volunteer Battalion of the Leicestershire Regiment, agreed to step in. Likewise, commanding officers for the two Leicestershire county battalions (2nd and 3rd Battalions), a number of company captains and a county adjutant for Leicestershire were not easily found. The 2nd, or Western, Battalion, began 1917 not only lacking a commanding officer, but also without a single officer of any military experience. Even by May both the Melton and the Market Harborough companies of the 3rd

Battalion were still without captains, a handicap which seriously retarded any progress towards military efficiency.[179]

What made the scarcity of suitable officers worse was the wide dispersal of the rural battalions. In February 1917 the county's Volunteers, outside Leicester itself, comprised only two infantry battalions, but they were so fragmented that there were 'something like 48 different units'. Rutland experienced the same problem, and her officers lamented their inability to concentrate their battalion with any ease, due to the dearth of railway links. In Leicester itself the officer problem was for a while given a rather different twist. It was comparatively easy to find officers, but the 1st Battalion became too unwieldy to run as a single battalion and its officers were overworked. Not until mid-1917, after two applications to the War Office, was permission received to subdivide it and finally distribute the work load over a greater number of officers.[180]

Discipline and training both suffered further from a certain confusion and laxity in punishing exempted men for truancy. The Volunteers themselves did not see this as their responsibility, but rather that of the tribunals and the recruiting officers (who had the power to report delinquents to the tribunals). The local tribunals were accused of being remiss in such cases, but tribunal members, several of whom were themselves members of the Leicestershire Territorial Association, pointed in turn at the recruiting officers, one of whom, it was claimed, had said that he had been instructed 'to be chary over taking action against a Volunteer for not attending his drills'.[181] But truancy was not the only difficulty with the exempted men. Such men were for the most part given exemption because their work was deemed to be of 'national importance'. On occasion they were simply not able to attend, as in the case of local munition workers who failed to appear for the Volunteers' instructional schools held over Easter of 1918.[182]

Apart from the exempted men of B category, the Volunteer Force also included a large number of men who were enrolled but 'who are either unwilling or unable as Special Constables or for other reasons to undertake a definite obligation'. In returns made for the Leicestershire and Rutland Associations such men were lumped together, rather disparagingly, as 'Remainder-men'.[183] Their numbers however were significant: in November 1917 they made up almost 46 per cent of the 2nd Battalion and just over 50 per cent of the 3rd. The presence of these Remainder-men, especially those of D category ('who refuse to accept any obligation'), had in Col Sarson's view meant that 'The men were rather the masters of us . . . '.[184] By the beginning of 1918 D category had been abolished, in Sarson's opinion shifting the balance back to the officers, but there remained the conflicting duties of those who were also

Special Constables, in category P, and the limited value of those such as railway workers who were in category R, and would not be available to the Volunteers in the event of a real emergency.

Competent instructors were in short supply, a deficiency felt most outside Leicester itself, where there were so many small and scattered detachments. By May 1917, however, each battalion had a permanent adjutant, with promise of a sergeant major and a sergeant instructor of musketry soon to be appointed. In addition to uniforms, there was also great need for modern arms and equipment. By the spring of 1917 the first modern rifles had been issued, 190 to each battalion (and four Hotchkiss machine guns approved for the Rutland Battalion), but older pattern weapons for drill purposes only continued to predominate in the Volunteer arsenal for some time to come. In the 1st Leicester Battalion shotguns outnumbered modern rifles, and the Rutland men too possessed a hundred of these stalwarts to set beside their modern strip-fed Hotchkiss guns. From mid 1917 matters began to improve, as the War Office authorized the issue of modern rifles and sets of equipment to each enrolled volunteer, up to 1,000 per battalion. Training and administrative facilities had also to be found for the Volunteers. In Leicestershire former Territorial premises were largely sufficient, but in Rutland new locations, apart from the old Territorial headquarters in Oakham, were needed to accommodate the Rutland battalion's many scattered detachments. Ranges had to be improved and new training grounds developed for the Volunteers.[185]

With so many disadvantages the Leicestershire and Rutland Volunteers made little headway in training prior to 1917, and even after the reordering of the force under the Territorial Associations, progress was slow. Until 1917 modern weapons were almost unknown in the Leicestershire battalions, unless borrowed temporarily from some obliging unit of the regular army. By that spring, however, the War Office seemed finally to be 'extremely anxious that the training of the Volunteers shall proceed as quickly as possible'.[186] Adjutants had been appointed to all battalions and were to be followed by permanent staff sergeant majors and sergeant instructors of musketry. The Leicestershire and Rutland battalions had also been affiliated to local training battalions of the regular army, a link which soon proved its value as Volunteers were able to attend special instructional classes given by officers and non-commissioned officers from those battalions. During the summer of 1917 a series of weekend camps were held regularly at Syston Range and elsewhere in Leicestershire, enabling a large number of men to complete their musketry and to pass the efficiency test. At Syston, the largest of the camps, the Volunteers were not only able to use the range facilities but were also provided with a drill ground, a bayonet fighting course and a dummy bombing ground, as well as another practice area for digging and live bombing. Travelling instructors also visited the county, and further afield classes were held at the Central Schools of Instruction at Cannock Chase. Officers could attend a Bombing School at Otley and a musketry course at Bisley.

Although some of the military authorities in London were pressing for their abolition, the final year of the war began under circumstances which, to the Volunteers, seemed more than ever to emphasize their importance, and the need for them to attain a creditable standard of training. The strain on the nation's manpower seemed enormous, yet the war appeared likely to continue 'to an indefinite period'. 'We cannot,' said the Duke of Rutland, 'get away from the fact that we are up against a very big thing.'[187] The next six months, he thought, would require every available man at the front, a fact which made the training of the Volunteers for home defence more urgent than ever. The result in Leicestershire was an expanded programme of training. In addition to the regular weekend summer camps within the county there were also week-long camps during the Whitsuntide and August Bank holiday weeks at locations as far away as Skegness and Mablethorpe on the Lincolnshire coast. Attendance at the camps, however, was no more than two to three hundred men per battalion, a small proportion of their total claimed strength in all categories. The number of men passed as efficient grew only gradually, and was continually cut back as men were called up for the regular army.[188] By the end of the war Leicestershire and Rutland had produced a total of only 2,365 efficients, but the standard achieved by some units received high praise. In 1918 Leicestershire units won both of the Volunteer competition trophies for the Northern Command, while the Rutland Battalion, despite its scattered nature, claimed to have had the highest proportion of efficients in England.[189]

In the first days of November 1918 the majority of the Leicestershire and Rutland Volunteers were reported to be clothed, their Permanent Staff complete and their mobilization stores nearly so. In categories A, B and C the five battalions mustered 3,729 other ranks, of whom 2,171 were efficients.[190] Only days later the war came to an end, and all drills and parades became entirely voluntary. It 'was practically left to the individual volunteer to decide his own attitude to the Force'.[191] After the armistice very little was done and by February 1919 the Volunteer Force was 'in a state of suspended animation'. Suggestions that the Volunteers might be retained as the basis of a National Reserve came to nothing, and in June the Volunteers took part in a final parade before the King. Disbandment began at the end of 1919 (except for the Motor Volunteers, who were retained a little longer, until 1921) and their financial accounts were finally cleared the following year.

During the war, 'very many thousands' of men had passed through the Leicestershire and Rutland Volunteer Corps, since their first appearance as Citizens' Training Corps.[192] Thirty per cent of the original Oakham company of the Volunteer Training Corps had joined the army and three of them had received commissions. The Rutland Volunteer Battalion as a whole sent 194 men into the armed forces and it was said 'that all found their previous training extremely useful'.[193] In their own counties the Leicestershire and Rutland Volunteers had played an active part in air defence, manning observation posts and guarding the Royal Flying Corps' emergency landing places. They were responsible for securing any hostile airships forced to ground (prior to the arrival of regular troops) and on several occasions protected the Royal Flying Corps' own planes when forced to land from engine trouble. Providing guards for vulnerable points (such as forage stores and ammunition dumps), and lines of communication in the event of an invasion was another very important part of their work. The Motor Volunteers, who in Leicester had originally been trained as a fighting unit, were charged with assisting the police in emergencies, providing transport for field ambulances and general conveyance and rationing for the Volunteer infantry battalions.[194] In the summer of 1918, when Special Service Companies were raised to do temporary duty on the coast in order to release regular troops for overseas service, the Leicestershire and Rutland battalions were able to send 162 officers and men. Considering the difficulties, principally the large number of exempted men who were reluctant, or unable, to go, Col Sarson thought it a satisfactory number – though it was in fact less than three-fifths of the quota originally asked for. The men spent two or sometimes three months on coastal duty, and following their return Sarson received a message of official thanks from the War Office. Their services had 'enabled the Government to meet a critical situation, and to rise over very difficult days in the history of the war . . . up to the limit of their powers they have directly contributed to the improvement of the Situation in France, and on more distant fronts.'[195]

This message and a general letter from the King in September the following year were the principal thanks which the Volunteers received for their efforts. If somewhat uncharitable, it was perhaps not so surprising for a force which throughout its existence had been so controversial. In Leicestershire and Rutland, as elsewhere, the management of the Volunteers had been a vexing problem for the Territorial Associations, and for many the memory seemed only further proof of the government's indifference towards the local amateur soldier.

CHAPTER ELEVEN

Between the Wars, 1920–39

Reconstruction

Reconstruction of the Territorial forces in Leicestershire and Rutland began in February 1920. After a break of nearly three years the Joint Association resumed a direct responsibility for the raising, equipping and maintaining of local Territorial units. Not all of the pre-war units were re-formed. The Leicestershire Yeomanry and the 4th and 5th Battalions of the Leicestershire Regiment were reconstituted, together with the medical and RASC support companies, but the Leicestershire Royal Horse Artillery was replaced by a field battery, the 239th Royal Field Artillery. The situation in 1920 was quite different from that which the Joint Associations had faced in 1908 at the birth of the Territorial Force, when units of the old Volunteer Force had provided a base to build on. Although the reconstituted units of 1920 were to be much weaker in strength, they would have to be created from scratch, and hopes of re-forming the Territorials in Leicestershire and Rutland rested heavily on enticing former members back to the re-established units. Such hopes were soon disappointed. In post-war Britain reconstruction proved a far more difficult task than anticipated. Recruiting became a perpetual problem for the best part of the next two decades.

The Yeomanry and the artillery were able to establish themselves relatively quickly – certainly by 1922 – and apart from some difficulty when the artillery became mechanized in 1932, both were able to sustain complete or near complete numbers throughout the inter-war period. The RASC companies enjoyed an even greater popularity and were soon filled, but by 1922 they had been disbanded in the financial cuts which stripped the Territorial Army of its supporting units.[196] The difficulty was principally one of finding infantrymen.

The Recruiting 'Head-Ache'

From the start, the raising of the 4th Battalion of the Leicestershire Regiment ran onto barren ground and, though the 5th Battalion did much better, neither seemed able to establish themselves so firmly as to relieve all doubts over their future for very long. By the end of 1923 they seemed well established and the future looked promising, but recruiting continued to be an irksome task, encouraging one year, dismal the next, at times seriously hampered by events quite beyond the Joint Associations' control. Time did not seem to bring any sustained improvement, and in 1935, after fifteen years of struggle, the Joint Associations of Leicestershire and Rutland still found themselves confronted by an 'inexplicable falling-off' in both infantry battalions, which 'if continued . . . must result in the gradual and early extinction of these units'.[197] The situation of the Territorial Army had become 'a national question' which in the view of the Joint Associations' members demanded effective action by the government and the War Office. From such despair, however, the fortunes of the Territorials soon revived, but not before the 4th Battalion was put through one final trauma: conversion into an anti-aircraft searchlight battery (44th (The Leicestershire Regiment) Anti-Aircraft Battalion Royal Engineers) at the end of 1936. The conversion resulted in the immediate loss of almost 75 per cent of the other ranks, the men taking advantage of the free discharges being offered on account of the conversion. The officers stayed with the battalion and had to begin the chore of virtual reconstruction all over again.[198]

A gradual improvement in recruiting in 1936 and 1937 was given a strong upwards push in 1938, especially in the 44th AA Battalion, by the Austrian and Czechoslovakian crises. Establishments were expanded and recruits continued to come forward. Women were also to be included in the expanding forces, and in September 1938 instructions were received to recruit four units of the new Auxiliary Territorial Service. In March 1939 it was announced that the Territorial Army was to be doubled in size. In Leicestershire the 5th Battalion was split into two units, the 1/5th and 2/5th. Supporting units, a casualty clearing station (3rd CCS), and a company of the RASC (906 Company) were again made part of the Leicestershire and Rutland Territorial establishment.[199] The 239th Battery RFA was expanded to regimental strength, becoming the 115th Field Regiment (consisting of a 238 Field Battery – later changed to 239 – and a 240 Field Battery). Recruiting continued apace, both to fill the new units and to increase numbers to war strength. In May 1937 there had been only 1,163 Territorials in Leicestershire and Rutland. A year later that figure had nearly doubled, and by 9 May 1939 it had almost doubled again to 4,143, with new men coming forward every day.[200] By the close of the 1930s, as the nation rushed to gather its strength on the brink of another war, the recruiting problem had finally been relieved, but only to be replaced by the frenzy of trying to cope with a sudden upsurge of recruits which soon swamped existing facilities.

Explaining the dearth of recruits had been as difficult as finding them. The 'slackness' in recruiting was soon seen as a phenomenon not confined to Leicestershire and Rutland. There seemed to be no easy answer, though in Col Sarson's opinion there was no doubt '. . . that a great deal must be put down to general weariness of matters military produced by the War, and a general indifference as to the future of the Military Forces of the Crown'. He did not see such attitudes as 'entirely confined to one section of society', and in 1922 was confident that 'in time the reaction will again set in and matters will be easier'.[201] Time, however, did not seem to make much difference. In 1935 the recruiting problem was as prominent as ever and its chief cause still as uncertain – whether due 'to the apparent dislike of Military Service generally' or simply to other attractions being so readily available. The Joint Associations' members complained of 'anti-army propaganda' but could not explain why it was that recruiting for the regular army in Leicestershire was very successful, indeed had 'not been so good for a very long time'.[202] When in the first months of 1938 recruitment began to rise sharply, members seemed just as baffled by the Territorial Army's sudden popularity.[203]

The attitude of local employers and their labour force, particularly in Leicester, the recruiting ground of the 4th Battalion, was crucial. Any industrial unrest seemed to check the flow of recruits, especially if the Territorials seemed likely to be involved in suppressing disorder.[204] In the first years of reconstruction the 4th Battalion found recruiting in Leicester extremely difficult. The city's work force was not interested, and those who did join the battalion showed a marked avoidance of the Defence Force of 1921 – a sharp contrast to the number of Territorials who did join it from the county's other units.[205] Managers and foremen were singled out as the real 'kill-crows' of Territorial recruitment. According to one employer who had tried to organize a machine gun troop at his works, '. . . there was some influence working against it, and that element was, he thought, largely Socialism. The older men discouraged the younger men from joining, if they did nothing more.'[206] Without encouragement from their managers and foremen, 'who quite naturally may not want their shops disrupted by the annual training period',[207] or because no assistance was offered to make up wages lost during training, many did not join.

The 'best material' for a Territorial was a 'man who is in good employment and constant work', and apart from the attitude of work-mates and shop foremen, the goodwill of employers was vital if such a man was to be recruited.[208] In Leicester the Joint Associations enjoyed a good relationship with both the City Council and the Chamber of Commerce, finding in both a willingness to co-operate whenever asked. The ties were particularly close in 1925 when Capt Simpson, himself an active recruiter as well as a city councillor and member of the Leicestershire Territorial Association, served a term as mayor. Appeals to employers usually met with at least a 'satisfactory' response and the great majority did co-operate, some even helping the men financially (by making up lost wages) so they could attend the annual camp. The assistance offered by Messrs W. & G. Bates was a worthy model. Men in regular employment were guaranteed a place after their return from camp and received up to twenty shillings if they attended for the full fifteen days of annual training.[209]

A few employers, however, were not only unsympathetic but also obstructive, and were thought 'to look on membership of the Territorial Army as a disqualification for employment'. Such negative attitudes were hardly new, but in the 1920s seemed more serious on account of the Territorial Army's increased importance in national defence and its perpetual recruiting difficulties.[210] From the spring of 1938, however, the fortunes of the Territorial Army underwent a dramatic improvement, especially in the new 44th AA Battalion. As fear increased over the threat of aerial bombardment, appeals to local firms brought in many new recruits, including older men (as the retirement age in the AA Battalion was fifty). In the months remaining before war finally broke out, whole searchlight teams enlisted together both from local businessmen's associations and from factories.[211]

At various times specific events dealt the Territorials some hard knocks. In the very first year of reconstruction industrial unrest checked the flow of recruits, and the following April (1921) it was 'brought to a standstill' in Leicestershire and Rutland by the creation of the Defence Force.[212] In all, 311 Territorials, over a quarter of the Territorial Army's strength in the two counties, joined the local Defence Force, making up almost one third of its total strength. When the force was disbanded in July only 283 men re-enlisted into the Territorial Army – but even so the full repercussions were not immediately felt. When the Defence Force was stood down, a number of new men from the force joined the

Territorials, and though not as many as had been lost to the Defence Force, the occasion was seen as a beneficial opportunity to get rid of Territorials who had proved unsatisfactory. But the retention of the Defence Force into early July, over what was the Territorial Army's best period of the year for recruiting, did much damage to the normal enlistments, and in time there were further problems. In 1922, just before their annual training camp, both the 4th and 5th Battalions lost a considerable number of one-year men who had joined from the Defence Force. The loss of such men during that year was a serious blow to the units who had recruited them, and 'for a long time recruiting and rebuilding became very slow'.[213] In February 1925, commanding officers were 'still handicapped by the number of undesirable men who joined the Force during the early part of reconstruction and after the demobilization of the Defence Force, and who now have to be discharged and got rid of as useless'.[214]

Organizational and major equipment changes caused further havoc. In 1932 recruiting for the 239th Battery RFA suddenly became much harder, as the battery was finally converted from horse draught to mechanized six wheel tractors. The changeover was made more difficult as the unit had then to look for motor drivers and other specialists, as well as new gunners. Its problems were to continue through the next two years.[215]

The annual training camps were the single most attractive feature to potential recruits, especially if they were held at a popular seaside resort. With the announcement of a popular venue, a large intake of new recruits was always expected. It was therefore a severe blow when in 1926 the camps were cancelled by the government. It 'had an immediate and disastrous effect' on both infantry battalions, though the Yeomanry, being always more popular, escaped unscathed. Not only did recruits stop coming, but most of those due to re-engage upon the expiry of their four years of service declined to do so. When it was understood that the neighbouring Notts and Derby Brigade, also in the North Midland Division, was intending to go ahead with its training as originally planned, men in the Leicestershire battalions clamoured for an immediate transfer.[216] The cancellations brought a most promising year to a shuddering halt and the effects were still being felt the following spring – by which time recruitment had been hurt further by the announcement that the bounty for men enlisting after 28 February was to be abolished (though there was to be Proficiency Pay available instead).[217] In 1932 the annual camps were again cancelled, with 'a generally adverse effect', which by the autumn had reduced units to a lower level than in 1931. The idea had '. . . got abroad, that owing to the abolition of Annual Camps in 1932, recruits are not required . . .'.[218]

Recruiting also suffered from 'leakage'. The number of men who registered for Leicestershire Territorial units in the early 1920s was claimed to be out of all proportion to those who were finally enlisted. Where twenty registered, perhaps only four enlisted, 'so it would appear that there is a great leakage between registration and attestation'.[219] Of those who presented themselves in the first months of 1922, from 25 to 33 per cent were rejected as medically unfit.[220] Rejections, principally on medical grounds, but also for other reasons deemed 'on primary examination' to make a candidate 'unsuitable', were a constant source of loss, most noticeably in the already hard pressed 4th Battalion. From November 1927 to February 1930 a total of 460 men offered themselves for enlistment in the battalion, but only 343 were accepted. Just over a quarter (25.4 per cent) were rejected – a proportion far greater than the 3.7 per cent rejected by the 5th Battalion, or the one man out of 131 who presented themselves to the Yeomanry over the same period. Only the 239th Battery RFA, which also recruited in the city of Leicester, had a comparable proportion of rejections: 21.8 per cent.[221] In the early thirties mass unemployment helped recruitment, but hard times also took their toll on the health of would-be recruits. Over the first months of 1931 the 4th Battalion had to turn away 'a very considerable percentage of those presenting themselves . . . for the most part being under weight'.[222]

If there was too much 'leakage' from prospective recruits, there was equally 'tremendous wastage' from within the ranks. It was an acute problem which outside the Territorial Army did not seem to be generally appreciated. Every year men dropped out to join the regular army, or to emigrate, or had to be discharged as unsuitable, having failed to fulfil their obligations. Every year too there were men lost whose time had expired and who chose not to re-engage. These were all 'sure and certain losses which take in themselves a fair recruitment to compensate for'.[223] Regardless of their success in recruiting, units were prevented from reaching their full strength. The reconstructed Territorials of 1920–1 were enlisting more men per quarter than the old Territorial Force, but even where units had enlisted over 100 per cent of their authorised numbers, they were unable to complete, having both to cover wastage and to re-form themselves at the same time. In the very first months wastage was already taking its toll. By November 1920 more than 8 per cent of the men enlisted by the Leicestershire and Rutland Associations had been discharged, chiefly to join the regular army. After the first two and a quarter years 22 per cent of the recruits had been discharged, and by July 1923, the figure stood at just over 37 per cent of the 2,030 men enlisted since the reconstruction had begun in February 1920.[224] In 1925 it was estimated that in order to cover the usual losses the Joint

Associations required 'about twenty five per cent of their Establishment as recruits each year'.[225] Admittedly the early 1920s were particularly troubled by the need to replace the many unsuitable men who had joined, and who came in from the Defence Force, by a better 'stamp of man'. There were also heavy losses from short-term enlistments, but even as these things improved, the basic problem of wastage remained. What made things worse was the enormous variance in the intake and losses which could happen from one year to the next. Even an improved year's recruiting could end up in a decline of strength. In 1937 the 5th Battalion did marginally better at recruiting than they had the previous year, but their losses through discharges were very heavy, 145 men, more than two and a quarter times the number lost in 1936. The result overall was a drop in strength, leaving them at less than three quarters of their authorized peacetime strength.[226]

The need to attract and retain recruits was all pervasive. It insinuated itself into the weekly social activities at the local TA club, and into the programme for the annual training. The clubs, especially in the smaller towns, were seen as a direct investment in the search for recruits, but they also paid a further dividend in staunching losses. The Leicester club's offer of regular smoking concerts, dances, skittles matches, whist drives, snooker and billiards tournaments attracted new members and did 'much to keep alive interest in things Territorial during the winter months'.[227] The competitions and prize draw held at Christmas were especially popular. The aim was to make the club a true social centre for Territorials and not merely a place to 'spend their time in consuming beer'.[228] The investment of sufficient time and money on the clubs was all the more pressing as Territorial recruitment was felt to be suffering from 'there being so many other attractions for the young man compared with 20 or 30 years ago'.[229] Since the war, this had become 'accentuated in the country districts owing to the cheap and convenient transport facilities which enable men to come into the towns after work in the evening'.[230] Yet, with economies and financial cuts also a fact of everyday life, the improvement of club facilities could not always progress as smoothly or as quickly as desired. The club clientele could also be a matter of concern. In 1935 there was a complaint that the Leicester club had become too much of a haunt for 'old soldiers', and was not used nearly enough by younger men who were actually serving Territorials.[231]

The attractions of the clubs, however, were enjoyed behind closed doors, and important as they were in sustaining the Territorial Army, they did not relieve the recurring anxiety that the local Territorials were not seen enough in public, that they were 'too much in the background'.[232] It was often insisted that the remedy for many Territorial ills, especially for the 4th Battalion, was more publicity, not only from notices and short articles in the local press, but particularly through public parades, band concerts, drills, route marches and ceremonials, blending self advertisement with a useful dose of discipline while under the public gaze. Territorials took a regular part in civic celebrations, and in the county the 5th Battalion staged special torchlight tattoos to stimulate interest in the Territorial Army. The venues of the annual training camps were well advertised, especially those held at the seaside, and even the training programme itself might be made to answer the needs of recruitment. In 1931 the Yeomanry set aside four days of their training time to carry out a route march in the eastern parts of Leicestershire and into Rutland, areas 'where recruits have not presented themselves so freely for enlistment . . .'.[233] More prosaically the Joint Associations put up posters in factories, enlisted the help of ex-servicemen's organizations, asked former officers to canvass in person and tried offering rewards for bringing in recruits. In the early thirties the 5th Battalion set up local recruiting committees of 'influential people'.[234]

Training for War?

Recruiting the necessary numbers was an interminable problem which defied a solution, but the ultimate goal, to 'make them satisfactory soldiers',[235] was no less of one. Critics even insisted that preoccupation with the former too often eclipsed the latter. In rough outline, Territorial life in the 1920s and 1930s appeared little changed from its antecedents in the old pre-war Volunteers and Territorial Force. At the reconstruction the terms and conditions of service were very little changed from those of the 1907 Act. Provision was made for annual training in camp of not less than eight or more than eighteen days. During the year a minimum of ten drills had to be attended, and there was an annual course of musketry in which a man could qualify merely by firing off a total of seventy-three rounds if he failed to meet the minimum standard in his first twenty-three. Weekly evening drills over the drab months of winter, 'usually regarded as more or less the dead time of the Territorial year',[236] were enlivened in the spring by the commencement of musketry practice, and then by weekend camps as the warmer days of summer approached. The climax of the training year came with a fortnight's Annual Training under canvas, usually in brigade or divisional strength for the infantry, who held theirs in August, but earlier, in May, for the Yeomanry. In the autumn the Rifle Association held its annual prize shooting. Interspersed were church parades, recruiting marches, special ceremonials and inspections, with sports, social gatherings, dances, dinners and suppers rounding off the Territorial calendar.

The Annual Training camp was both the Territorial Army's trump card in bidding for recruits – for it offered a holiday with some pay – and also its most important opportunity for military training. Many a raw recruit, typically in his late teens, still feeling awkward in his new uniform, arrived at camp with a military career behind him which could be measured only in weeks. His tent might well be shared with complete strangers. Having seen little more than the activities of the local drill hall, where he signed on, he now saw his assembled unit in its entirety for the first time. In the Yeomanry it might also be his first encounter with riding and caring for a horse – regardless of what he might have told the squadron officers when enlisting! In 1931 only 35.8 per cent of the Leicestershire Yeomanry was made up of 'real yeomen or other riding classes', i.e. farmers, farmhands, grooms and stablemen. Of the other groups in the regiment the most numerous were clerks and men engaged in the local shoe and leather trade.[237]

As ever, camp life in the twenties and thirties was a mix of duties, training, sports and socializing. In the Yeomanry the day began shortly after five with early morning 'Stables'. By 8 a.m. horse and man were to be fed, groomed and on parade, ready for a morning's exercise, which in the first week was usually 'elementary': mounted drill in squadron, or perhaps practice at 'dismounted actions'. By noon the exertions of the morning were ended and an hour taken for mid-day Stables, to groom, attend to minor injuries, check horseshoes and saddlery – all to a musical interlude provided by the regimental band. At one o'clock, on the trumpet's call, the horses were fed, the band striking up the national anthem to bring mid-day Stables to a close. Dinner followed, after which the afternoon could be spent in a variety of ways: saddle cleaning, a map reading class, a lecture on horse care, or tent-pegging practice for the sports competitions. At four o'clock the day's duties were brought to a close with evening Stables. 'Teas' were 'the final military responsibility for almost everyone', and as the day ended officers began leaving by car to scour 'the drowsy countryside for cocktails and baths', while the rest of the regiment donned their blue 'patrols' for a stroll into the nearby town. By eight all the officers who had left were back in camp for a formal mess dinner, complete with candles, the regimental silver and a final performance by the band. When the formalities of dinner were ended, the night was then their own 'for howling round the piano: for playing with cards or dice: for fabulous trials of strength or agility: or for ski-joring in a tin bath towed by a motor car – the wise ones well cushioned against the angry heat engendered by their lunatic progress across the field'.[238]

Other days in camp were given over to day-long schemes, route marches, night manoeuvres, an inspection, a church parade or a regimental parade at the Yeomanry's war memorial, set up in 1927 in Bradgate Old Park near Loughborough. Towards the end of camp, on Whit Monday, the regiment held an afternoon of 'Yeomanry Sports', a display to which the public were invited, and which was an important source of income for the regiment, three or four hundred pounds in admissions often being taken. The Whit Monday events of the 1929 camp at Stoughton, near Leicester, included wrestling on horseback, section jumping over hurdles, tent-pegging, 'musical chairs' and a 'V.C. race', this last being a precarious performance by teams of two men riding bareback on a horse excited by the close discharge of blanks 'within a inch of its nose'. The displays were completed by the intricate steps of a musical ride, performed by the non-commissioned officers.[239]

Some camps were especially memorable: that of 1929 saw the visit of the Yeomanry's Colonel-in-Chief, the Duke of York, who shared the bad weather of a stormy night in camp with the officers and non-commissioned officers of 'his' regiment. The Duke took part with his officers in the 'time honoured competition' of lighting a candle while seated on a bottle, drank ale in the Sergeants' Mess and applauded the efforts of the sergeants' burlesque jazz band, 'a strange combination of art and determination'. The next day he inspected the regiment and personally presented a number of long service awards.[240] The camp of 1934 was remembered for a very different reason: a daring theft of the regimental safe from the officers' mess tent. Some £500, most of it gate money from the Whit Monday displays, went missing – a serious blow to regimental finances. The police pronounced it the work of a slick London gang, who had spirited the near 5 cwt safe away by motor car. No sooner was the story splashed across the local newspapers than both safe and money were recovered – in a refuse heap not fifty yards away. The 'London gang' had got no further than the next field, their 'motor' turning out to be that most pedestrian of vehicles, a wheelbarrow![241]

The boisterous pranks and good humour were often the best remembered moments of the annual camps, but the underlying purpose was of course military training, and there was also hard work and occasionally serious injuries. Many camp competitions were directed at more than simply entertainment. Competition was recognized as an essential ingredient in fostering general proficiency, discipline and esprit de corps. At the end of the 1920s the Yeomanry were competing among themselves for thirteen different regimental prizes, awarded variously for excellence in mounted sports, weapons handling, tactics and general all round proficiency. To encourage men in the winter months, three prizes were specifically awarded for excellence during winter training.[242] Col John Jamie, who commanded the 5th Leicesters in the 1930s, developed the idea of competition to a high degree. During the battalion's Annual Training 'all parts of the soldier's day were woven into the general pattern of competition for the Colonel German Efficiency Shield, from individual saluting to mass cross-country running . . .'. Jamie also introduced a Lines Cup, awarded for extreme cleanliness in camp. Match sticks, cigarette ends and 'less salubrious finds' were all accounted for before announcing the winner.[243]

At all levels, individuals and units were proud of their successes. In 1928 the 5th Leicester's Market Harborough platoon won the North Midland Division's St Quentin Canal Cup. In 1933 the Yeomanry's signallers were placed seventh in the Lord Dartmouth Cup, a competition open to the whole Territorial Army. The next year the Yeomanry won the 6th Cavalry Brigade's Machine Gun Cup, while the same year the artillery won their brigade's Section Turnout Prize, and the cooks of the 4th Battalion took a divisional cooking prize. In the early 1930s the 4th Battalion, under the prompting of Col Halkyard, did particularly well in shooting competitions, having a number of places in the final hundred of the Queen Mary competitions, and helping to win the China Cup at Bisley in 1933 and again in 1936. In 1933 RQMS Ball won the Warrant Officers and Sergeants Championship of the Territorial Army.[244]

Success in competitions and the general commendations of inspecting officers were gratifying, but too often the overall standard of training was a poor one. In retrospect it seemed that the Yeomanry were training in a 'world of make-believe', while the 4th Battalion were only 'adequately trained to the standards of the time'.[245] Another world war was to make 'those happy carefree days' of the 1920s and 1930s seem distinctly unrealistic. That the requirements set down for Territorials were hardly rigorous was not surprising, for in 1922 a War Office conference had concluded that, while the training standards of Territorial officers and non-commissioned officers should be maintained, training for the men in peacetime was 'not essential'. Territorial officers of the 'old Volunteer type' were censured for putting sports and competitions ahead of serious training at the annual camps. Their priorities gave their men very little time for anything more than the most elementary training. One former Territorial characterized the infantry training as generally 'dull, unimaginative and unilluminating'. Maj-Gen Sir John Kennedy went further. Territorial training he said 'is largely a veneer – which the rough usage of war destroys almost at once – unless it is carefully preserved until war experience gradually produces the real fighting soldier . . . '.[246]

Few seem to have seriously disagreed. Territorial training left much to be desired, but matching peacetime training to the rigours of real service has always been a problem for every peacetime soldier; and the Territorials had more reason than most to plead extenuating circumstances. Lack of sufficient time to learn the details of the military profession and to practise them was an inherent deficiency in part-time soldiering and was made worse by the growing sophistication of military technology, but Territorial problems did not end there. The Territorial Army's recruiting problems had serious consequences for any training programme. Training was most effective when units were at full strength 'than when men who did not exist had to be imagined',[247] but for lack of numbers and the presence of too many new recruits, the annual camp, the one opportunity for more advanced training at battalion, brigade or divisional level, could not be put to the best use. An annual turnover of up to one quarter of the men meant that an unacceptably high proportion of inexperienced men was bound to be present, and the situation was made worse by the highest intake of recruits being always in the months, and often only in the weeks, immediately preceding the camp. There were too many who would achieve little until the following year. Commanding officers were 'very hard put to it to advance their Scheme of Training beyond a certain point'. The constant changes in personnel made it 'necessary to go frequently over the same ground and it is only with a strong complete Battalion for the second week of the Annual Training that definite progress in the more advanced stages can be made'.[248] But not all men could attend for the full two weeks, while others never appeared at all. The 4th Leicesters had the worst of it. As a result of absenteeism from the four annual camps held from 1929 to 1933 (that of 1932 being cancelled), no less than ninety-five men were dismissed, seventy-nine of them being prosecuted for their failure to fulfil their obligations.[249] As in recruitment, employers had a crucial role to play in the success of the Annual Training of local units. Here at least many Leicestershire employers were sympathetic. In 1924 and 1925, with the close co-operation of the Leicester Chamber of Commerce, a very high turn-out was achieved for the camps of the 46th North Midland Division. In 1924 Leicestershire's three divisional units, the 4th and 5th Battalions of the Leicestershire Regiment, and the 239th Battery RFA, managed an attendance of 90.7 per cent, which helped their division attain the best attendance for the whole country that year. At other times, however, things did not go so well. In the twenties the Yeomanry could expect at best only three quarters of its other ranks to attend the Annual Training, most of the absentees being men who were refused leave from their employers.[250]

The 'unimaginative' training complained of was not a little related to the Territorial Army's embarrassment over manpower, but poor facilities, lack of equipment, and above all poor funding, also played a part.

The amount of machine gun and automatic rifle shooting done by the new post-war Territorials soon required considerable alterations in the existing Leicestershire ranges, but until the new range at Kibworth was opened in 1930, firing was carried on under 'very great difficulty'.[251] To complete the annual course it was necessary to use ranges belonging to neighbouring Associations, in Staffordshire and Nottinghamshire. In 1923 the Leicestershire artillery battery rejected the idea of mechanization for its guns and wagons because it already experienced great difficulty in obtaining the use of local fields for riding and driving practice with its horses. The officer commanding 'was quite sure that it would be absolutely impossible to obtain a field for the purpose of training if mechanised traction were used'. The immediate problem of practice with horses was finally relieved the next year, when the War Office sanctioned the renting of a twenty-acre field close to the newly opened Leicester Territorial riding school. The battery was then able to practise driving drill before their annual camps, something they had 'greatly missed in the past'.[252]

Both Leicestershire infantry battalions had not only to use their imaginations for 'men who did not exist', but also for non-existent weapons and vehicles. In exercises, supporting weapons such as mortars, heavy machine guns and anti-tank weapons were nearly always represented by flags. While the tactics themselves were 'not much different' from those later evolved by the Battle Schools of the 1939–45 war, 'Individual, section, platoon and company training could not under that system be good enough to give proper value to higher training, and every year training had to begin from the beginning all over again'. In the spring of 1939 the Yeomanry had to use flags to mark its non-existent bren guns. Swords, however, never seemed to be in short supply![253]

The approach of war, after the Munich crisis in September 1938, brought improvements. Recruiting picked up quickly and the 5th Battalion began to receive new vehicles, anti-tank weapons and bren guns, while the former 4th Battalion, on account of its conversion to anti-aircraft troops at the end of 1936, had already been enjoying a sudden embarrassment of riches, at one point even having more lorries than drivers. The good times however did not last. In the spring of 1939 the doubling of the Territorial Army, on a spur of the moment decision by the Prime Minister, hit the 5th Battalion like a 'bomb-shell'. Having reached a peak of efficiency from which they could fairly claim to need very few months' training 'to be fit for war', they were thrown into confusion, broken up to form the nuclei of two struggling battalions, which were filling rapidly with recruits.[254] Such was the lot of the inter-war Territorials. Years of neglect by both the public and the government were now ended in sudden panic. At times one might wonder if the true testing time for the amateur soldier was war, or merely enduring the peace.

CHAPTER TWELVE

The Second World War, 1939–45

The 'Terriers' Abroad

By the spring of 1939 the continuation of peace in Europe seemed very much in doubt. In the towns and villages of Leicestershire and Rutland the Territorials were looking for recruits to fulfil their part of the announced expansion of the Territorial Army. That summer the 44th AA Battalion did not hold an annual training; instead, its companies were called out on a rota system to man war stations with other units of the Anti-Aircraft Command. On 24 August the entire battalion was embodied. The old Magazine in Leicester buzzed with the talk of war, just as it had twenty-five years before, and on the afternoon of Friday 1 September the order to mobilize was received. Two days later the nation was again in 'a state of war with Germany'.[255]

At mobilization the Leicestershire Yeomanry could muster 620 other ranks, half of them recruited since the beginning of the year.[256] After embodiment in the squadron areas, the regiment moved on 22 September to its concentration area at Rufford Abbey in Nottinghamshire, where it received horses and began to train in earnest for its expected role in the First Cavalry Division. However, on 25 November, any expectation of mounted service was brought to an abrupt end by War Office instructions that the regiment was to be converted into Royal Artillery. Worse still, the regiment was split in two, becoming the 153rd (Leicestershire Yeomanry) Field Regiment, RA, and the 154th (Leicestershire Yeomanry) Field Regiment, RA. Early in the new year the drafts necessary to make up the new numbers began to arrive, and soon 'completely swamped' the original men of the regiment.[257] In April 1940 the two regiments parted company. The 153rd remained in Britain until June 1944 when it was sent to Normandy as part of the Guards Armoured Division, to which it had been posted in October 1941. Thereafter the regiment took part in the Liberation of France and Belgium, and the final advance into Germany. By contrast, the 154th left Britain at the end of July 1942 and, sailing round the Cape of Good Hope, eventually joined Montgomery's Eighth Army in North Africa, just in time for the great battle of El Alamein. From there its travels continued into the Middle East, as far as Persia (Iran). In April 1944 the 154th again went into action, in Italy, and continued with the allied forces there until the close of the Italian campaign. In July 1945 the regiment was moved to Austria where it was finally disbanded in October. Its sister regiment, the 153rd, was to continue a little longer, ending its days in Holland early the following year.[258]

The 5th Battalion of the Leicestershire Regiment, Leicestershire's Territorial infantry, fared far worse. The very sudden doubling of the Territorial Army in the spring of 1939, which had resulted in the division of the battalion into the 1/5th and 2/5th, greatly increased the number of men under arms, but cost much in individual unit proficiency and equipment. The Leicestershire battalions which confronted the German Wehrmacht in the spring of 1940 were but partially trained and very poorly equipped. Both battalions were decimated before the war was nine months old. In mid April 1940 the 1/5th left Scotland, with the 148th Infantry Brigade, as part of a hastily contrived expeditionary force to counter the German attack on Norway. After landing south-west of Trondheim on 18 April, they were directed towards Oslo and early on the morning of 21 April were attacked at Lake Mjosa by German troops advancing northwards. The men of A and D companies became the first men of the Leicestershire Regiment to see action against the Germans. By the evening of 23 April this first encounter with the enemy was over. Only six officers and 150 other ranks managed to reach Scotland again. Most were taken off by the Royal Navy, but others escaped on their own in small fishing boats, while still others struggled through thigh deep snow into Sweden. Without motor transport (which had been sunk at sea), with insufficient ammunition, no anti-aircraft defences, and nothing beyond anti-tank rifles to oppose the enemy's armour, they had been immediately forced into a fighting withdrawal by a rapidly advancing and victorious enemy who enjoyed both air and armoured support. The 1/5th was reformed at Hawick in Roxburghshire, but was to see no further action. After a tour of duty in Ireland, the battalion returned to Great Britain in 1942, where it was assigned a training role. The remaining years of the war were spent at Wrotham, in Kent, in the training of over 25,000 officer cadets. In August 1946 the battalion was disbanded.[259]

Even as the drama in Norway was coming to its sad conclusion, the men of the 2/5th Leicestershire Regiment were themselves preparing for active service. On 26 April 1940 they left Leicester, sailing for France from Southampton as part of the 139th Infantry Brigade, in the 46th North Midland Division. It was initially intended that the battalion should remain in Brittany, assisting in railway construction while also continuing their training. They were not designated as a fighting formation, but on 15 May they were ordered suddenly to the front, which by that time was collapsing in an increasingly chaotic retreat. At first deployed on traffic duty to control the flood of refugees and soldiers, they were soon caught up in the retreat themselves. On 26 May the battalion was attacked and overwhelmed at the Canal de la Haute Deole, while trying to make a stand against the enemy advance. Only B company, which had been in reserve, managed to withdraw to Dunkirk; the majority of the battalion were left behind, either dead or as prisoners. The reconstituted battalion did not leave Britain again for active service until December 1942 when it embarked for North Africa. Almost immediately it was thrown into action in Tunisia, losing half its strength in helping to stem the German breakthrough after the American defeat at the Kasserine Gap. Subsequently the battalion saw service in Italy, with a respite to refit and reorganize in the Middle East, and in December 1944 was sent to Greece to oppose the communists. In April 1945, at the close of the European war, the battalion was withdrawn and sent on to Weisskirchen. A year later, in May 1946, it was disbanded.[260]

The 4th Battalion of the Leicestershire Regiment had of course ceased to be infantry well before the war, and its new role as anti-aircraft troops saved it from the fate which overtook the 5th Leicesters. As the 44th (The Leicestershire Regiment) AA Battalion RE (TA), the old 4th Leicesters had been called out during the Munich crisis in 1938, and through the summer of 1939 were again called to war stations. A major air attack was expected at any moment, but apart from some later action against German coastal raiders, the regiment was to see no combat until the summer of 1944. In the intervening five and a half years the regiment remained in Britain, first becoming the 44th Searchlight Regiment, RA, and from January 1942, the 121st Light Anti-Aircraft Regiment, RA. As a light anti-aircraft regiment, armed with Bofors guns, the regiment was sent to Normandy as part of 8th Corps in 1944. After taking part in the final drive into Germany, the regiment ended the war at Lubeck. Early in 1946, after a stint at occupation duties in the Kiel area, the regiment was put into 'suspended animation'.[261]

Like the infantry of the 1/5th and 2/5th Leicesters, Leicestershire's Territorial gunners were destined for early service against the enemy. In

1939 the men of the new 115th Field Regiment, RA, attended their August camp as usual, but a week after their return, the country was at war. The regiment was embodied and new drafts taken in, and in October it left for training at Bordon. Five months later, in March 1940, they proceeded to France and on 19 May saw their first action, and casualties, at St Maur, while covering the approaches to the River Escaut. Falling back under the pressure of the German attack, the regiment was successfully withdrawn to England through Dunkirk. Early in May 1941 the regiment was re-equipped with 25-pounder guns and a third battery, 480 Field Battery, was added. In March 1942 it embarked for an arduous journey round the Cape of Good Hope to Bombay, arriving at its destination that May. Sixteen months were spent in Ceylon, training in 'jungle warfare', and in November 1943 the regiment was returned to India to join the 19th Indian (Dagger) Division. Finally, in September 1944 it was ordered to join the Fourteenth Army in northern Burma, and on Christmas Eve 1944 fired its first shots against the Japanese enemy. Hard fighting followed through January and February 1945 and into March, when it took part in the prolonged battle which finally captured Mandalay. The campaign however continued, the regiment going south to assist in clearing the Mandalay–Rangoon road. During this period it suffered more casualties than at any other time, battling against both the Japanese and the torrential rains of the monsoon season. In July it finally reached the River Sittang, its final objective. The war against Japan, however, was still not over and the regiment was redeployed for its final task of preventing the remnants of the enemy's army from escaping across the Mandalay–Rangoon road and into the hills. Hostilities ceased in mid-August and in September 1945 the regiment was sent to Rangoon, where it embarked for the return journey home. At the end of October it arrived at Southampton and the men were sent to demobilization centres.[262]

The Home Guard

Once hostilities began the Territorials had soon disappeared into the National Army, but as in the Great War of 1914–18, there emerged in the towns and villages which they had left a new force of Volunteers whose sole regard was local defence. 'In order to volunteer, what you have to do is to give in your name at your local police station, and then, as and when we want you, we will let you know'. The words of the newly appointed Secretary of State for War, Anthony Eden, met with an immediate response from great numbers of local men who 'had been waiting and hoping for just such an opportunity'.[263] His words gave birth to a new army of part-time amateur soldiers, which in the North

Midland Area was based at first on companies, with the intention of creating battalions as arms became available. In directing these new 'Local Defence Volunteers' to police stations, the Secretary's instructions also gave the new force its initial basis of organization. In Leicestershire the 'groups', or battalions, were at first assigned according to police districts: two for Leicester and district, five for the rest of the county, based on its principal towns.

By the beginning of August 1940, just ten weeks after Eden's radio appeal, 18,495 men in Leicestershire and 604 in Rutland had enrolled themselves in what had by then become known as the 'Home Guard'. In Leicester alone 8,283 men had come forward, an overwhelming response which was met by doubling the number of battalions in the city: three based geographically on different residential quarters of the city, and a fourth, the Central Battalion, 'to deal with the Factory and Public Utility works,' which drew on no particular area. Ultimately, with the addition of a 'Post Office Battalion' and a 'Motor Reconnaissance' battalion, the city would sustain six battalions of the Home Guard, totalling 12,000 men. Elsewhere in the county, the original five battalions was soon expanded to seven. In Rutland, what started as a single company grew quickly into a battalion of 850 men.[264]

The menace of imminent invasion by an army already flushed with success brought out Volunteers on a scale not seen since the threat of attack by Napoleon. Called into being, literally overnight, before any arrangements for staff, funds or facilities could be made, the force relied heavily on local initiative to improvise what was needed. Finding suitable premises from which to operate was a top priority, but for the first five months or so of its existence the Rutland battalion had no satisfactory headquarters. Arms, ammunition and equipment were at first dumped at the old police station in Oakham, and though permitted to use the Oakham Territorial Drill Hall from June 1940, this was for some time on sufferance only, the Home Guard being allowed officially only one of its rooms. Former naval officer, Wing Commander J.W. Ogilvy-Dalgleish, the battalion's commander after July, kept two headquarters: one at the drill hall and the other in his own home 'where there was plenty of space and whence we should not be turned out by Authority'. To cope with the ever growing mass of paperwork, especially on matters of supply, he had neither an adjutant or a clerk to assist him until June 1941. Administration generally, especially of such a scattered rural battalion, was a major problem, but with the friendly assistance of others the necessary letters and orders were sent out.[265]

As in the previous war, overall responsibility for the administration, records, finance and supply of the new Volunteers was placed on the shoulders of the Leicestershire and Rutland Territorial Associations under the chairmanship of the Lord Lieutenant of Leicestershire, then Sir Arthur Hazlerigg. The Joint Associations suddenly became answerable for the collection, distribution and accounting for, of the arms, ammunition, equipment and clothing for a force which by November 1940 numbered over 22,000 men in the two counties. Finding accommodation was another duty which, for such a large and scattered force, was 'a complex question' involving the provision of office, store and training facilities. In November 1941 the Home Guard were occupying 'over 250 buildings that the Secretary [of the Association] knows of', but two years later the list covered 241 requisitioned premises, 210 hirings for winter training, 70 explosive stores, 2 huts and a further 9 premises belonging to the Joint Associations themselves.[266]

The active support of the government, inspired by a sense of real urgency, transformed the new mass of Volunteers into an armed and uniformed force with remarkable speed. The contrast with the tortuous progress of the local VTC of the Great War could not have been greater. In November 1940 it was reported that every Volunteer had by then received a suit of uniform, either the loose canvas 'denims' used by the regular army as a working dress, or the smarter 'battledress'. Despite having to withdraw an original supply of P14 Lee Enfield rifles for issue to regular troops in September, arming the Home Guard was by then well in hand, and improved as time went on. At the final disbandment of the force, the Joint Associations returned 11,758 rifles, 5,947 sten guns and 399 light machine guns which they had drawn for the Home Guard.[267] In Rutland the first quota of 135 rifles (P14 Lee Enfields) arrived at Oakham police station by the end of May, followed a little later by a further 85 Canadian Ross rifles. When withdrawn, the Lee Enfields were soon replaced by a more generous issue of Ross rifles, which in turn were replaced in November by 610 American P17 Springfields. In addition, the battalion made use of 30 12-bore shot guns, eighteen Lewis light machine guns and an assortment of Mills grenades and AW bombs. The small arms were all of Great War vintage, but the only serious handicap was the meagre supply of ammunition, a mere sixty rounds per rifle for their Springfields (apart from practice rounds). Nevertheless, Ogilvy-Dalgleish thought 'that so far as the Territorial Army Association was concerned Home Guard matters had gone very smoothly . . . '.[268]

Through the summer of 1940 all of Leicestershire's 'vulnerable points', together with chosen observation posts, and in some cases barricades, were manned at night by the Home Guard. Everywhere they stood 'in readiness for the possible arrival of German Parachute Troops'.[269] The intended role of the LDV had not gone much beyond the early and accurate reporting of the enemy, but 'The most effective operational use of what was then, an ill-armed, semi-trained but enthusiastic body of men, spread over a large area, was a debatable subject . . . '.[270] Opinions differed not only on the proper role of the new force, but also on what constituted a 'vulnerable point'. Unguarded aerodromes, of which Leicestershire had four and Rutland three, were easily identified as danger spots, but the immediate decision on the actual deployment of the men could be an intensely local one. In Rutland, the thirty-five Defence and Observation Posts manned by the Rutland Home Guard in the summer of 1940 were selected by local platoon commanders. At key positions, like the unfinished air station at North Luffenham, a night guard was kept, with all men standing to at dusk and again at dawn, the periods felt most likely for an attack. Dawn patrols walked the high ground of the county and a night patrol kept watch on the Welland Railway viaduct. Enemy agents and saboteurs were another concern, and for several months a nightly guard was mounted at Oakham post office to protect telephone communications.[271]

By its very nature the Home Guard was a very parochial force, deployed according to the chances of demography, rather than to any deliberate plan. In calling the LDV into being the government had succeeded, far beyond its hopes, in creating a comprehensive network of local observers, but the fact that each one of these new Volunteers was tied to his own particular locality greatly constrained their use in too active a military role. Nnetheless, from simply spotting and reporting the enemy in their own area, plans naturally evolved to include the actual defence of those areas, the intention nation-wide being to provide defence in depth, everywhere. The operational role of the Home Guard was thus defined geographically and came under the control of various area commanders, whose responsibilities changed with the periodic re-alignment of the different 'sectors'. At first, Leicestershire and Rutland each constituted a distinct 'zone', both being part of a larger sub-area which included Northamptonshire. Subsequently, in 1941, North-ampton dropped out, leaving a 'Leicester Sub-Area' (later 'sub-district') which comprised Leicestershire and Rutland only and was divided into three 'sectors', viz. Oakham/Melton, Bosworth and Leicester. This arrangement lasted almost one year, which was longer than most, and was succeeded by others.[272]

Although naturally suited to some form of static defence, the proper operational role of Home Guard units, within their own particular areas, was seen increasingly to include aggressive tactics. In the defiant words of the Leicester sector defence scheme, 'The enemy WILL BE exterminated from whatever direction he may come and whatever mode of transport he may use'.[273] Not content with merely giving 'early, accurate and continuing information' on any invader, Ogilvy-Dalgleish and the Rutland battalion were determined both to defend their positions and 'To attack and harass the enemy . . . '. Early in 1941 a defence scheme was drawn up for the whole county of Rutland, which 'implied not static defence only, but also aggressive and mobile defence'. In Oakham a small mobile fighting patrol of twenty men and a machine gun was trained, ahead of official orders from higher authority, and by the winter of 1941/42 the other companies had similar patrols. Training exercises put more emphasis on mobility, and in 1942 one complete platoon of C company became mobile, for use anywhere in the battalion area.[274] In Leicestershire the Home Guard had already formed a 'Mobile Column' in 1940, which by early 1941 had become their 12th Battalion, a motorized reconnaissance unit organized as lorried infantry.[275]

Training, as always for the part-time soldier, had to be fitted into a normal working life. Weekday nights for lectures, classes, drill and small exercises, and Sundays for longer exercises, became a standard routine which for many, particularly in isolated rural areas, demanded considerable personal effort just to attend. Whenever possible, training was done in conjunction with regular troops in the local area. During the spring and summer of 1941 the Rutland Home Guard gained experience in tactical exercises which pitted them against regulars. The men of D company confronted 'enemy' airborne troops ('borrowed' from the regulars) in Wardley Wood. Later the Home Guard itself were cast in the role of the enemy, for an attack on the defences of the North Luffenham air station, then held by partially trained men from the RAF Regiment. In June and July, regular troops probed the Home Guard's own defences for Uppingham and a number of Rutland villages.[276]

The summers of 1940 and 1941 came and went, and still the enemy did not come. Time to prepare was the one thing that was most needed, and with the passage of time the Home Guard became better trained and better equipped, and its plans matured. In August 1942 new instructions envisaged the use of many Leicestershire and Rutland towns in a web of 'Tank Keeps'. By blocking the roads and streets, when required, with anti-tank rail (or 'asparagus'), and covering the obstructions with rifle, machine gun and mortar fire it was hoped to deny the enemy access to the towns. The Home Guard would defend such 'keeps' and other defended localities as long as they could, enabling a counter-attack by more mobile forces, both from the Home Guard and the regulars. Exercises continued throughout the year, but by December 1942 the fear of invasion was beginning to recede, and the following year the pace of activity slackened. Field exercises became fewer, and later that summer Ogilvy-Dalgleish recalled that 'most of the Rutland HG were busy getting in a good harvest'. In December 1944 the Home Guard was finally stood down, and disbanded a year later.[277]

The Home Guard, like all its Volunteer predecessors, was subjected to a certain amount of ridicule, but its portrayal as 'a collection of elderly and rather futile men' was vigorously denied by the commanding officer of the Rutland battalion. Such descriptions, he said, were simply ignorant, for his own battalion, and others, 'were a cross-section, similar to that in full-time paid units'. Most were young, with no previous military experience – the raw material of all armies. The Uppingham School Cadet Corps provided many of its older boys, but the majority of those who enrolled were fully employed in work deemed to be of national importance. There were

> . . . numbers of young men awaiting call-up . . ., and many more aged from thirty to forty in reserved occupations, such as agriculture, engineering and other work essential to keep the country going; then came those in their early forties and fifties, often as tough as any and including veterans of World War I, whose services were quite invaluable. Finally, there were a few older men for whom there were plenty of important, but less physically exacting jobs, available at 'stand to'.[278]

The makeshift and often idiosyncratic force of 1940 left many amusing anecdotes to posterity, but in finding humour in its inadequacies it is too easy to overlook the serious intent, the fears, and the urgency which created it. Nor should it be forgotten that all who joined the LDV so enthusiastically were exposing themselves to great personal risk, as the German enemy made it clear that any civilian who took up arms would be summarily shot, if apprehended. In this light the LDV's lack of uniform was no joking matter and the men of the Rutland battalion breathed a distinct sigh of relief when full army battledress began to appear, replacing their armbands and an inadequate supply of denims. Volunteer discipline has always been ridiculed, and the Home Guard, like many of its predecessors, could, until 1942, resign on fourteen days' notice. With no power to punish beyond discharging a defaulter, the authority of officers 'rested largely on the good will and self discipline of all ranks'. Although subject to military law under the Army Act when training or on parade, or if action stations were ordered, no man could actually be ordered to attend. Even after the introduction of penalties for non-attendance (once the Home Guard was made compulsory in 1942), the means of enforcement was left in civilian hands, and was 'ponderous to a degree'. How reliable could such a force be? Ogilvy-Dalgleish was emphatic that it did 'not imply that there was a lack of discipline . . . quite the contrary, it was just a matter of mutual confidence and co-operation. In emergency, civilian commitments, with certain exceptions, went by the board and all became full-time soldiers.'[279]

The Home Guard of 1940 could have done little to repel a determined German onslaught, and even a year later, although much better organized and equipped, it was still a rather feeble opponent. Yet the Home Guard had been given better and more immediate assistance by the government than any previous Volunteer Force – a clear measure of the perceived danger. Even so, its battalions, like those in Leicestershire and Rutland, had much to contend with. At the outset, the old bugbear of the part-time amateur, finding adequate time to learn and to practise the soldier's trade, had never been more pressing as the whole force was expecting 'immediate action'. Lack of accommodation was a major difficulty, much exacerbated by the wide dispersion of the rural battalions. The Rutland battalion, for example, was distributed over an area of 287 square miles, among forty-seven towns and villages – which often meant hours of arduous cycling just to attend training. It was also a considerable headache for the battalion adjutant, and yet for the first year of its existence the battalion had no adjutant at all! Training, not to mention effectiveness in actual combat, was greatly handicapped for some time by a lack of appropriate small arms ammunition, and of support weapons. The latter was only partially met by the issue of spigot mortars and the incredible smooth-bore Smith gun, which had to be turned on its side before firing! But even as the force's younger men were trained and became proficient, they were lost to the Home Guard by being called up for regular service. As early as May 1941 it could be seen that the Home Guard would experience great difficulty in keeping up its numbers by voluntary enlistment alone. When, in May 1942, the 'wastage' problem was countered by the implementation of compulsory service, the battalions had then quickly to create new and more intensive training schemes. Under compulsory enrolment the Rutland battalion found its authorized strength jump to 1,100 men, an increase which demanded more instructors, new plans and new training facilities. The battalion not only coped, but produced such a successful scheme that it was adopted as the basis for training throughout the North Midland District.[280]

To make up for their shortcomings, rural battalions like that in Rutland were relying on their vastly superior local knowledge.[281] Despite everything it was hoped that this would allow them to surprise and harass the enemy. Fortunately the call to 'action stations' never came. As so many Volunteers before them had done, the Home Guard battalions of Leicestershire and Rutland made plans, trained, and waited, but saw no action. Their assistance to the police, the capture of the odd German airman and the manning of traffic check points could appear little enough in the way of concrete achievement, but their efforts were not in vain. The real contribution was more intangible. By signalling defiance at a moment of peril, the Volunteers of the LDV and the Home Guard raised morale and reasserted the nation's belief in itself, and in the very values which for so long had nurtured the tradition of the British Volunteer.

Appendices

Appendix 1: Leicestershire and Rutland Volunteers, 1794–1828

The precise titles used by the Volunteer infantry corps and companies, and troops of cavalry of the Napoleonic era are somewhat problematic, appearing variously in different contemporary sources. This applies to all sections in Appendix 1.

1. Leicestershire Volunteer Cavalry and Artillery, 1794–1815

(a) 1794–1802

	First commissions
Ashby de la Zouch Cavalry Association	25 July 1798
Loyal Leicestershire Volunteer Cavalry	9 May 1794
Lutterworth Loyal Troop of Volunteer Cavalry	19 July 1798

(b) 1803–15

	Date accepted	Establishment Dec 1803	Disbanded
Attempt to raise a troop in Ashby failed			
Leicestershire Regiment of Yeomanry Cavalry	5 Sept 1803	450	Continued in service – see Appendix 2
Lutterworth Independent Troop of Yeomanry	11 Sept 1803	42	Feb 1807
Loddington Volunteer Artillery	7 Sept 1803	2 curricle guns	c. April 1805

2. *Leicestershire Volunteer Infantry Corps, 1794–1813*

(a) 1794–1802

	First commissions
Ashby de la Zouch Infantry Association	25 July 1798
Hinckley Volunteers	20 June 1798
Loyal Corps of Leicester Volunteer Infantry	28 May 1794
Loyal Loughborough Volunteer Infantry	22 Aug 1794
Melton Mowbray Volunteer Infantry	1 Jan 1795
Wymeswold Armed Association	accepted 6 Aug 1798

(b) 1803–13

	Date accepted	Establishment Dec 1803	Disbanded	Notes
Ashby de la Zouch Volunteer Infantry	5 Sept 1803	120	March 1809	
Allexton Independent Company of Infantry	15 Sept 1803	120	May 1805	
Appleby Volunteer Infantry	20 Oct 1803	60	May 1809	
Belvoir Castle Volunteers	5 Sept 1803	400	Sept 1806	
Coleorton Independent Company of Infantry	15 Sept 1803	120	June 1807	
Donington Park United Volunteers	6 Oct 1803	186	Jan 1807	
Great Glen & Stretton Independent Company of Infantry	15 Sept 1803	120	March 1813	
Loyal Harborough Volunteer Infantry	6 Sept 1803	120	Aug 1809	
Ibstock Independent Company of Infantry	6 Oct 1803	120	Aug 1809	
Loyal Leicester Volunteer Infantry	5 Sept 1803	480	Nov 1808	250 men to Local Militia
Loyal Loughborough Volunteer Infantry	31 Aug 1803	140	Nov 1808	150 men to Local Militia

Melton Mowbray Volunteer Infantry	16 Aug 1803	120	Nov 1806	Disbanded by June 1804, re-raised in July
Lutterworth Independent Company of Infantry	7 Sept 1803	120	Nov 1808	71 men to Local Militia
Scraptoft Independent Company of Infantry	15 Sept 1803	120	Nov 1808	60 men to Local Militia
Sheepshed & Garendon Independent Company of Infantry	6 Sept 1803	120	Nov 1806	
West Leicestershire Regiment of Loyal Volunteers[1]	31 Oct 1803	480	Nov 1808	384 men to Local Militia

1. The West Leicestershire Regiment was formed from the Hinckley Battalion of Infantry; the Market Bosworth Volunteers; the Kirkby Mallory, Peckleton, Thurlaston, Desford, Barwell and Stapleton Loyal Volunteers; and the Earl Shilton company.

3. Rutland Volunteer Corps, 1794–1828

(a) 1794–1802

	First commissions
Oakham Armed Association	24 July 1798
Rutland Volunteer Infantry	25 July 1798
Rutland Yeomanry Cavalry	25 April 1794

(b) 1803–28

	Date accepted	Establishment Dec 1803	Disbanded
Rutland Volunteer Infantry	22 Aug 1803	240	June 1810
Rutland Yeomanry Cavalry, part of Rutland Legion	Renewed service 3 Aug 1802	160	1828

Dismounted Rifle Company, Rutland Legion	22 Aug 1803	95	March 1813

Appendix 2: Lineage of the Leicestershire Yeomanry, 1794–1985

April–May 1794	Raised as The Loyal Leicestershire Volunteer Cavalry
1802	Disbanded
Sept 1803	Re-raised as The Leicestershire Regiment of Yeomanry Cavalry
Feb 1844	Given additional title 'Prince Albert's Own'
April 1901–8	'Imperial' added to title, becoming 'Prince Albert's Own' Leicestershire Imperial Yeomanry
April 1908	Transferred to Territorial Force, title 'Imperial' dropped
Feb 1920	Reconstituted in Territorial Army as Leicestershire (Prince Albert's Own) Yeomanry
Nov 1939	Divided into 153rd (Leicestershire Yeomanry) Field Regiment, RA, and 154th (Leicestershire Yeomanry) Field Regiment, RA
Jan 1947	Reconstituted as the Leicestershire (PAO) Yeomanry, Royal Armoured Corps, TA
Feb 1957	Amalgamated with the Derbyshire Yeomanry, RAC (TA), to form the Leicestershire and Derbyshire (Prince Albert's Own) Yeomanry
1967	Reduced to cadre strength
April 1971	Re-established as Leicestershire and Derbyshire Yeomanry Squadron, 7th Battalion, Royal Anglian Regiment
Successors (1985)	The Leicestershire and Derbyshire Yeomanry (Prince Albert's Own) Company, 7th (Volunteer) Battalion, The Royal Anglian Regiment, and B (Leicestershire and Derbyshire Yeomanry) Company, 3rd (Volunteer) Battalion, The Worcestershire and Sherwood Foresters Regiment

Appendix 3: The Leicestershire Rifle Volunteers, 1859–83[1]

Official date of formation	Original title	Designation on full territorialization in 1883 as 1st Vol Battn, Leics Regt
31 Aug 1859	1st Leicestershire Rifle Vols (1st Leicester Town Rifles)	A Company
13 Feb 1860	2nd Leicestershire Rifle Vols (Duke of Rutland's Belvoir Rifles)	B Company
2 March 1860	3rd Leicestershire Rifle Vols (Melton Mowbray Rifle Corps)	C Company
4 March 1860	4th Leicestershire Rifle Vols (2nd Leicester Town Rifles)	D Company E Company
3 March 1860	5th Leicestershire Rifle Vols (3rd Leicester Town Rifles)	F Company G Company
7 July 1860	6th Leicestershire Rifle Vols (Loughborough)	H Company
6 Oct 1860	7th Leicestershire Rifle Vols (Lutterworth)	Disbanded 1873
16 Sept 1860	8th Leicestershire Rifle Vols (Ashby de la Zouch Vol Rifles, Hastings Company)	I Company
24 Dec 1860	9th Leicestershire Rifle Vols (4th Leicester Town Rifles)	K Company
27 Nov 1860	10th Leicestershire Rifle Vols (Hinckley)	L Company
April 1880	Market Harborough Company	M Company

1. Nationally, the Leicestershire Rifle Volunteers ranked as the 31st regiment of Volunteers accepted by the War Office. In July 1860 all of the Leicestershire corps were grouped together as the 1st Administrative Battalion Leicestershire Rifle Volunteers. In February 1880 the 1st A B Leicestershire Rifle Volunteers was consolidated as the 1st Leicestershire Rifle Volunteers. In February 1883 the 1st Leicestershire Rifle Volunteers became the 1st Volunteer Battalion, The Leicestershire Regiment. In April 1908 the 1st V B The Leicestershire Regiment transferred to the Territorial Force, its companies creating the 4th and 5th Battalions, The Leicestershire Regiment.

Appendix 4: Leicestershire and Rutland Territorials, 1908–39

1. Territorial Establishment, 30 September 1910

	Officers	Men
Leicestershire Yeomanry	21	426
Leicestershire Royal Horse Artillery[1]	7	166
4th Battalion Leicestershire Regiment	22	923
5th Battalion Leicestershire Regiment	22	954
Lincoln & Leicester Brigade Coy ASC[1]	2	88
North Midland Mounted Brigade T & S Column[1]	3	100
2nd North Midland Field Ambulance	8	203
5th Northern General Hospital[1]	3	42
Total	88	2,902

1.   Raised after April 1908.
     Source: LRO, DE 819/1.

2. Units raised and administered by Leicestershire and Rutland Territorial Associations, April 1915

	Officers	Men
1/1st Leicestershire Yeomanry	28	500
2/1st Leicestershire Yeomanry	26	507
3/1st Leicestershire Yeomanry	5	254
1/1st Leicestershire Royal Horse Artillery	10	222
2/1st Leicestershire Royal Horse Artillery	5	212
1/4th Leicestershire Regiment	30	995
2/4th Leicestershire Regiment	30	993
3/4th Leicestershire Regiment	–	495
Depot 4th Leicestershire Regiment	1	9
1/5th Leicestershire Regiment	29	985
2/5th Leicestershire Regiment	33	1342
3/5th Leicestershire Regiment	3	44
Depot 5th Leicestershire Regiment	1	6
1/2nd North Midland Field Ambulance	9	236
2/2nd North Midland Field Ambulance	7	220
3/2nd North Midland Field Ambulance	–	38

1/5th Northern General Hospital	21	161
1/1st North Midland Mounted Bde T & S Column	(not received)	
2/1st North Midland Mounted Bde T & S Column	3	22
3/1st North Midland Mounted Bde T & S Column	1	15
1/1st Lincoln & Leicester Bde Coy A S C	5	103
2/1st Lincoln & Leicester Bde Coy A S C	6	105
3/1st Lincoln & Leicester Bde Coy A S C	1	64
North Midland Divisional Ambulance Column	–	34
Railway Detachment ASC	–	61
North Midland Div Casualty Clearing Stn	8	77
No. 1 Coy Super Coy 4th Leics Regt	5	228
No. 1 Coy Super Coy 5th Leics Regt	3	134
No. 2 Coy Super Coy 5th Leics Regt	3	125
No. 2 Coy Super Coy 4th Leics Regt	3	120
No. 3 Coy Super Coy 4th Leics Regt	2	57
Total	368	8,274

Source: LRO, DE 819/1.

3. Leicestershire and Rutland Territorial Units, 1920–39

	Establishment 30 June 1922	Strength
Leicestershire Yeomanry[1]	248	239
239th Battery RFA[2]	101	96
4th Battalion Leicestershire Regt[3]	637	394
5th Battalion Leicestershire Regt[4]	637	533
Total	1,623	1,262

5th Cavalry Mobile Veterinary Section, RAVC	Disbanded 1922
No. 3 Coy 2nd Cavalry Div. Train, RASC	Disbanded 1922
No. 4 Coy 2nd Cavalry Div. Train, RASC	Disbanded 1922
No. 3 Coy 46th North Midland Div Train, RASC	Disbanded 1922
No. 5 Coy 46th North Midland Div Train, RASC	Disbanded 1920
2nd North Midland Field Ambulance, RAMC	Disbanded 1922
5th Northern General Hospital	Disbanded 1922

1. Divided into 153rd (Leicestershire Regiment) Field Regiment RA and 154th (Leicestershire Regiment) Field Regiment RA, 25 Nov 1939.

2. Expanded to become 2/60th Field Regiment RA, 7 April 1939, and shortly after re-designated 115th Field Regiment RA.
3. Became 44th (The Leicestershire Regiment) Anti-Aircraft Battalion, RE (TA), 10 December 1936.
4. Divided into 1/5th and 2/5th Leicestershire Regiment, 31 March 1939.

Source: LRO, DE 819/3.

4. Leicestershire and Rutland Auxiliary Territorial Service Units, Sept 1938

	Officers	Members	To be affiliated with
1st Leicestershire Coy (Leicester)	2	53	44th AA Bttn
10th Rutland Company (Oakham)	1	23	Leics Yeomanry
11th Leicestershire Coy (Loughborough)	1	23	5th Bttn Leics Regt
40th Leicestershire Coy (Leicester)	2	53	Leics Yeomanry
Unit HQ Leicester	1	1	—
Total	7	153	

Source: LRO, DE 819/5 and 819/19.

Appendix 5: Leicestershire and Rutland Volunteers – the Home Front in the World Wars, 1914–18 and 1940–4

1. Leicestershire and Rutland Volunteer Force, February 1917

1st Battalion Leicestershire Volunteer Regiment[1]
('Leicester Battalion' – city of Leicester)

2nd Battalion Leicestershire Volunteer Regiment[1]
('Western Battalion' – Loughborough, Ashby de la Zouch and Hinckley)

3rd Battalion Leicestershire Volunteer Regiment[1]
(Syston, Narborough, Melton Mowbray and Market Harborough)

Mounted Section[1]

Leicester Motor Volunteers

Pharmacists Section (working with Leicester Battalion)

1st Battalion Rutland Volunteer Regiment
(originally Rutland Volunteer Training Corps, until May 1916)

1.   Started as the Leicester and Leicestershire Volunteer Training Corps.
Source: LRO, DE 819/2.

2. Leicestershire and Rutland Volunteer Force, May 1918

	Officers	Other ranks	To be renamed from May 1918 as
1/1st Bttn Leics Vol Regt	37	1,188	1st Vol Bttn Leics Regt
2/1st Bttn Leics Vol Regt	23	1,067	4th Vol Bttn Leics Regt
2nd Bttn Leics Vol Regt	28	1,257	2nd Vol Bttn Leics Regt
3rd Bttn Leics Vol Regt	17	998	3rd Vol Bttn Leics Regt
Leicestershire Motor Vol Corps	10	365	Leicestershire ASC, MT(V)
1st Bttn Rutland Vol Regt	25	624	unchanged
Total	140	5,099	

Source: LRO, DE 819/2.

3. Leicestershire Home Guard, January 1941

Leicester Group
1st (North Leicester) Bttn, Leicestershire Home Guard
2nd (South Leicester) Bttn, Leicestershire Home Guard
3rd (West Leicester) Bttn, Leicestershire Home Guard
4th (Leicester Central) Bttn, Leicestershire Home Guard
Melton Mowbray Group
5th (Belvoir) Bttn, Leicestershire Home Guard
6th (Quorn) Bttn, Leicestershire Home Guard

Harborough/Bosworth Group
7th (Market Harborough) Bttn, Leicestershire Home Guard
8th (Market Bosworth) Bttn, Leicestershire Home Guard

Loughborough Group
9th (Loughborough) Bttn, Leicestershire Home Guard
10th (Charnwood) Bttn, Leicestershire Home Guard
11th (Ashby de la Zouch) Bttn, Leicestershire Home Guard
12th (Motor Reconnaissance) Bttn, Leicestershire Home Guard

Extra-Zone Unit
13th (Post Office) Bttn, Leicestershire Home Guard

Source: LRO, DE 819/22.

4. Rutland Home Guard, 1940–4

May 1940
The Rutland LDV were started as a company, with each of its four platoons allotted an area of the county:

No. 1 Platoon (north-eastern): Belmisthorpe, Casterton, Empingham, Essendine, Exton, Greetham, Pickworth, Ryhall, and Whitwell

No. 2 Platoon (central): Hambleton, Ketton, North and South Luffenham, Market Overton, Thistleton and, at first, Langham

No. 3 Platoon (Oakham and district): Braunston, Brooke, Burley, Egleton, Lyndon, Manton, Oakham and, later, Langham

No. 4 Platoon (Uppingham and district): Ayston, Belton, Bisbrooke, Caldecott, Glaston, Lyddington, Morcott, Preston, Ridlington, Seaton, Uppingham, Wardley, and Wing

July 1940
The LDV were renamed the Home Guard, and the Rutland company was expanded, each of its platoons becoming a company of the new 1st Rutland Battalion, Rutland Home Guard, with a total strength of 850 men.

A Company (formerly No. 1 Platoon), Platoons 1–4

B Company (formerly No. 2 Platoon), Platoons 5–8

C Company (formerly No. 3 Platoon), Platoons 9–12

D Company (formerly No. 4 Platoon), Platoons 13–16

June 1943
B Company was divided into two smaller companies, with Platoons 5 and 6 being kept in B Company, while 7 and 8 went to a new E Company.

Source: Ogilvy-Dalgleish 1955.

References

The following abbreviations are used:
LRO Leicestershire Record Office
PRO Public Record Office, Kew

CHAPTER 1
1 Letter from Duke of Newcastle, 1 June 1745, quoted in Montefiore 1908, 65.
2 Norfolk 1965, 7–8.
3 Montefiore 1908, 73–4.
4 Western 1965, 117.
5 Appeal 1746.
6 Id.; Montefiore 1908, 79–80.
7 Norfolk 1965, 8.
8 Montefiore 1908, 73–5.
9 Ibid., 72, quoting letter from Duke of Newcastle, 14 Oct 1745.
10 Appeal 1746; Montefiore 1908, 78.
11 Montefiore 1908, 73–5, 78.
12 Western 1965, 104–5.
13 Montefiore 1908, 44–5.
14 Western 1965, 161.
15 Ibid., 142; Montefiore 1908, 47–8.
16 18 Geo III c.59, quoted in Montefiore 1908, 48–9.
17 Western 1965, 211–14.
18 Montefiore 1908, 50–3; Western 1965, 215.
19 Montefiore 1908, 105–8, 52.
20 Ibid., 108.
21 McDowell 1979, 256–7.
22 LRO, LM 8/8/1–9, circulars and letters re proposal that principal towns raise their own corps, 1782; Western 1965, 217–18.

CHAPTER 2
23 Emsley 1979, 38.
24 Montefiore 1908, 56–8.
25 34 Geo III c.31.
26 Montefiore 1908, 169.
27 Western 1956, 603–14; Dickinson 1989, 103–25.
28 Western 1965, 220, 222, 224.
29 Montefiore 1908, 189–90, 192, 200–1, 224.
30 Ibid., 220.
31 Quoted in ibid., 230.
32 Ibid., 234.
33 Montefiore 1908, 265–6.
34 Glover 1973, 141–2.
35 Ibid., 133–5.
36 Montefiore 1908, 299–300.
37 Glover 1963, 250.
38 Quoted in ibid., 240.
39 Quoted in ibid., 246.
40 Ibid., 249–52.
41 Fortescue 1909, 269–70.
42 Montefiore 1908, 264–5.
43 Ibid., 236–7, 264–5.
44 Western 1965, 250.
45 Fortescue 1909, 90.
46 Windham and Castlereagh quoted in Montefiore 1908, 337–8 and 344–5 respectively.
47 Fortescue 1909, 199.
48 Montefiore 1908, 236, quoting letter from Duke of Richmond, 8 Aug 1802.
49 Montefiore 1908, 56, 74–5.
50 Quoted in ibid., 170–1.
51 Ibid., 166–7, 199, 207–8, 211–13.
52 Ibid., 213–14.
53 Glover 1973, 141–2.
54 Fortescue 1909, 172.
55 Montefiore 1908, 345–50; Glover 1963, 251.

CHAPTER 3
56 Darvall 1934, 306; Mather 1959, 1–6, 12–16.
57 Mather 1959, 38, 49, 52–4, 142–3.
58 Ibid., 142–3, 145.

59 Ibid., 142, 146–8.
60 Teichman 1940, 75–90.
61 Mather 1959, 143–4.
62 Ibid., 90–3.
63 Ibid., 149–50.
64 Teichman 1940, 140–3.

CHAPTER 4
65 *Volunteer Service Gazette*, 12 Feb 1861, quoted in Beckett 1982, 1.
66 Cunningham 1975, 5–11; Beckett 1982, 13–16, 34.
67 Quoted in Cunningham 1975, 1.
68 Ibid., 46–9.
69 *The Times*, 27 May 1872.
70 Beckett 1982, 138.
71 See Cunningham 1975 and especially Beckett 1982.
72 Quoted in Beckett 1982, 42.
73 Ibid., 41.
74 Ibid., 43, 52–4, 61–7.
75 Ibid., 70–3.
76 Cunningham 1975, 25, 41–2; Beckett 1982, 43, 58, 67–70, 73–5;.
77 Beckett 1982, 98–101.
78 Quoted in Cunningham 1975, 55.
79 Cunningham 1975, 108–123; Beckett 1982, 107–18.
80 Beckett 1982, 48–50, 113, 128.
81 Cunningham 1975, 2, 26–7, 89–90; Beckett 1982, 116–17, 125.
82 *The Times*, 25 Dec 1869, 21 Sept 1864, 9 Oct 1866, quoted in Cunningham 1975, 87–9.
83 *Wimbledon Annual* (London 1869), 8.
84 Cunningham 1975, 90–1; Beckett 1982, 129–31.
85 Beckett 1982, 132–5, 185–8.
86 Cunningham 1975, 2, 49–50, 68, 86–7, 91; Beckett 1982, 103–6.
87 Cunningham 1975, 128; Beckett 1982, 195–6.
88 Cunningham 1975, 128–9; Beckett 1982, 106, 214. The precise numbers are uncertain.
89 Cunningham 1975, 127–9; Beckett 1982, 214, 216–18.
90 Beckett 1982, 143–67.
91 Beckett & Simpson 1985, 6–7, 128; Dennis 1987, 13–14, 19.

92 Beckett & Simpson 1985, 128–30.
93 Ibid., 129.

CHAPTER 5
94 Beckett & Simpson 1985, 139.
95 Ibid., 71, 131–3; Dennis 1987, 30–2.
96 Beckett & Simpson 1985, 13, 132, 152.
97 Ibid., 15; Beckett 1985a, 77; 1985b, 27–9; Osborne 1988, 64–7.
98 Beckett & Simpson 1985, 15–16; Beckett 1985b, 30–1.
99 Beckett & Simpson 1985, 15–16; Beckett 1985b, 31–2, 34, 37–8; Osborne 1988, 70–1.
100 Dennis 1976, 207.
101 Dennis 1987, 126–7, 131–2, 134–9, 244.
102 Dennis 1976, 199; 1987, 65–70, 73–5, 81–2.
103 Dennis 1987, 77–8, 83–4, 90, 106, 124, 127–30, 147, 155–9, 165–6.
104 Quoted in ibid., 189.
105 Ibid., 124, 220.
106 Ibid., 95, 101, 164, 180–1, 205.
107 Ibid., 191–3, 196, 199–201, 219–20, 231–4, 237–8, 251–2.
108 Ibid., 247–9, 256.
109 Details on the Home Guard are taken largely from Longmate 1974.

CHAPTER 6
1 Throsby 1791, III, 151–2.
2 McLynn 1983, 127; White 1877, 532.
3 *Leicester Journ*, 1 and 29 June 1782.
4 Ibid., 21 and 28 Feb 1794.
5 Ibid., 4 and 18 April 1794.
6 Ibid., 9 May 1794; *Leicester Herald*, 14 June 1794.
7 *Leicester Journ*, 9 and 16 May, 27 June 1794.
8 Ibid., 23 May, 20 June, 11 July, 5 Sept, 10 Oct 1794.
9 Ibid., 11 and 18 July, 15 and 29 Aug 1794, 3 April, 23 Oct 1795.
10 Hind 1899, 380–2; *Leicester Journ*, 10 Oct, 19 Dec 1794, 16 Jan 1795; Read 1881, 131.
11 List 1800; Patterson 1954, 81–2; Read 1881, 131, 155–6.
12 Patterson 1954, 82, 84.

13 PRO, HO 50/77, Rutland to Yorke, 25 Aug 1803, and Mansfield to Yorke, 6 Sept 1803.

14 Ibid., Keck to Rutland, 14 Aug 1803, enclosed in Rutland to Hobart, 20 Aug 1803.

15 LRO, DG 39/1595 and 1596, Peach to Turvile, 13 and 17 Aug 1803.

16 LRO, DE 836/29, broadsheet of Duke of Rutland's address, 1 Sept 1803; PRO, HO 50/77, Rutland to Yorke, 25 Aug 1803, and Winstanley to [Yorke], 26 Aug 1803.

17 PRO, HO/111, Rutland to Yorke, 1 Sept [1803]; HO 50/77, Winstanley to Yorke, 1, 10, and 31 Oct 1803.

18 PRO, HO 50/77, General Return of Leics Vols [29 Sept 1803], and Winstanley to Yorke, 31 Oct 1803; HO 50/111, Rutland to Yorke, 1 Sept 1803.

19 PRO, HO 50/111, Rutland to Hawkesbury, 29 May, 8 June, 11 and 15 July 1804; HO 50/155, Rutland to Spencer, 11 Nov 1806.

20 PRO, HO 50/77, Winstanley to Yorke, 7, 25 and 29 Nov 1803; HO 50/138, Rutland to Hawkesbury, 3 May 1805.

21 PRO, HO 50/111, Winstanley to Hawkesbury, 5 July, 8 Sept 1804; HO 50/138, Boott to Winstanley, 10 Dec 1805.

22 PRO, HO 50/155, Rutland to Spencer, 10 Sept 1806.

23 Ibid., Winstanley to Spencer, 17 Oct, 18 and 24 Nov, 29 Dec 1806; HO 50/171, 17 Feb 1807.

24 PRO, HO 50/195, Cooke to Hawkesbury, 10 Dec 1808.

25 Ibid., Rutland to Hawkesbury, 27 Nov 1808; HO 50/223, Rutland to Liverpool, 8 and 27 March, 5 June, 12 Aug 1809; WO 13/4427.

26 PRO, HO 50/195, Rutland to Hawkesbury, 19 Sept, 17 Nov 1808; HO 50/223, Rutland to Liverpool, 27 Jan 1809.

27 LRO, DE 1797/1/154, broadsheet of meeting at Oakham Castle, 22 March 1794; *The Times*, 21 April 1794; *Leicester Journ*, 18 April 1794, has meeting to appoint officers on 12 April and Oakham meeting on 21 March.

28 *Journ Soc Army Hist Res*, VIII (1929), Replies, 145–6; LRO, DG 7 Rut 5, Finch MSS, Dundas to Winchelsea, 26 May 1796.

29 PRO, HO 50/342, Winchelsea to Hobart, 29 Sept 1801; List 1797; *Gentleman's Mag*, Nov 1795.

30 PRO, HO 50/342, Winchelsea to Portland, 30 June 1797, and Winchelsea to Hobart, 29 Sept 1801; HO 50/83, Winchelsea to Hobart, 19 Aug 1803, General Return, sent 6 Oct 1803, and Winchelsea to Yorke, 27 and 31 Aug 1803; HO 50/201, Abstract of Muster Rolls, 9 Dec 1808; HO 50/228, Winchelsea to Liverpool, 27 Sept 1809; LRO, DG 7 Rut 5, Finch MSS, Infantry Account from August 1803; PRO, WO 13/4524.

31 PRO, WO 13/4030; Robinson 1978, 92–3.

32 PRO, HO 50/342, Winchelsea to Dundas, 25 June 1798, 8 Nov, 19 Dec 1799; List 1800, 1801.

33 Ibid., Winchelsea to Dundas, 25 June 1798, 19 Dec 1799; HO 50/83, Winchelsea to Yorke, 17 and 19 Oct 1803.

34 PRO, HO 50/83, Winchelsea to Yorke, 27 and 31 Aug, 1 Sept, 4 and 9 Nov 1803; HO 50/228, Abstract of Muster Rolls, 29 April 1809; HO 50/249, Winchelsea to Ryder, 1 Jan, 19 June, 9 Nov 1810.

35 PRO, HO 50/249, Winchelsea to Ryder, 9 Nov 1810; HO 50/271, Winchelsea to Ryder, 4 March, 28 June 1811; LRO, DG 7 Rut 5, Finch MSS.

36 *Leicester Journ*, 9 May 1794.

37 Ibid., 9 Sept 1803.

38 Ibid., 4 July, 22 Aug, 24 Oct, 28 Nov 1794.

39 LRO, DG 7 Rut 5, Finch MSS, Infantry Account from August 1803.

40 *Leicester Journ*, 23 May, 27 June 1794, 30 March 1798; PRO, HO 50/77, General Return of Leics Vols, 29 Sept 1803.

41 Patterson 1954, 81–2; PRO, HO 50/77, Smith to King, 6 Nov 1803; HO 50/138, Chessher to Neapean, 12 Aug 1805.

42 Hind 1899, 380–1.

43 Address 1797, 17; PRO, HO 50/77, Rutland to Yorke, 25 Aug 1803.

44 Robinson 1795, 8, 12.

45 *Leicester Journ*, 24 July 1795.

46 Ibid., 7 and 14 Aug, 29 Sept 1795; LRO, Barrow-on-Soar burial register, 8 Aug and 2 Oct 1795; Nichols 1800, III.i, 69; Patterson 1954, 76–7.

47 Hillier 1984, 59; *Leicester Journ*, 9 Sept 1803.

48 PRO, HO 50/111, Rutland to Hawkesbury, 8 June 1804, with enclosures.

49 Id.

50 Ibid., Morgan to Hawkesbury, 12 June 1804.

51 PRO, HO 50/77, Mansfield to Yorke, 6 Sept 1803, and Winstanley to Yorke, 23 Oct 1803, with enclosures.

52 Hind 1899, 380.

53 PRO, HO 50/77, Ryder to Winstanley, 17 Aug 1803, enclosed in Winstanley to [Yorke], 26 Aug 1803.

54 Francis 1930, 122.

55 Hind 1899, 381; *Leicester Journ*, 29 May 1795.

56 Robinson 1795, 11.

57 *Leicester Journ*, 11 and 18 Dec 1795.

58 Ibid., 12 and 19 Dec 1794.

59 PRO, HO 50/138, Fleetwood Churchill to Hawkesbury, 24 June 1805.

60 PRO, HO 50/111, Winstanley to Hawkesbury, 8 Sept 1804.

61 PRO, HO 50/138, Fleetwood Churchill to Hawkesbury, 24 June 1805, and Rutland to Hawkesbury, 16 Aug 1805, with enclosures.

62 PRO, HO 50/155, Winstanley to Spencer, 17 Oct, 18 and 24 Nov 1806, with enclosures.

63 PRO, HO 50/77, Rutland to Yorke, 27 Aug 1803; HO 50/195, Rutland to Hawkesbury, 17 Nov 1808.

64 PRO, HO 50/77, Rutland to Yorke, 31 Oct 1803.

65 LRO, DG 36/185, order to pay drill instructor of Melton Mowbray Vol Infantry, 1804; PRO, WO 134/4426, Certificate of Drill Serjeants of Leicester Regt of Vol Infantry, 20 March 1804.

66 PRO, HO 50/111, Rutland to Hawkesbury, 7 June 1804, with enclosures.

67 Quoted in Francis 1930, 122.

68 *Leicester Journ*, 11 May 1804; PRO, HO 50/111 and 138; WO 13/4427.

69 PRO, HO 50/138, Fleetwood Churchill to Hawkesbury, 24 June 1805.

70 PRO, HO 50/300, Hoyland to Sidmouth, 9 Nov 1813.

CHAPTER 7

71 Patterson 1954, 110, 112–14, 119, 127–8.

72 PRO, HO 52/14, Mundy to Undersecretary of State, 16 Oct 1831.

73 Id.

74 Ibid., Mundy to [Melbourne], 12 Oct 1831.

75 *VCH Leicestershire* II, 130–1.

76 PRO, HO 52/14, Burbidge to Melbourne, 11 Oct 1831.

77 Patterson 1954, 377.

78 *Leicestershire Mercury*, March 1838.

79 Read 1881, 158; Patterson 1954, 324–40.

80 Read 1881, 161; Patterson 1954, 360–1.

81 Read 1881, 161.

82 List 1850, 19; Read 1881, 157–60.

83 List 1850, xxvii, 19; Read 1881, 147; PRO, WO 27/474 and 475, Inspection Reports, Leics Yeomanry, 1853, 1854.

84 LRO, DE 40/46/4, regimental register, Leics Yeomanry, 1849–70.

85 List 1850, xxvii, 19; Patterson 1954, 180, 186–7; LRO, DE 40/46/4, regimental register, Leics Yeomanry, 1849–70.

86 Patterson 1954, 180, 187; *VCH Leicestershire* II, 133–4.

87 List 1850, xxxii, xxxv; PRO, WO 27/474, Inspection Report, Leics Yeomanry, 30 Sept 1853.

88 PRO, WO 27/474 and 475, Inspection Reports, Leics Yeomanry, 30 Sept 1853, 30 Sept 1854; LRO, DE 40/46/4, regimental register, Leics Yeomanry, 1849–70.
89 Id.
90 Ellis 1935, 187.
91 Id.
92 Gladstone 1953, 52, 98, 121–3.
93 Read 1881, 197.

CHAPTER 8
94 Richardson 1910–11, III, 3–4.
95 LRO, 16 D 35/2, oath roll, 1st Leics Rifle Corps, 3 Nov 1859.
96 LRO, LM 4/6–7, muster rolls, Leics Rifle Vols, 1861, 1862; Read 1881, 186.
97 LRO, LM 4/6–7, muster rolls, Leics Rifle Vols, 1861–2.
98 Ibid.; Read 1881, 171, 175–6.
99 LRO, 3 D 67/III/873, C.S. Smith Papers, details of Guarantee Fund for purchase of uniform, *c.* 1860–1; LRO, 3 D 67/III/699–708, printed vouchers for supply of articles of uniform 1864.
100 List 1860; LRO, 22 D 63/75, Rules of 10th Leics Rifle Vol Corps, 18 March 1861; LRO, Misc 320/9.
101 *Leicester Journ*, 2 Nov 1860.
102 Quoted in Westlake 1982, x.
103 *Melton Mowbray Times*, 8 Nov 1860.
104 Id.
105 *Leicester Journ*, 2 Nov 1860.
106 Read 1881, 181.
107 Ibid., 89–92.
108 Westlake 1982, 94–5; Wright 1881, 1898, 1904; Kelly 1900, 1908.
109 LRO, Misc 320/6, proposed rules for Hastings Coy, Ashby de la Zouch Vol Rifles, 2 July 1860; 22 D 63/75, Rules of 10th Leics Rifle Vol Corps, 18 March 1861; Read 1881, 174.
110 LRO, 3 D 67/III/998–9, 1002–3, 1021–7, 1112, C.S. Smith Papers, company order, 5th Leics Rifle Vols, Feb–June 1872.
111 Read 1881, 175–81.
112 *Melton Mowbray Times*, 8 Nov 1860.
113 Read 1881, 184.

114 *Leicester Daily Mercury*, 7 Aug 1879.
115 LRO, DE 2237/3, concert programme, 1st A B Leics Rifle Vols, 6 Aug 1879; DE 2237/4, sports programme, 1st A B Leics Rifle Vols, 4 Aug 1879.
116 *Midland Jackdaw*, no 41, vol 1, 8 Aug 1879; *Leicester Daily Mercury*, 7 Aug 1879.
117 Freer 1899.
118 LRO, Misc 320/8, Regulations to be observed at Ashby de la Zouch Rifle Range . . . , Aug 1861.
119 LRO, 22 D 63/86, Jubilee Programme, M Coy, 1st V B Leics Regt, 1887.
120 Read 1881, 182–3.
121 Ibid., 179–80.
122 Davies 1981, 75.

CHAPTER 9
123 Richardson 1910–11, vol III, 5.
124 LRO, P39, transcript of Harrison's diary.
125 LRO, pamphlet, transcript of Evans-Freke's diary.
126 LRO, P39.
127 LRO, pamphlet, notes with Evans-Freke's diary.
128 Gilbert 1901, 267.
129 Ibid., 147–53.
130 Ibid., 283.
131 Ibid., 284–5.
132 LRO, DE 1309/1, letter from George (no surname).
133 Gladstone 1953, 167–8.
134 LRO, DE 819/27, minutes, Finance Committee, 1st V B Leics Regt, 20 May 1901, 20 Dec 1905, 11 Jan 1906.
135 LRO, DE 819/1, 1–2, minutes, Leics County Association, 24 Oct 1907.
136 Ibid., 52–6, minutes, Joint Committee, 6 May 1909.
137 Ibid., 36–7, minutes, Leicester Employers in Conference, 15 May 1908.
138 Ibid., 132, minutes, Joint Committee, 27 Nov 1913.
139 Ibid., 124, minutes, Joint Committee, 3 July 1913.

140 Ibid., 77, minutes, Joint Committee, 3 Nov 1910.
141 Ibid., 113–14, 124, minutes, Joint Committee, 6 Feb, 3 July 1913.
142 Ibid., 37, minutes, Leicester Employers in Conference, 15 May 1908; Syllabus for Training Recruits of Territorial Infantry, 1910.
143 LRO, DE 2472/16, Leics Imperial Yeomanry, outline for forthcoming training, May 1907.
144 *Loughborough Monitor*, 10 June 1909.
145 Id.
146 LRO, 22 D 63/110 and 115, programme of regimental sports, 4th and 5th Battalions, Leics Regt, 1910–11; Hills 1919, 1.

CHAPTER 10
147 Milne 1935, 1.
148 Moore 1982, 120.
149 Hills 1919, 3–4.
150 LRO, DE 819/1, 161–71, minutes, 21 Sept 1914.
151 LRO, DE 819/2, 183, minutes, 10 Dec 1914.
152 LRO, DE 819/1, 200–2, 233, minutes, 15 April, 23 Sept 1915.
153 Ibid., 166, 180, 183–5, minutes, 21 Sept, 10 Dec 1914.
154 Armitage 1933, 25.
155 LRO, DE 819/1, 180, 183–5, minutes, 10 Dec 1914.
156 Codrington 1955, 24–5.
157 'The Experiences of the Leicester Yeomanry during the European War 1914', undated typescript, Rutland County Museum.
158 Id.
159 Phillips 1920, 14–15.
160 'The Experiences of the Leicester Yeomanry . . . '; Phillips 1920, 15.
161 'The Experiences of the Leicester Yeomanry . . . '.
162 Codrington 1955, 27–9; LRO, DE 2472/29, 'Records of Leicestershire Yeomanry on the nights of May 12th and 13th 1915', undated typescript; copies of various contemporary newspaper cuttings from Rutland County Museum.
163 Codrington 1955, 29–8.
164 Milne 1935, 157.
165 LRO, DE 819/2, 184–5, minutes, 2 May 1918; for service details see Anon (nd).
166 Jamie 1931, 34.
167 Armitage 1933, 249.
168 LRO, DE 2472/41, Muir to Codrington, 6 Feb 1928; Codrington 1955, 26.
169 LRO, DE 819/1, 186, minutes, 10 Dec 1914.
170 Phillips 1920, 236–7.
171 Ibid., 175; Armitage 1933, 24, 31, 166.
172 LRO, DE 819/1, 186–7, minutes, 10 Dec 1914.
173 Phillips 1920, 175.
174 LRO, DE 819/1, 303–13, minutes, 4 May 1916.
175 LRO, DE 819/2, 25–8, 235, minutes, 8 July 1916, 4 July 1918.
176 LRO, DE 819/1, 303–13, minutes, 4 May 1916; DE 819/2, 25–8, 48–56, minutes, 6 July, 2 Nov 1916.
177 LRO, DE 819/2, 72–80, 106–19, minutes, 1 Feb, 5 July 1917.
178 Ibid., 169–76, 191–4, minutes, 7 Feb, 2 May 1918.
179 Ibid., 48–56, 72–80, 96, minutes, 2 Nov 1916, 1 Feb, 3 May 1917.
180 Ibid., 77–8, 99, 106, minutes, 1 Feb, 3 May, 5 July 1917; Phillips 1920, 181.
181 LRO, DE 819/2, 173, minutes, 7 Feb 1918.
182 Ibid., 192, minutes, 2 May 1918.
183 Ibid., 96, minutes, 3 May 1917.
184 Ibid., 171, minutes, 7 Feb 1918.
185 Ibid., 91–2, 106–7, minutes, 3 May, 5 July 1917.
186 Ibid., 91, minutes, 3 May 1917.
187 Ibid., 153, minutes, 1 Nov 1917.
188 Ibid., 227, minutes, 4 July 1918.
189 Phillips 1920, 175.
190 LRO, DE 819/2, 257, minutes, 7 Nov 1918.
191 Ibid., 285, minutes, 6 Feb 1919.
192 LRO, DE 819/3, 26, minutes, 13 Nov 1919.
193 Phillips 1920, 175.
194 LRO, DE 819/2, 74–5, 93, minutes, 1 Feb, 3 May 1917.

195 Ibid., 233, 258–9, minutes, 4 July, 7 Nov 1918.

CHAPTER 11
196 LRO, DE 819/3, 106, 152, 166, minutes, 5 May 1921, 4 July, 7 Nov 1922.
197 LRO, DE 819/4, 290, minutes, 12 Nov 1935.
198 Underhill 1958, 6.
199 LRO, DE 819/5, 15, 20–1, 24, 33, 35, 40, 45–6, 51–2, minutes, 8 Feb, 10 May, 3 Oct, 8 Nov 1938, 14 Feb, 9 May, 19 Sept 1939.
200 Ibid., 45, minutes, 9 May 1939.
201 LRO, DE 819/3, 126, minutes, 7 Feb 1922.
202 LRO, DE 819/4, 269–74, minutes, 12 Feb 1935.
203 LRO, DE 819/5, 21, minutes, 10 May 1938.
204 LRO, DE 819/3, 73, minutes, 4 Nov 1920.
205 Ibid., 104, minutes, 5 May 1921.
206 Ibid., 255–6, minutes, 12 May 1925.
207 Ibid., 289–90, minutes, 2 Feb 1926.
208 Ibid., 253, minutes, 12 May 1925.
209 Ibid., 164–5, 231, 256, minutes, 7 Nov 1922, 11 Nov 1924, 12 May 1925.
210 Ibid., 232, 252–3, minutes, 11 Nov 1924, 12 May 1925.
211 Underhill 1958, 6.
212 LRO, DE 819/3, 103, minutes, 5 May 1921.
213 Ibid., 127, 150–1, 167, 200, minutes, 7 Feb, 4 July, 7 Nov 1922, 13 Nov 1923.
214 Ibid., 242–3, minutes, 10 Feb 1925.
215 LRO, DE 819/4, 195, 233, 243, minutes, 9 Feb, 9 May, 12 Nov 1932.
216 LRO, DE 819/3, 311, 313, minutes, 13 July 1926.
217 Ibid., 324, minutes, 9 Nov 1926; DE 819/4, 9, minutes, 10 May 1927.
218 LRO, DE 819/4, 194–5, 207, 215, minutes, 9 Feb, 12 July, 8 Nov 1932.
219 LRO, DE 819/3, 127, minutes, 7 Feb 1922.
220 Ibid., 140, minutes, 2 May 1922.
221 LRO, DE 819/4, 41, 51, 61, 76, 91, 103, 110, 122, 131, minutes, 14 Feb, 8 May, 10 July, 13 Nov 1928, 12 Feb, 11 May, 9 July, 12 Nov 1929, 11 Feb 1930.
222 Ibid., 163, minutes, 10 Feb 1931.
223 Ibid., 209–10, minutes, 12 Feb 1924.
224 LRO, DE 819/3, 151, 200, minutes, 4 July 1922, 13 Nov 1923.
225 Ibid., 242–3, minutes, 10 Feb 1925.
226 LRO, DE 819/5, minutes, 8 Feb 1938.
227 LRO, DE 819/3, 74, 219, minutes, 4 Nov 1920, 13 May 1924.
228 LRO, DE 819/4, 192–4, minutes, 9 Feb 1932.
229 Ibid., 29, minutes, 8 Nov 1927.
230 Ibid., 233, minutes, 9 May 1933.
231 Ibid., 272, minutes, 12 Feb 1935.
232 LRO, DE 819/3, 243, minutes, 10 Feb 1925.
233 LRO, DE 819/4, 164, 173, minutes, 10 Feb, 12 May 1931.
234 Ibid., 221, minutes, 14 Feb 1933.
235 LRO, DE 819/3, 251, minutes, 12 May 1925.
236 LRO, DE 819/4, 220, minutes, 14 Feb 1933.
237 LRO, DE 3765, Regimental Diary, Leics Yeomanry, 1920–50, 116, 125.
238 Bouskell-Wade 1948, 5–12.
239 *Leicester Mail*, 17 May 1929; Bouskell-Wade 1948, 13.
240 *Leicester Mercury*, 15 May 1929.
241 *Leicester Evening Mail*, 22–3 May 1934.
242 Standing Orders 1928, 80–1.
243 LRO, DE 63/17/1–3, typescript, '5th Battalion TA', nd, 2.
244 LRO, DE 819/4, 73, 243, 264, 320, minutes, 13 Nov 1928, 12 Nov 1933, 13 Nov 1934, 10 Nov 1936.
245 Bouskell-Wade 1948, 4; Underhill 1958, 5.
246 Dennis 1987, 26, 94, 110–11, 218, 253.
247 LRO, DE 819/3, 242, minutes, 10 Feb 1925.
248 Ibid., 128, 253–4, minutes, 7 Feb 1922, 12 May 1925.
249 LRO, DE 819/11–12.
250 LRO, DE 3765, Regimental Diary, Leics Yeomanry, 1920–50.
251 LRO, DE 819/4, 30, minutes, 8 Nov 1927.

252 LRO, DE 819/18, minutes, 19 March 1923; DE 819/3, 218–19, minutes, 13 May 1924.

253 LRO, 22 D 63/16/1–2, typescript, 'History of the 4th Battalion 1927/1939', nd, 1; LRO, 22 D 63/17/1–3, typescript, '5th Battalion TA', 3–4; Bouskell-Wade 1948, 4.

254 Underhill 1958, 8–9.

CHAPTER 12

255 LRO, DE 819/22, minutes, 6 Sept 1939.

256 LRO, DE 819/5, 52, minutes, 19 Sept 1939.

257 LRO, DE 2473/99, Cuckson to Sanders, 15 Aug 1940.

258 Codrington 1955, 43–59. See also Bouskell-Wade 1948, Brassey & Winslow 1947.

259 Underhill 1958, 19–26.

260 Ibid., 27–35, 130–66.

261 Ibid., 231–2.

262 Anon (nd).

263 Ogilvy-Dalgleish 1955, 5.

264 LRO, DE 819/22, minutes, 30 July 1940; DE 819/5, 67–8, minutes, 9 Aug 1940; Ogilvy-Dalgleish 1955, 6, 13.

265 Ogilvy-Dalgleish 1955, 24.

266 LRO, DE 189/5, 93, minutes, 11 Nov 1941; DE 819/6, 12, minutes, 9 Nov 1943.

267 LRO, DE 819/6, 29, minutes, 13 Nov 1945.

268 Ogilvy-Dalgleish 1955, 6, 13, 23, 30; LRO, DE 819/5, 77, minutes, 15 Nov 1940.

269 LRO, DE 819/5, 77, minutes, 15 Nov 1940.

270 Ogilvy-Dalgleish 1955, 13.

271 LRO, DE 819/5, 77, minutes, 15 Nov 1940; DE 819/22, minutes, 28 May 1940; Ogilvy-Dalgleish 1955, 9–10.

272 Ogilvy-Dalgleish 1955, 12, 43.

273 Underhill 1958, 234.

274 Ogilvy-Dalgleish 1955, 8, 33–4, 49.

275 LRO, DE 819/5, 84, minutes, 28 Feb 1941; Underhill 1958, 234.

276 Ogilvy-Dalgleish 1955, 38, 41–2.

277 Ibid., 55–7, 59.

278 Ibid., 7, 27, 52–3.

279 Ibid., 8, 12, 54.

280 Ibid., 36, 38, 53.

281 Ibid., 18.

Bibliography

The number of serious studies on the auxiliary forces (Militia, Yeomanry and Volunteers) is still very limited. Since this study was completed, Dr Ian Beckett has produced a most important general history, *The Amateur Military Tradition, 1558–1945* (Beckett 1991), but much remains to be examined. While the Rifle Volunteers of Victorian Britain have recently received detailed attention from Ian Beckett (1982) and Hugh Cunningham (1975), their eighteenth and early nineteenth century predecessors have not. For these latter, recourse must still be made to the much earlier work of Cecil Sebag Montefiore (1908) and Sir John Fortescue (1909), and to the relevant sections of Richard Glover (1963) and J.R. Western (1965). Notwithstanding the number of regimental histories which have been written, the history of the Yeomanry has been similarly neglected. The Volunteers of the twentieth century have fared little better. The Territorial Army between the world wars has been the subject of investigation by Peter Dennis (1976, 1987), but the Volunteer Training Corps of the Great War remains in almost complete obscurity, and the much better known Home Guard of the Second World War is as yet unexamined in any depth.

The following list of sources is intended only as a rough guide to those works and collections found to be most useful; it is by no means exhaustive. A great many more sources are listed by Beckett (1991). For all periods the would-be student of the auxiliary forces will find local newspapers to be an essential source.

Unpublished Primary Sources

Leicestershire Record Office (LRO)
Eighteenth century:
LM 8/8/1–9   Circulars and letters re proposal that principal towns raise their own corps, 1782.

The French Wars, 1793–1815:
109'30/9   Loyal address to George III from Loyal Leicester Vol Infantry, expressing concern over recent attack on him, 9 Nov 1795.

109'30/4/38	Letter from War Office informing late paymaster of Leicester Vol Infantry that his accounts for 1805 are now closed, 14 Sept 1814.
DE 750/33	List of Newbold Verdon residents willing to bear arms, serve as pioneers, drovers, guides, cavalry, etc, 1797.
DE 836/29	Broadsheet of Duke of Rutland's Address, Statherine Hill, 1 Sept 1803.
DG 7 Rut 5	Finch MSS, items on Rutland Yeomanry, 1794 and 1796; Rutland Legion, 1803–13; and Rutland Local Militia, 1812–13.
DG 36/185	Order for payment of drill instructor of Melton Mowbray Vol Infantry, 1804.
DG 39/785	Letter of resignation from Lutterworth Troop, April 1799.
DG 39/1439–53	Letters re Lutterworth Troop, 1798–9.
DG 39/1595–6, 1605	Letters re raising of Leics Yeomanry, 1803.

Nineteenth century:

DE 40/46/4	Regimental register, Leics Yeomanry, 1849–79.
DE 2237/1–23	Items re Leics Rifle Vols, 1859–80.
DE 2472/3	Record of Officers' Service, Leics Yeomanry, *c.* 1890–1901.
DG 7 Rut 5	Finch MSS, items re Rutland Yeomanry, 1820–6.
LM 4/5	Record of Officers' Service, 1st V B Leics Regt, 1860–1916.
LM 4/6/1–10	Muster rolls, Leics Rifle Vols, 1861.
LM 4/7/1–10	Id., 1862.
LM 4/8	Nominal roll, Leics Rifle Vols, 1880.
LM 4/9	Id., 1884.
LM 4/10	Id., 1885.
LM 4/11	Id., 1886.
3 D 67/111/53 etc.	Papers of C.S. Smith, 5th Leics Rifle Vols, *c.* 1860–80.
16 D 35/1–4	Oath rolls, 1st Leics Rifle Vols, 1859–64.
16 D 35/4/1–4	Items re 1st Leics Rifle Vols, 1869–71.
22 D 63/53/19/1–2	Newspaper cuttings re S.H. Gilbert.
22 D 63/74	Newspaper cuttings, Rifle Vols, 1860.
22 D 63/75	Rules of 10th Leics Rifle Vol Corps, 1861.
22 D 63/86	Jubilee Programme, M Coy, 1st V B Leics Regt, 1880.

22 D 63/98/1–2	Address to Hinckley Vols upon their return from South Africa, 1901.
P39	Transcript, Diary of R. Harrison, South Africa, 1900–1.
Misc 320	Broadsheets, 1853–63, including items re Leics Rifle Vols.
(Pamphlets)	Transcript, Diary of the Hon P.C. Evans-Freke, South Africa, 1900.

Twentieth century:

DE 819/1–33	Records of Leics and Rutland Territorial Association 1907–68 (incl. Finance Committee minutes and Offence Report Register, 1st V B Leics Regt 1901–8, items 27 and 28).
DE 2472	Records of Prince Albert's Own Leics and Derbyshire Yeomanry Coy, 7th (Volunteer) Battalion, Royal Anglian Regt (largely items re 20th century service of Leics Yeomanry and its descendants).
DE 3765	Regimental Diary, Leics Yeomanry, 1920–50, and other papers.
22 D 63	Records of Leics Regt (incl. items re 4th and 5th Battalions).

National Army Museum

Archives 7808–50	Items on Donington Park Vols, 1803–5.

Public Record Office, Kew (PRO)

HO 50/77	Home Office correspondence, internal defence, Leics, 1803.
HO 50/111	Id., 1804.
HO 50/138	Id., 1805.
HO 50/155	Id., 1806.
HO 50/171	Id., 1807.
HO 50/195	Id., 1808.
HO 50/223	Id., 1809.
HO 50/245	Id., 1810.
HO 50/266	Id., 1811.
HO 50/300	Id., 1813.

HO 50/338	Id., 1794–1813.
WO 13/4010	War Office muster rolls and paylists, Leics Yeomanry, 1804–31.
WO 13/4426	War Office muster rolls and paylists, Leics Vols, 1794–1808.
WO 13/4427	War Office muster rolls and paylists, Leics Vols, 1803–12.
HO 50/83	Home Office correspondence, internal defence, Rutland, 1803.
HO 50/117	Id., 1804.
HO 50/142	Id., 1805.
HO 50/157	Id., 1806.
HO 50/176	Id., 1807.
HO 50/201	Id., 1808.
HO 50/228	Id., 1809.
HO 50/249	Id., 1810.
HO 50/271	Id., 1811.
HO 50/288	Id., 1812.
HO 50/302	Id., 1813.
HO 50/342	Id., 1794–1813.
WO 13/4524	War Office muster rolls and paylists, Rutland Vols and Rifles, 1798–1812.
WO 13/4030	War Office muster rolls and paylists, Rutland Yeomanry, 1803–27.

Published Primary Sources

Address 1795, *Address to the Yeomanry of England, by a Field Officer of Cavalry* (London).

Appeal 1746, *The Disbanded Volunteers Appeal to their Fellow Citizens: being an Impartial Account of the Proceeding at Exeter against a Set of Gentlemen, who had formed themselves into a Volunteer Company for His Majesty's Service* (Exeter).

Ellis, I.C., (ed.) 1935, *Records of Nineteenth Century Leicester* (privately published).

Exercise 1795, *Exercise for the Rutland Yeomanry Cavalry* (London) (copies in LRO DG7/3/84).

Gilbert, S.H., 1901 *Rhodesia – and after: Being the Story of the 17th and 18th Battalions of Imperial Yeomanry in South Africa* (London).

Harrod, W., 1808, *The History of Market Harborough, in Leicestershire, and its Vicinity* (Market Harborough).

Hind, W.H., 1899, 'A Declaration and Resolutions of the Loyal Loughborough Volunteer Infantry, 22nd October 1794; 1794 Muster Roll of the Loughborough Company of Loyal Volunteer Infantry', *Trans Leicestershire Archit Archaeol Soc*, VIII (1899) 380–2.

Kelly, 1900, 1904, 1908, *Kelly's Directory of Leicestershire and Rutland* (Leicester).

List 1797, 1800, 1801, *A List of the Officers of the Several Regiments and Corps of Fencible Cavalry and Infantry; of the Officers of the Militia; of the Corps and Troops of Gentlemen and Yeomanry; and of the Corps and Companies of Volunteer Infantry* (London).

List 1803, 1805, 1807, *A List of the Officers of the Militia; and the Gentlemen and Yeomanry Cavalry; and Volunteer Infantry* (London).

List 1804, *List of the Volunteer and Yeomanry Corps of the United Kingdom of Great Britain and Ireland* (London).

List, Local Militia 1811, *A List of the Officers of the Local Militia of Great Britain* (London).

List 1820, 1825, *A List of the Officers of the Militia and of the Yeomanry Cavalry and Volunteer Infantry of the United Kingdom* (London).

List 1850, *Royal Militia and Yeomanry Cavalry List* (London).

List 1860, *The Volunteer Army List* (London).

Melville & Co, 1853, *Directory and Gazetteer of Leicestershire* (Leicester).

Read, R., 1881, *Modern Leicester* (Leicester and London).

Richardson, W., 1910–11, *His Majesty's Territorial Army*, 4 vols (London).

Robinson, T. 1795, *Address to the Loyal Leicestershire Volunteer Infantry, at the Presentation of the Colours, in the Parish Church of Saint Martin, Leicester, October 19, 1795* (Leicester).

Standing Orders 1928, *Standing Orders of the Leicestershire (Prince Albert's Own) Yeomanry* (London).

White, 1863, 1877, *White's Leicestershire and Rutland Directory* (Leicester).

Wright, 1881, 1882, 1884, 1890, 1898 and 1904, *Wright's Leicester Directory* (Leicester).

Published Secondary Sources

Anon (n.d.), *315 Medium Regiment RA (TA)* (Leicester).

Armitage, F.P., 1933, *Leicester 1914–1918: The Wartime Story of a Midland Town* (Leicester).

Barker, S., 1984, 'The Loyal Harborough Volunteer Infantry', *Harborough Historian*, 1 (May 1984) 4–5.

Beckett, I.F.W., 1982, *Riflemen Form: A Study of the Rifle Volunteer Movement 1859–1908* (Aldershot).

Beckett, I.F.W., 1985a, *Call to Arms: The Story of Bucks' Citizen Soldiers from their Origins to date* (Buckingham).

Beckett, I.F.W., 1985b, 'Aspects of a Nation in Arms: Britain's Volunteer Training Corps in the Great War', *Rev Internat d'Hist Milit*, 63 (1985) 27–39.

Beckett, I.F.W., 1986, 'The Amateur Military Tradition in Britain', *War & Society*, 4.26 (Sept 1986) 1–16.

Beckett, I.F.W., 1991, *The Amateur Military Tradition, 1558–1945* (Manchester).

Beckett, I.F.W., & Simpson, K. (eds), 1985, *A Nation in Arms: A Social Study of the British Army in the First World War* (Manchester).

Berry, R.P., 1903, *A History of the Formation and Development of Volunteer Infantry* (London and Huddersfield).

Bond, B. 1980, *British Military Policy between the Two World Wars* (Oxford).

Bouskell-Wade, Lt-Col G.E., 1948, *'There is an Honour Likewise . . .' The Story of 154 (Leicestershire Yeomanry) Field Regiment RA* (Leicester).

Brassey, Lt-Col B.T., & Winslow, Maj P.D., 1947, *153rd Leicestershire Yeomanry Field Regiment RA, TA, 1939–1945* (Hinckley).

Codrington, Col Sir G., 1955, *An Outline of the History of the Leicestershire (Prince Albert's Own) Yeomanry* (London).

Cousins, G., 1968, *The Defenders: A History of the British Volunteer* (London).

Cunningham, H., 1975, *The Volunteer Force: A Social and Political History 1859–1914* (London).

Darvall, F.O., 1934, *Popular Disturbances and Public Order in Regency England* (Oxford).

Davies, J.C., 1981, *Yesterday's Town: Victorian Harborough* (Buckingham).

Dennis, P., 1976, 'The Reconstitution of the Territorial Force 1918–1920', in A. Preston & P. Dennis (eds), *Swords and Covenants* (London). 190–215.

Dennis, P., 1987, *The Territorial Army 1906–1940* (Woodbridge).

Dickinson, H.T., 1989, 'Popular Conservatism and Militant Loyalism 1789–1815', in H.T. Dickinson (ed.), *Britain and the French Revolution 1789–1815* (London) 103–25.

Emsley, C., 1979, *British Society and the French Wars 1793–1815* (London).

Fortescue, J.W., 1909, *The County Lieutenancies and the Army 1803–1814* (London).

Francis, H.J., 1930, *A History of Hinckley* (Hinckley).

Freer, W.J., 1899, 'Col Sir Henry St John Halford, Bart, CB, VD', *Trans Leicestershire Archit Archaeol Soc*, VIII (1899) 291–303.

Gladstone, E.W., 1953, *The Shropshire Yeomanry 1793–1945* (Manchester).

Glover, R., 1963, *Peninsular Preparation: The Reform of the British Army 1795–1809* (Cambridge).

Glover, R., 1973, *Britain at Bay: Defence against Bonaparte 1803–1814* (London).

Hillier, K., 1984, *The Book of Ashby-de-la-Zouch* (Buckingham).

Hills, Capt J.D., 1919, *The Fifth Leicestershire: A Record of the 1/5th Battalion, the Leicestershire Regiment, TF, during the War 1914–1919* (Loughborough).

Jamie, Lt-Col J.P.W., 1931, *The 177th Brigade 1914–1918* (Leicester).

Longmate, N. 1974, *The Real Dad's Army: The Story of the Home Guard* (London).

McDowell, R.B., 1979, *Ireland in the Age of Imperialism and Revolution 1760–1801* (Oxford).

McLynn, F.J., 1983, *The Jacobite Army in England 1745* (Edinburgh).

Mather, F.C., 1959, *Public Order in the Age of the Chartists* (Manchester).

Matthews, B., 1984, *By God's Grace . . . : A History of Uppingham School* (Maidstone).

Mileham, P.J.R., 1985, *The Yeomanry Regiments: A Pictorial History* (Tunbridge Wells).

Milne, Capt J., 1935, *Footprints of the 1/4th Leicestershire Regiment, August 1914 to November 1918* (Leicester).

Montefiore, C.S., 1908, *A History of the Volunteer Force: From the Earliest Times to the Year 1860* (London).

Moore, A., 1982, *A Son of the Rectory: From Leicestershire to the Somme* (Gloucester).

Nichols, J., 1800, *History and Antiquities of the County of Leicester*, III (London).

Norfolk, R.W.S., 1965, *Militia, Yeomanry and Volunteer Forces of the East Riding 1689–1900* (E Yorks Local Hist Soc).

Ogilvy-Dalgleish, Wing Cdr J.W., 1955, *The Rutland Home Guard of 1940–44* (Oakham).

Osborne, J.M., 1988, 'Defining their own Patriotism: British Volunteer Training Corps in the First World War', *Journ Contemporary Hist*, 23 (1988) 59–74.

Patterson, A.T., 1954, *Radical Leicester: A History of Leicester 1780–1850* (Leicester).

Phillips, G., 1920, *Rutland and the Great War* (Salford).

Robinson, A., 1978, 'The Regiments of Rutland', in Traylen, A.R. (ed.), *The Services of Rutland*, Rutland Local Hist Soc, In Rutland Series, 2 (Oakham).

Sainsbury, J.D., 1969, *Hertfordshire's Soldiers from 1757* (Hitchin).

Spiers, E.M., 1980, *The Army and Society 1815–1914* (London).

Teichman, O., 1940, 'The Yeomanry as an aid to Civil Power 1795–1867', *Journ Soc Army Hist Res*, XIX (1940) 75–91, 127–43.

Throsby, J., 1791, *The History and Antiquities of the Ancient Town of Leicester*, III (Leicester).

Underhill, Brig W.E., (ed) 1958, *The Royal Leicestershire Regiment, 17th Foot: A History of the Years 1928 to 1956* (Leicester).

VCH Leicestershire, 1954, *Victoria History of the County of Leicester*, II (London).

VCH Rutland, 1908, *Victoria History of the County of Rutland*, I (London).

Western, J.R., 1956, 'The Volunteer Movement as an Anti-Revolutionary Force 1793–1801', *Engl Hist Rev*, 71 (1956) 603–14.

Western, J.R., 1965, *The English Militia in the Eighteenth Century: The Story of a Political Issue, 1660–1802* (London).

Westlake, R.A., 1982, *The Rifle Volunteers 1859–1908* (Chippenham).

Westlake, R.A., 1985, *The Territorial Battalions: A Pictorial History 1859–1985* (London).

Index